IT for Property People

Andrew Waller

2005

EG Books

A division of Reed Business Information

Estates Gazette
1 Procter Street, London WC1V 6EU

Typeset by FiSH Books, London.
Printed by Bell & Bain Ltd, Glasgow

Contents

Foreword

Ten years ago, how many of us made regular use of e-mail? Yet, which of us could live without it now? There are few senior property figures, from *Estates Gazette's* editor, to any number of developers and senior partners, who leave their desks without a Blackberry to hand.

For some reason technological change is always both over-hyped and under-hyped. It is over-hyped because change never happens as fast as people predict; under-hyped because the change is, in the long-term, more radical than people predicted.

The evidence that change has been dramatic within business in general is hard to ignore. There are those ever-present Blackberries in meetings, and it's all but impossible to go into a coffee shop or airport departure lounge without tripping over half a dozen business people using wireless internet access on their laptops. Indeed, I'm drafting this in Edinburgh airport, using wireless broadband. Looking at the property industry specifically, property management systems, listings sites and electronic links with government departments have joined e-mail as a regular part of day-to-day business.

Let's face it. Five years ago, senior partners would proudly boast that their secretaries printed out e-mails for them, so they didn't need to touch a computer. Nowadays, such a senior partner would be treated with pity, not respect, and might be looking at an unexpectedly early retirement.

But they were right in one sense. The significant part of "Information Technology" is not the technology – it's the information. It is said that information is power but the key to this is using that knowledge effectively. Too much information can be just as dangerous as too little, and the development of so many sources of data for the property industry has often played into the hands of traditionalists. Too often old fashioned, inefficient ways of managing contacts and data win and IT just delivers simple data, not knowledge. Technology beats out information.

Outside the property sector there are obvious examples of industries where information has created huge market advantage. Take Tesco, which uses its Club Card information as part of its strategy to claim an eighth of all spending in the UK. On the other hand, too much unstructured data contributed in part to the downfall of businesses such as Enron.

The changes in the industry clearly create huge opportunities for those who know how to get the best information from their technology and there is evidence that these opportunities are being taken. Andrew's book is the culmination of a decade of advising people within the property industry on how best to run their business better, both in person and on paper. Since *EG* shifted its IT coverage from a technology to a business focus five years ago, Andrew has been an integral part of that process.

As a result, the book is loaded with practical examples of how real property firms have used technology to give them the information to beat the marketplace.

This is not a book for IT people. This is a book for business people. In fact, this is a book for *property* business people.

It's your chance to take advantage of the future, before your competitors use the future to take advantage of you.

Adam Tinworth
Features Editor
Estates Gazette
May 2005

Acknowledgements

The book would not have been finished and, in a few cases even started, without the help of the following people who have, in turns, helped out, supported and pointed me back in the right direction.

Melita Thomas and Mark Jones, my partners in Remit Consulting have helped through the whole process both by taking on more in Remit while I took days out on the manuscript and by providing large amounts of content for the book. Mark gave the original presentation at PCS-Expo about running IT without an IT team on which Chapter 9 is largely based. Mark also wrote the discussion paper about web-based applications in Chapter 8.

Melita wrote the test scripts in Chapter 5 and they both vigorously challenged the drafts and corrected my grammar.

Martin Farncombe, founder of Theopraxis and joint author of *The Atomic Corporation* and *Atomic*, kindly went beyond the call of duty by reviewing and commenting on the entire manuscript leading to much useful debate about the various methods described. Martin also provided helpful comment about the concepts in his book, *Atomic*, which are discussed in Chapter 10.

Robert Shooter of Field Fisher Waterhouse provided a lot of help on Chapter 6 particularly in writing the section on the technicalities of buying IT.

The case studies could not have been written without the help of the following people. In particular, I would like to thank Stephen Spooner of British Land; Antony Slumbers of Vicinitee and Bob Flood of Broadgate Estates; Alison Warburg, Richard Shepherd-Cross and Richard Auterac of Jones Lang LaSalle; Tony McDonagh and Caron Jawed of Mayfield Property Consultants; Mick Flynn of Trace Solutions; Philip Doyle of Peel Holdings; Carol Ledwidge of Intuit MRI; David Baruch at Equity Office Properties and Mark Watts at Realm Ltd.

Keith Jones of Performent Consulting gave me good advice about the current and future issues affecting the public sector and Angus McIntosh of King Sturge helped me prioritise the main influences on the future needs for information in the property world.

Much of this book depends on thoughts and ideas developed over the last 10 years. Rob Oldham, my boss at Ernst & Young and now head of Corporate Consulting at DTZ Pieda, gave great support to our team at Ernst & Young and, together with the then Head of Department, Eugene Bannon, encouraged the Real Estate Information Solutions service to flourish.

I also need to thank Adam Tinworth of the *EG* who published my thoughts on IT in property each month for many years and who persuaded EG Books to consider this manuscript.

Lastly, my thanks to my wife, Yvonne, and children, Jonathan, Julia and Sarah, who have put up with the inevitable missed weekends while I have typed away. I am now looking forward to spending more time with them.

Introduction

In the summer of the year 2000, I facilitated a workshop of 20 senior professionals in a European property agency. The daylong workshop was intended to define the company's approach to using technology. As an introduction I presented a number of the ideas that were in the market at the time. For example, Yahoo! had recently launched a US property brokerage online and was showing that the majority of profit for them was in commission from financial services, insurance and fit-out. Elsewhere, an enormous amount of detailed property information was becoming available over the internet for free.

"If all property information is available online", I asked, "what services will you provide which will add value to your client and for which you can charge fees?" The responding silence was deafening. As one observer put it later, you could hear the wind whistling through the gaps in the windows and imagine tumbleweeds blowing down the large central boardroom table.

I genuinely thought that the workshop had come to an end and that our team would be escorted from the room. The panic in the eyes of our sponsor said it all but over the next 10 minutes we managed to coax the agents into teams of three or four and they set about discussing a "distant future" when clients would already know what deals were happening and they could take their pick of experienced brokers.

The problem with my question was that it had made real the fear of all the agents in the room. For so long they have controlled information in real estate. They make the market they work in and no single client has sufficient property to take that from them. Certainly they are beholden to clients for the agency instructions, but clients need agents just as much to tell them what deals are being transacted and how that affects their own property.

Indeed, in 2005, it is still a requirement in the UK that a company wishing to advise on the value of buildings for a RICS Red Book valuation must have sufficient current local market knowledge; this phrase is usually interpreted that the valuing firm must have an agency department from whom market comparable evidence can be obtained. How 20th century is that?

Many of their investment clients also believe they have much to gain from this lack of transparency in the market. One portfolio manager who is responsible for over £1bn of real estate told me, "It is the opacity of the market which allows me to make money. I profit from the arbitrage in information – I sell well if I know bad things about the property which are unknown to the buyer; I buy well if I know the opposite. I can't do that if everyone has the same information".

Our agents in the year 2000 had heard about independent online property portals being set up by people outside the main surveying firms. Research portals were giving away information about new developments for free. However, if these ideas were to be extended, the information now held by agents would be freely transferred to the investors, and agents would have nothing of their own on which to base their advice.

Little wonder that there was mistrust of new technology. It threatened to take away the very livelihood of surveyors. They would have no monopoly on market information; there would be no need for clients to use agents to transact the deals, and no need for valuers except in an independent capacity. The property profession would be left with property management, an undervalued and low margin business that is still unattractive to the dealmakers in agency.

Furthermore, the new technology seemed out of their grasp. The failure of online ventures such as Pathway, Zethus and Constellation showed that the surveying firms could not take control of this new phenomenon. Therefore the internet, and by extension information technology (IT) in all its guises, was something which they were eager to ignore.

What was missing at that stage was an understanding of what value real estate agents add to transactions. Our workshop participants caught onto this over the next 30 minutes and started creating lists of services they could offer which used their skills and knowledge but did not rely on control of the underlying information.

What they realised was that even if nothing changed, they would make money from their skills in using the information, not from hoarding it. If information did not become freely available on the internet, they could sell their information at a premium to augment their fees; or they could give the information away to undermine the value of the services provided by their competition. Either way they would win.

Essentially, we managed to move the discussion away from IT and onto how the agents do business; which market do they really want to earn fees from and what services does that market require? What processes do they go through each day that could be improved? Where should property people spend their time most effectively and where do they make the most profit?

IT and property

Many property people like to ignore IT. If it works, it becomes another chore that runs your life. If, or in many cases *when*, it doesn't work, it is more of a problem than it is worth. A few recognise IT as a useful, but often frustrating, tool.

The real estate world briefly flirted with IT in the dotcom boom and many online companies were started. I suspect that the majority of those from mainstream real estate became involved because of their love of the deal and the buzz of investing in rapidly growing stock rather than because of a deep-seated desire to change the way in which the industry works.

Following the demise of many of the original dotcoms, most of the industry went back to the way it used to work. Some, including those in the case studies in this book, persevered. They have contributed to changes in the industry and we can see the results of many different technology changes around us.

- Real estate particulars are sent as PDF files by e-mail and websites for individual properties are common.
- E-mail now accounts for the majority of written information received by professionals.
- Professionals are demanding mobile devices such as Blackberrys to keep in touch with their e-mail.
- Corporate estates departments rely on large "Enterprise" finance systems to deal with rental and service charge payments.

However, many of these changes are not real estate specific. E-mail and the onward march of enterprise finance systems have developed despite the industry rather than because of our own needs.

Other examples show how real estate is lagging behind.

1. There is no reason why 70-80% of information shouldn't be available (not free, but available) to everyone – clients and agents alike. As more information becomes available online from both government and private research companies, those who try to hoard information will be ignored.
2. In many areas, our industry is seriously falling behind others. For example, the widely promoted 50% cost reductions in back office processing in India and China is providing many companies with significant opportunities. Corporates, whose main business is not real estate, expect to rollout cost savings across all departments – not just all those except real estate.

Effective use of IT helps companies to adapt to many new opportunities. This begins to refine the question I seek to answer in this book – how do I harness the good parts of IT?

Successful resolution of this question will lead to better efficiency, cost savings and greater productivity. Above all, it gives you control and reduces the number of your sleepless nights.

What is the aim of the book?

Assuming that you have decided to use IT more effectively as part of your efficiency drive, this book will show you how to approach the whole project, not just the technology.

It is tempting to approach an IT project from the wrong end. Often people consider the systems available and then work out what they need. The result is a badly drafted specification and the resulting tender can never provide an answer because there is no clearly defined question.

My approach starts with the business and those elements of day-to-day work that need to be improved. Thus, the business case will be based on business improvements and the resulting specification and tender will solve the particular problem.

As a result of this clearer definition, it is easier to source the most appropriate IT for the problem. This might not be a traditional software solution sitting in a box in your office. The software might be hosted away from your offices, or you might decide to outsource the whole business function to someone who provides the service and software combined.

We have therefore turned the IT solution into a business issue, rather than one of technology. The benefit is that we can start comparing the investment of time and money with other business initiatives and the problem of understanding the technology itself becomes less important.

My aim is therefore to reduce the fear of dealing with IT and to answer many of the most common questions I am asked.

The structure of the book

The first thing to note is that the chapters do not read like a recipe book; the approach cannot be applied chapter by chapter in chronological order. This is because I have tried to isolate the various factors involved in defining, selecting and implementing systems. By doing this I have attempted to discuss each aspect in sufficient detail to be useful and so that the different elements can be put together logically to deal with different organisational requirements.

Thus, several of the chapters need to be considered in parallel. Many people would start at specifying the system, and this is dealt with relatively early. The book progresses, in a logical sequence, to the tender process straight afterwards.

However, without applying the approaches in Making it Work (Chapter 7), from the beginning of the project, the project is unlikely to be a success. This chapter concentrates on the elements of the project that are often overlooked; it is attention to the matters such as project management, change management and communications that will lead to a successful result.

To explain this more clearly, I have used the diagram in Figure 1.1 that is based on the Remit Process Model (RPM) used extensively in this book. More detail of how the model is used can be found in Chapter 5, but essentially the RPM here divides the book into several sections. In each section are relevant issues and subsections. The diagram groups various chapters together and you can see that the book needs to be viewed as a whole before embarking on the project – just as most projects benefit from a holistic approach.

Looking at the structure in more detail, the book deals with the following topics.

Setting the Scene (Introduction, and Chapters 1 and 2) deals with the way in which information is needed and used in the real estate industry. It also shows a number of case studies which I hope will inspire readers to experiment – if only because other people in the industry are already using much of what you might be thinking about doing.

The next two sections, Prioritising the Need (Chapters 3 and 4) and Specification and Tender (Chapters 5 and 6) are grouped together to make the point that they should be indivisible. It is not possible to successfully select and implement new software if the business need is not fully developed, scoped, and understood.

Many companies lose focus on the original specification during the tender process. It is common for preferred systems to lack critical requirements or for the scope to increase to include an attractive new feature. The approach set out here should keep everything tightly concentrated on the defined business need.

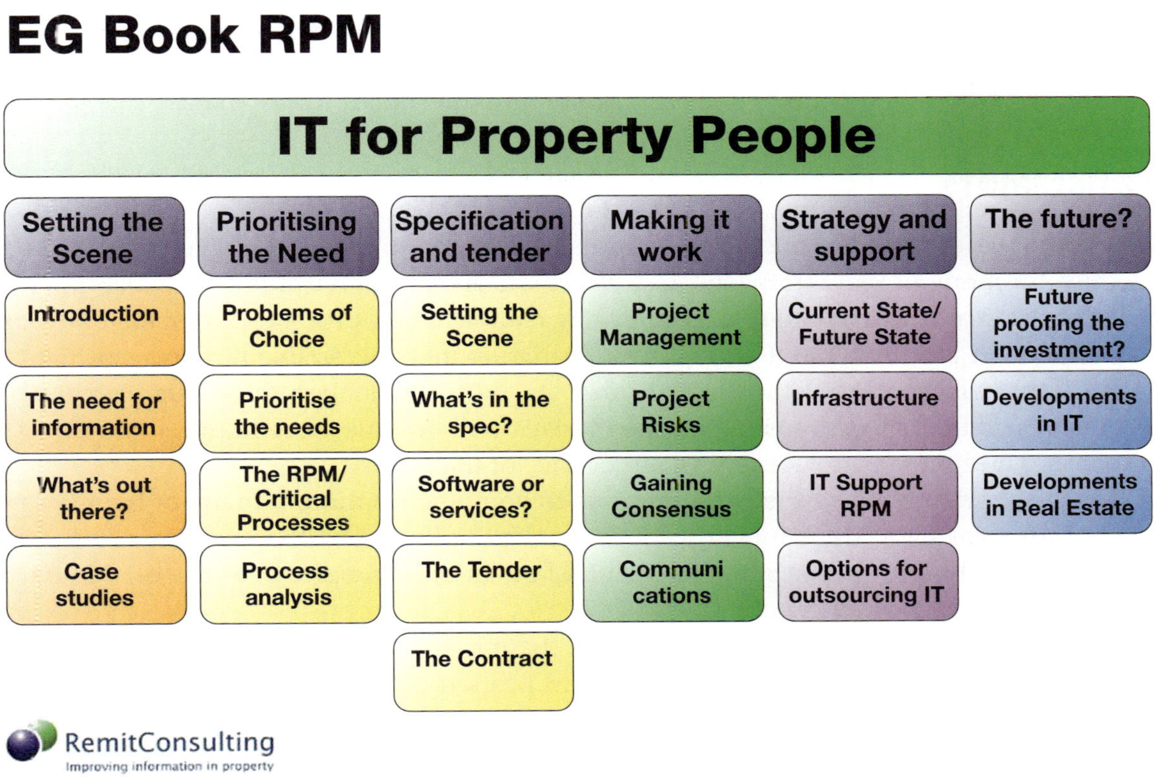

Figure I.1 RPM for the book structure

Making it Work (Chapter 7) deserves a book to itself and this is the first break with chronological sequence; it supports and underlines every aspect of the project and its suggestions should be applied from the beginning of the project. The topics in Making it Work have their own section so that I do not give the impression that, for example, Project Management only becomes necessary when the software needs to be implemented. The same applies to the other disciplines in this chapter: Risk Management, Gaining Consensus, and Communications.

Chapter 7 is not optional – if you want the project to succeed its principles must be applied from the start.

Having completed your first IT project, you will be tempted (encouraged, maybe) to look at other areas of business needing improvement. You should make time for putting together a strategy (Chapter 8) and you will come up against the constraints of the organisation's infrastructure. If you need to develop overall IT support for the business, Chapter 9 will take you through the essentials using the same structures you will have seen in the rest of the book. Again, these chapters can be taken out of sequence.

And what of the future? Questions about such topics as future-proofing your IT often arise, and Chapter 10 allows us to do a bit of future gazing: both in respect of technology and about the real estate industry. Who knows if the predictions will turn out correct, but I look forward to debating some of the more controversial points in due course. By all means start here if you want to stimulate some thoughts about future plans.

Constraints

As mentioned at the start, one of the reasons that many in real estate have ignored IT is because for many of real estate jobs, free information reduces the ability to make money. It is therefore not in the interest of many in real estate to promote the availability of information. It is agued that if you make information more accessible it reduces profits.

The longer-term view, of course, is that as information becomes more available, decision-making is more transparent; the markets will become more liquid, more capital is invested and most people receive a larger slice of the pie.

It is the short-term view that will continue to hamper adoption of many of the market facing innovation and thus, much of the technology adopted by the real estate industry has been to automate property management. Many of the examples in this book therefore focus on property management.

You will find that in the following chapters there is an unconscious focus on packaged systems and particularly those that automate property management. I have included examples of agency systems where possible; the case study of Jones Lang LaSalle is a very good example and many more systems are now available online or off-the-shelf. Hopefully over time a balance will emerge.

There is also a tendency to focus on packaged solutions because these are widely available and provide a lot of functionality out of the box. However, there will be increasing numbers of companies going down the enterprise finance system route and the principles in this book are sound for these as well.

In situations where your company has selected an enterprise finance system and the intention is to include the estates team, it would usually be unwise to fight against it. In common with best business politics, don't fight for a property system if you are ultimately going to lose the battle – put your energy into making sure the system you get will work. Use the techniques outlined here to promote the specific business needs of your team.

Another option for new technology is bespoke software. Again, this is touched upon and the same principles apply, particularly in the section about "Making it Work". However, bespoke software is difficult to specify correctly and tricky to implement effectively. It is usually not a good idea to start here unless you really cannot satisfy the business need in another way.

The thing to remember whatever route to new software you choose is that the principal cause of software failure is poor adoption and management of change in the business – not the software chosen. This why such a large number of chapters deal with the changes to business, not with the technology.

Summary

This book is not about technology, it is about how IT can be used by business to make better returns on investment. Neither will it tell you which systems to buy. Every organisation will have its own criteria for assessing the worth of a new system.

Technology has become, and will remain, a commodity. New developments will put companies ahead for some months, maybe years, but if the technology has general application the price will fall and it will become a commodity.

My hope is that after reading this book you will be able to implement whatever technology you choose effectively because you have the business case, the buy-in from the business and the corporate sponsorship to make it happen.

Please let me know how you get on.

1 The need for information in property

The essence of dealing in property is information. Information about what will soon come to the market. Information about what has been on the market too long. Why certain properties sell quickly and what price can be achieved. Importantly, how much of this information do I know that my competitor doesn't?

The valuation of properties relies on information. Which properties have recently sold and for how much? Which features of the property are of benefit and which will reduce the price?

Information is also key in property management. Increasingly, legal precedent and statute dictate how property is managed. In the UK the Disability Discrimination Act, asbestos regulations and general health and safety regulations have made property management vital for occupiers, more risky for practitioners and more expensive for landlords. Having the right information available saves time, cost and lowers the risk of ownership.

What influences property decisions?

To get a picture of the information requirements in each sector of the industry we can look at the stakeholders in each type of organisation. Many of these will have radically different objectives and their decisions will be made on different information.

This is not just down to the different goals of landlords and tenants, although this represents a significant variation in priorities. In the UK, where the traditional lease structure has put these parties in opposition, the differing information requirements are at their most extreme.

Landlords traditionally let properties on Full Repairing and Insuring (FRI) leases, meaning that the tenant must keep the property in good repair regardless of the cost; the landlord theoretically takes back a building requiring no further work at the end of a lease. The landlord's income has virtually no deductions and his investment is easy to value. The landlord traditionally needs little direct information about his property.

The tenant, on the other hand, is keen to understand every aspect of the running of a building so as to minimise his liabilities, both financial and statutory. He will need far greater detail about the structure, repair and layout.

This is a key, but traditional difference. As leading practice investment ideas are adopted worldwide, so UK landlords are finding that more information about their estate produces stronger growth and greater profitability in the longer term.

Other differences in information requirements appear when looking at trends in the property market; while different types of landlord have always needed different information, the differences are becoming more exaggerated.

Trends

For example, the owner of a private property company may not have any natural inclination to invest in environmentally sustainable transport initiatives. A local authority, on the other hand, will have responsibility for a share of the £100bn of property in local government, and environmental and local concerns will be far higher on their list of priorities.

It is often this weight of property owned by the public sector that determines trends in the property market. A good example is in the outsourcing of property portfolios.

Outsourcing

The property industry woke up to where outsourcing could lead in 1997 when the UK government tendered the PRIME contract. More than just transferring the services to manage the property, PRIME transferred the whole estate, including freehold and leasehold property to Trillium, one of a new breed of property companies set up to take advantage of these deals.

This is genuine transformational outsourcing. The idea of ordering 1500 desk spaces for the next year in, say, Hemel Hempstead and letting the service provider work out how best to provide it removes all of the need for property expertise from the occupier. The service provider is an expert in managing property and can reduce costs throughout a far larger managed estate than the occupier could do on their own. This is somewhat theoretical in that some management costs are often necessarily duplicated but the principle is driving much of the occupier market's current thinking.

The PRIME contract was followed by STEPS (Inland Revenue property estate), Abbey and BT among others. One of the main advantages of this approach cited by proponents is that by transferring property to another organisation, the capital locked up in the property portfolio of corporate occupiers can be released to the company, thus, in theory, improving shareholder value. It has certainly released substantial sums into the Treasury coffers and to companies taking this route.

This is just one example of the trends in property ownership and use that significantly changes the requirement for information. The involvement of third parties in a company's property processes requires a far greater understanding of what the company needs. Firstly, this type of project focuses the collective minds of the organisation on what they expect property to provide. A focus on business benefit is essential so that the outsourcing team can set appropriate service levels with the supplier and determine the measures to be used in assessing the performance of the supplier and the portfolio.

As more organisations seek to improve their overall performance by outsourcing non-core activities, so the need to report information about property and measure changes becomes more important. This is the same for landlords wishing to outsource their rent and service charge collection, and for tenants wanting to establish benchmarks for their property costs.

A further complication of this increasingly sophisticated approach to outsourcing is that the information required to report performance measures is generated both inside the property organisation and at their supplier.

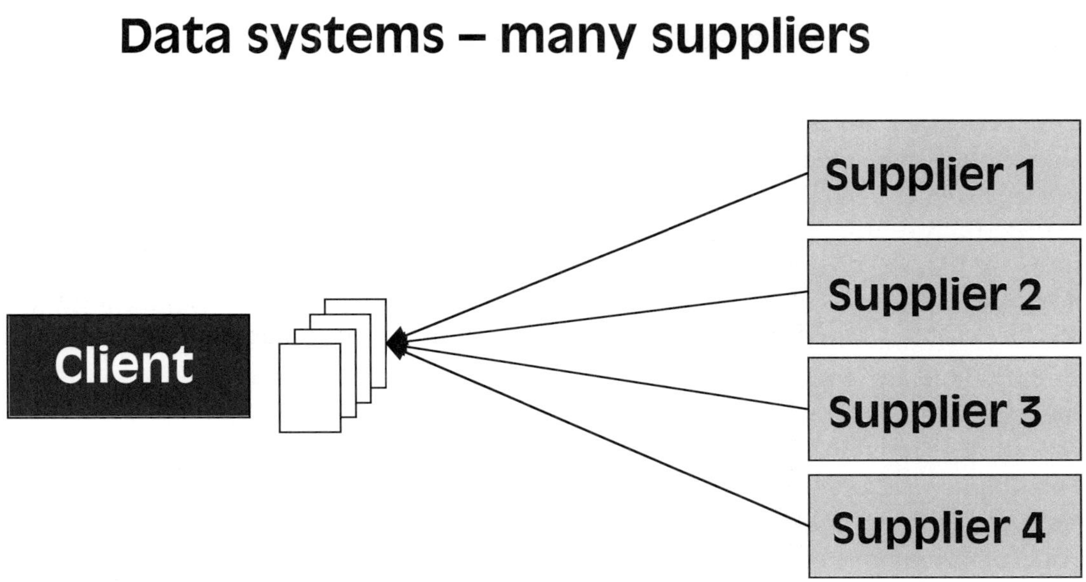

Figure 1.1

In Figure 1.1 above the client receives a number of different reports from his suppliers in different formats. Some may be in MS Word; some in MS Excel and some may by in a Portable Document Format (PDF) such as Adobe Acrobat. Even if all the reports were in Excel, the different formats are time consuming and costly to integrate into one report.

For the supplier, things are no easier. Fifteen clients are likely to run at least 10 different systems and it is difficult for the supplier to convince all his clients to accept the same format of report.

Furthermore, the supplier is privileged to the same information he has always had but now, with an effectively integrated management system in his office, he can easily compare costs across several clients and, potentially sell this information externally. Many clients are uncomfortable with this ability to use their data for separate gain and we will see increasingly lengthy negotiations on this subject in the market.

Thus the increased demand for information about property portfolios due to more sophisticated outsourcing contracts has brought about significant new challenges.

Investor relations

Another trend to affect the way information is held and processed is the increasingly widespread ownership of prime commercial property among high net worth individuals. The lack of transparency in the property market has scared off many private investors in the past.

A fun benchmark is the number of celebrities buying commercial property as investments. Time was when agency pub talk always covered the rare occasions when celebrities were in the market. Now most of these situations are unremarkable as these property transactions are too numerous even for agency gossip.

The recent surge in buy-to-let investment is also spilling over into commercial property. UKPiP, a UK based investment property portal has 10,000 subscribers to its newsletter giving details of new investment properties on the market; Primepitch, another portal has a similar number of subscribers. Both portals deal with properties of between £1m and £5m.

Additionally, in the UK, the increasing frustration with pension returns and the lack of growth in the equities market over the last few years have further emphasised the attractions of property as a long-term investment. The possibility of the introduction of Real Estate Investment Trusts (REITs), modelled on the REITs in the US, is another factor that may lead to increasingly diverse property ownership. UKREITs will be tax transparent vehicles for holding property, shares of which will be widely available and which will be tradable.

The upshot of these trends is that commercial property is now an increasingly popular investment among non-professional investors and the market can no longer rely on opaque practices and information hoarding if it is to encourage and grow this wave of new money into the sector. Investors will go to the funds with the friendliest, most transparent portals.

All these investors are seeking enough information to understand their investment without relying on agents. Compare, for example, these market changes with the popularity of the website The Motley Fool[1] where individual investors can exchange their own information about the market without paying advisory fees. Will a similar site be successful in property?

If the UK market follows the success of REITs in the US, and of similar vehicles in Australia and elsewhere, increasing numbers of REITs owners will want to know every last detail of their investment, not just the year-on-year return.

Managing the expectations of retail investors, whose main contact with the fund manager is by telephone call centre or over the internet, represents a major change in customer relationship management for the UK property industry.

The websites of the REITs in the US are very rich in detail. You only have to look at the website of one of the largest US REITs, Equity Office Properties[2] to see how much detail the site provides about the properties in which they invest.[3]

Some UK property companies are already improving investor access to their sites to prepare themselves for REITs. Hammerson, for example has an easy to use website with details of their key property holdings together with their financial results.

This information is not difficult or risky to display but it can be time consuming to research and present. Companies wishing to attract highly mobile investors will need to decide what performance indicators to present, find where that information currently sits, automate the collection of the data and keep that data up to date. No mean feat for many property investors who typically take three weeks to prepare a presentation for analysts.

Property sector requirements

To give an idea of the breadth of information required by property organisations, we can look at the following examples from across the sector.

- Property companies – private and public.
- Institutions – investment companies and venture capitalists.
- Property agents and consultants.
- Corporate occupiers.
- Government – central and local.

Property companies

Property Companies are unusual businesses. They outsource many of the management responsibilities of their core business such as market knowledge, managing their

1 www.fool.com
2 www.equityoffice.com
3 See EOP case study, page 45

buildings and developing their investments. They also have small teams in comparison with their capital value.

British Land, for example, had revenue in 2003 of £551m and their net asset value in excess of £4,300m but their head office team was only 160 employees[4]. This small number of direct employees compared to the high income and worth of the company is rare for companies with fixed assets outside the property sector. This is not a resource intensive business and until the last few years, information requirements were limited.

The drivers for a property company are capital growth and income. Traditionally this translates into the fact that they need to own the right property in an improving location and need to secure their rent on good quality tenants who will continue to pay the rent for a long lease.

The information they need, at its most basic level, will be:

- sufficient details of the tenant, the lease and the building to ensure that the rent can be collected
- the knowledge that the tenant is not in difficulties
- the knowledge that any landlord's obligations are satisfied.

Many property companies rely on external agents for the management of the properties but often retain control of the rent collection because of the importance of controlling the cash flow. The information will therefore be generated both inside and outside the company and integrating that information is a further challenge.

If the company develops property, it will need information about the current market for the buildings being developed and the future trends. It will need to integrate information from its contractors and project managers into budgets, and report consolidated views of how projects are running.

However, property companies make their real money by gearing. If they only use their own money for 10% of the cost of the property and borrow the rest, any capital gain in the overall property is 10 times more profitable for them. This means that they are beholden to external investors and banks, which provide the other 90% of the property value.

Whereas a private property company might only need to gather sufficient data to satisfy its auditors, banks and investors, a publicly quoted company has a further set of issues to deal with. Traditionally, a quoted property company's shares trade at a discount to the company's Net Asset Value (NAV). By reducing this discount the company can improve its value by many millions and most property companies have been looking at ways to do this.

One factor that contributes to the share price is the view of sector analysts and it follows that if the analyst clearly understands the underlying company data, they will reduce the discount to NAV.

4 British Land – Annual Report & Accounts 2003

It is this fact and the possibility of REITs that are driving property companies to improve the integration of their systems and, in particular, the quality of their reporting.

A significant difference between public and private property companies is therefore the need to show how well they perform. Private property companies are reliant on funds from private investors and Joint Venture (JV) partners, and their banks.

Since most of their finances will be largely hidden, they are less inclined to expend valuable resources on outwardly impressive reporting systems. More important to them will be ensuring that the basics are covered. This will normally include:

- rent accounting
- managing and reconciling recoverables and non-recoverables, eg service charges and insurance
- managing capital projects, ie new developments.

The majority of private property companies are relatively small and as a result, many have been able to manage these areas without sophisticated systems. They have relied on their JV partners to provide systems support and the necessary reports.

However, with the reduction in cost of many of these systems and the ability to access quite sophisticated functionality over the Web, they now have an opportunity to improve the way in which they use systems to support their business and many are taking this opportunity.

Institutions

Institutions have long been one of the mainstays of the UK property market, whether homegrown, or from continental Europe, the Far East or the US. Typically in the UK insurance companies and pension providers invest about 15% of their assets in property and therefore influence a considerable proportion of the property market.

Unlike property companies, many of which wish to show their investors how well they are performing in an increasingly public way, the main business of the institutions is providing insurance or assurance cover, or providing pensions. The management of

Finance	Asset and Governance
Statutory Financial Reporting	Property Management
Performance Measurement	Performance Measurement
Cash Management/Transfers	Supply Chain
Client Financial Reporting	Meetings and Reports
Document Management	Statutory Records
Business Policies and Procedures	Customer Relationship Management

property is a relatively small part of their work and most of the actual management is outsourced to property agents.

The majority of institutions concentrate on strategic management of assets and many even allow the area of stock selection to be undertaken outside the organisation by asset managers. This table shows the typical information requirements for funds.

From this list, the elements that are most different from the requirements of property companies are Performance Measurement and Cash Management.

Performance Measurement

The aggregated returns are compared against industry benchmarks such as Investment Property Database (IPD) and general pension fund benchmarks such as Russell/Mellon CAPS, and there is a requirement for information to be gathered to support these benchmarks. This is usually provided by their managing agents and is often time-consuming for the organisation to co-ordinate but since it happens relatively infrequently, there is often limited pressure from the institution to automate this procedure.

Improvements in information flow among property investors and the further integration of currently disparate property systems will significantly improve the ability of institutions to collect and distribute their property information. This will greatly ease data collection for benchmarking and may lead to clearer reporting in other parts of these businesses.

Cash Management

Much of the opportunity to use information more effectively within institutions comes from the sheer scale of capital that needs to be moved to support the transactions in which they become involved. For example, Morley Fund Management, the institutional asset management business of Aviva plc, is one of the largest managers and invests approximately £12bn in property[5]. The lot sizes of their investments are correspondingly larger than most other players in the property market and this is true for many of the household names in this sector, whether in the UK or from overseas.

Depending on the fund, the holding structures for property are often dictated by the most efficient way to reduce the tax liability on the holding. There are many countries such as the Netherlands, Luxembourg and Japan that allow companies to hold property in a tax efficient way and, by structuring a fund across several of these countries, significant savings on tax can be achieved upon disposal.

This can mean that the capital for a transaction needs to travel across the globe from company to company several times before ending up paying for a new property.

5 Morley Fund Management website information. www.morleyfm.co.uk

Cash management in these large transactions is of prime concern. Despite the increasingly global nature of banks, the process of moving money from one account to another still needs to be tracked accurately and until recently, many funds did not have adequate controls on these movements. However, the internet has allowed much more accurate tracking and remote authorisation of funds from account to account which means that, in addition to the advantages of control, the true value of actually setting up these complicated structures can now be measured. It can now be calculated whether the cost of setting up the staffing of local offices, with the allied complications of many different companies and banking costs, outweighs the tax savings through the arrangement.

Property agents

Of all the players in the property market, property agents have probably changed the most over the last 10 years. Originally starting out in the 18th and 19th centuries as "the Landlord's men", responsible for rent arrears and often seen in the same light as tax collectors, the profession has developed into many different specialisms. It is still common to mock the estate agent, without whom many jokes about unprofessional practice would have no punch line, but the increasingly global nature of property investment has led to the rapid development of the profession and an exponential growth in the need for information.

In their attempts to differentiate their firm from the competition, the terms used to describe what agents do varies enormously. The traditional way that UK agencies have described themselves, Chartered Surveyors, has in many cases given way to Property Consultants or Advisors as firms have become global. However, in the US for example, companies trade as "brokers", and "appraisers" deal with valuations.

Regardless of the terminology used, the basic property advisor types remain similar across most markets. Let's look at the most usual split of disciplines within commercial agents and consultants.

Agency/Brokerage

Traditionally it is the agents (brokers), especially the investment agents, who provide the super profits for firms in the good years of frequent transactions[6]. Good agents are worth their weight in gold but often need teams of slightly less talented colleagues as support to their large deals.

Often difficult to manage, agents are the prima donnas of the business. Good agents rely on their own knowledge and contacts and many, many projects to capture some of this knowledge for the good of the firm have failed because agents are often disinclined to write things down.

6 Interestingly, this may be changing in the global advisory companies where corporate occupier account managers now often gain more prestige for their annuity management contracts.

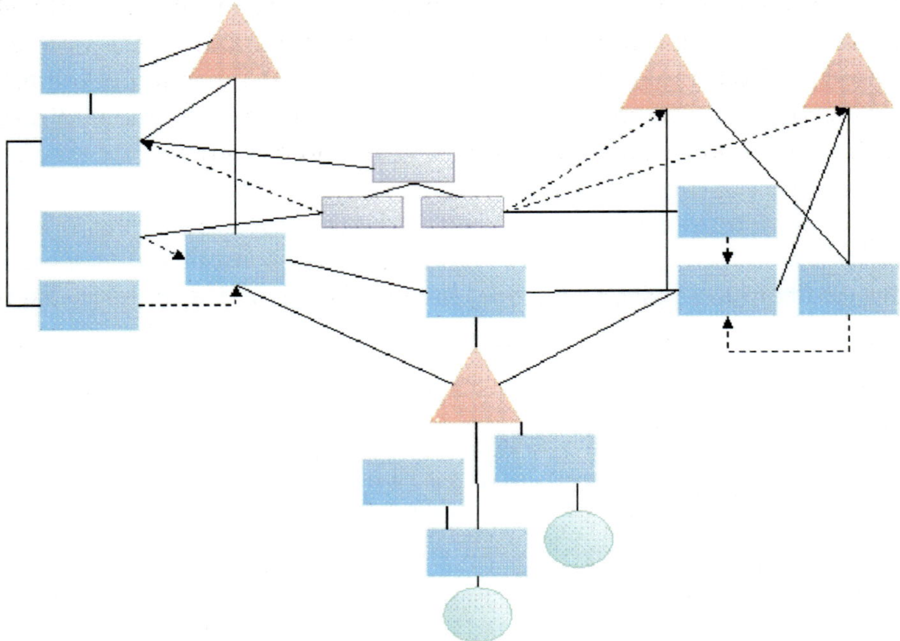

Figure 1.2 Example tax structure for a property fund. Each cash transfer between blocks and triangles needs to be monitored.

The information requirements for letting agents and investment agents differ slightly. For example, letting agents, once instructed, will want to get the details of the property to as many people in the market as possible. The circulation of brochures and requirements sheets to 500 London agents which used to be done by Estate Agents Clearing House each day is now more efficiently carried out over the internet. PRIDE, Prime Pitch, UKPiP and Estates Gazette Property Link (EGPL) provide online property registers for commercial lettings.

The investment agents will tell you, however, that the act of publicising an investment too widely will put off the best buyers who will pay top dollar for a property that is not widely marketed. Introduction sites such as Propex cater for this by supplying an environment where an introducing agent can select his targets carefully and other agents can register the investment with buyers knowing that if they are first, their fee will be recognised if the transaction is successful.

The advance that the use of Propex has made in the investment agency business is that it has used one of the few drivers of the investment agent to get him to log property details in an electronic format – the agents desire to get introductions, and hence fees, registered with a potential buyer has led to agents preparing electronic particulars which can be used on Propex. Once the details are in a standard electronic form, they can be used elsewhere and the problems of inaccurate data and duplicate entry of information can start to be addressed.

Other advantages of electronic data can be found in setting up the original instruction. The information can be transferred directly from the property management system of the agent or his client without retyping. This can reduce the time taken to get the property to market and can form the basis for online collaboration tools which allow all parties to a transaction to access the most up-to-date information and documents.

Property Management

There are many definitions of property management. The following are the most common.

1. Asset Management – usually the management of property at a portfolio level, often looking at strategic goals and defining the type of investment to be made.
2. Estate Management – this is the function that deals with lease management and property management accounting. This is the traditional view of property management in the UK because most commercial properties are let on FRI leases and the property maintenance requirement is limited.
3. Facilities Management – which has developed largely out of the occupier sector, deals with much more detail of property ownership and occupation and will cover both planned and reactive maintenance as well as functions such as move management and Health and Safety.
4. Fixed Asset Management – often confusingly called Asset Management, this deals with non-real property. For example, the utilities companies own large numbers of assets such as pumping stations, pumps and a pipe network. Corporate occupiers also often have a far greater value of plant to manage than the buildings are worth in their portfolio. These assets need to be labelled, logged and maintained and Fixed Asset Management deals with these types of assets.

All these types of property management need systems and processes but in the UK the two definitions still most relevant to the work of property consultants are the first two: Asset Management and Estate Management. We have covered the information requirements of asset management above and therefore cover estate management here.

As the most intensive users of business applications the estate management team will have automated systems for collecting rent and service charge, a terrier of property lease details and a diary system to remind them when to schedule tasks.

We should expect that the basic functions of collecting rent, managing and reconciling the service charge and accounting to clients will be done effectively but this is not always the case. Often dissatisfaction with a firm's performance in these areas is a prime reason for clients switching to another agent. For example, many clients are now imposing a deadline of 12 weeks on their agents to close the service charge accounts each year. However, anecdotal evidence suggests that the average is still 20 weeks.

Estate management is considered to be a low margin, labour intensive business, and traditionally, many firms have admitted to supporting property management teams only because they are a source of agency and rent review instructions. One story tells of an agent who offered to take on the estate management of a portfolio of 20 properties for £1 pa on the condition that they received all the rent review, lease renewal and agency work from the portfolio.

If this is the general view of property management, it makes sense to minimise the cost of this function by automating the processes as much as possible and reducing the headcount necessary to run the service. This is possible but rarely done because of the capital investment and upheaval required.

Alternatively, or additionally, the estate management team can be seen as a sales division for the firm since they have regular contact over a five-year period with a significant number of buyers or influencers in key clients. Here is a prime opportunity for a firm to use its inside knowledge of their regular clients to keep in regular contact with relevant information and manage the relationship to gain an increased share of the client's business.

There is little time left for the traditional property agents to address this. The market is beginning to see specialists in particular aspects of estate management enter the market and the all-in-one approach of many agents may be slowly unravelled as clients choose one company to deal with service charges and another to host their property information. Yet another will deal with treasury and all these will work together over the internet using integrated management systems.

Valuation and professional services

One of the most obvious parts of the property industry to benefit from improved information flows is the valuations team. This team receives large quantities of data about property portfolios, updates the details and valuations and passes the data back to the client.

This data can be passed backwards and forwards electronically and it is not surprising to learn that some of the first uses for PISCES (Property Information Systems Common Exchange Standard) was within the field of valuation programs and their link to property management systems.

Unfortunately, this useful first step has not been exploited in other parts of the property firms. The existence of so much property information in an electronic format which is checked for accuracy each year should be an excellent basis for developing a property terrier of all of a firm's client property holdings.

The same applies to the professional teams, those teams that deal with rent reviews and lease renewals. Here the comparable information they use to support their valuations within negotiations and in court are more accurate and more comprehensively detailed than that of their agency colleagues. This again can form the basis for an invaluable databank of property knowledge.

There is always an argument that much of the information used in litigation is privileged but it would be easy to build in safeguards for this type of data.

A sadly lost opportunity in the West End occurred at one large firm that held details on paper of every property inspected over the previous 40 years. The switch to digital systems elsewhere in the firm left this archive behind. The data has never been adequately replaced. For companies whose main reason for existence is their in-depth knowledge of property, the general lack of co-ordinated databases of basic property information is a woeful oversight.

Corporate occupiers

The last 10 years has seen an enormous increase in the property market's concentration on corporate occupiers. This sector comprises companies which need to occupy property for their business but which do not make money primarily from trading in property. Technology companies need offices where their software designers can work, pharmaceuticals companies need manufacturing facilities and retailers need shops in every high street from which to trade.

Clearly, new technology such as the pervasive internet and mobile communications is changing companies' requirements for occupational property but the need for someone at the company to understand, and arrange the management of, the property holdings remains intact.

The major difference between investors and occupiers is that investors see property as an asset to be improved; occupiers see property as a liability to be minimised. There are many examples of retail companies developing freehold portfolios and office based companies that have put their property into their pension fund for well thought out tax reasons. However, this takes nothing away from the argument that the over-riding requirement for a property manager of an occupational estate is to minimise the risk and cost in using property. The ownership presents complications that should not distract the managers from their basic role.

My stand that occupiers seek to minimise liability usually elicits a long argument from property managers who claim that they can enhance asset values while building a portfolio specifically for their retailer/manufacturer, etc. That is an argument for another essay. However, property investment requires a different set of skills to retailing, for example, but the basic principle of "sticking to the knitting" in both cases holds true.

Let's take a retailer as an example to see what information he will require. His property selection will be driven by the market for the goods he sells. If the company's stock sells well in northern market towns, he will seek the best positions in northern market towns and will, if necessary, outbid competition for the best trading pitch. Market knowledge from local agents is important, as is the business model of competing retailers who may want that site. If the site is within a shopping centre, the bid may include an element of turnover rent and regular trading information will also be required at a unit level.

The new site needs to be fitted out and this capital project needs to be procured and project managed. The information from the project needs to be fed back to the budgets that were prepared by the retailers driving this acquisition.

Once the store is open, there will be no property manager on site and therefore the store manager needs a central call centre / help-desk through which he can report damage to the store or new works that need to be undertaken. The manager will need to arrange regular cleaning and minor electrical works and the property manager may be responsible for centralised contracts on each of these items.

The occupier property manager will also be far more interested in keeping a record of tenant's improvements so that these do not become part of the rent at the next review and in keeping the property in good order so that the Landlord cannot sue for dilapidations at lease end. He is therefore closely involved in facilities management and the crossover to capital projects and construction.

Office occupiers will be interested in the layout of their offices and calculations about space use. Useful tools for this include Computer Aided Design (CAD) systems and Computer Aided Facilities Management (CAFM) systems. These systems are generally different from estate management systems and they are rarely integrated with traditional lease management and billing systems. Several suppliers are now seeking to address this and better solutions will emerge over time.

Property management teams within corporate occupiers are often relatively small and they rely to a great extent on external consultants and contractors. The gathering of information from these external parties is time consuming and, despite the increasing capability of systems to exchange data, the majority of occupiers still do not have direct data integration with their suppliers. Here is a significant opportunity for the suppliers of professional services to the corporate occupier sector. If they could minimise the detailed data management for their corporate client, the client could spend more time managing the portfolio strategically with their retail managers, thus improving their position in the company.

The provision of this type of service need not be through becoming a software developer or a Value Added Reseller (VAR) of systems – few property advisors have the experience or expertise to operate as a software company. Simply by providing well thought out reports, complete transparency of information and the ability to easily transfer data should provide compelling differentiation in the current market.

Recent research by Gerald Eve[7] showed that the majority of corporate occupiers who outsource the management of their portfolio do so to free up their time to concentrate on strategic matters. They cannot spend more time on strategic management if the information that is sent to them is in several parts and requires re-keying to become part of management reports.

A further development in the last five years is that many larger occupiers have outsourced not only the provision of property services to an external organisation, but

7 Gerald Eve – Outsourcing Corporate Property Management, April 2004

also the provision of the property itself. This was pioneered by Central Government in the UK as a means to take property assets off the balance sheet and is discussed in more detail in "Government" below. Private sector companies that have followed this route include BT, Aviva and Abbey.

The implication of passing the provision of property to an external provider is that the corporate occupier has to be much clearer about the space needs of the business over five, 10 and 15 years, the service provision required in that time, and how to measure the performance of property in the business. This same rigour can be and, in some cases has been, applied to portfolios which have not been outsourced and has led to an increased understanding of how corporate portfolios work.

This comes at a time when technology is enabling companies to use far less office space, send production and call centres overseas and take retailing online. Now, more than ever before, property liabilities need to be minimised and direct investment in property as a user is considered to be a rather short-term approach. Is new technology enabling this change or being used as a result of the changes? It is, as ever, a combination of both and the pioneers in using technology effectively are, as we shall see, beginning to stretch their lead over the competition.

Government – central and local

Central and local government are both owners and users of property although, in the UK, recent years have seen a massive divestment of freehold property by local government because each council has been allowed to keep a substantial portion of property sales to balance their budgets.

Property types within this sector are diverse ranging from traditional office buildings to educational, recreational and community uses. Many information management initiatives have started in one sector of their holdings and spread to the others.

There has been increasing emphasis on the effective management of property assets and the introduction of Asset Management Plans (AMPs) and, until recently, their annual review has at the very least provided an understanding of what assets local government owns and manages.

Local government is changing in several ways.

1. Much investment is being made in the configuration of front and back office functions. Most of this concerns improvements in the efficiency of dealing with customers and call centres; enquirer self-service and IT are all reducing face to face enquiries where possible.
2. The actual offices are changing as customer service points become more diverse and decentralised.
3. Flexible working is not yet widespread but will develop, changing the way in which information is stored and distributed internally.

4. There is a transfer of expenditure from the property portfolio to IT. The repairs backlog will not go away entirely but the reduction in the need for a centrally located property portfolio is slowly diminishing.

Central government is changing in many similar ways although decentralisation of operations receives far higher exposure in the press because of its larger scale and scope for radical change.

Although asset management is key to these changes, the key constraint in this sector is still cash. Even if a sound business case can be formulated to spend money on improving asset management, the case needs to compete with other, more public facing requirements for funding. Even with the direct encouragement of Central Government, annual reviews and ratings tables for the quality of AMPs have achieved only patchy improvements in asset management.

Local government, like corporate occupiers, usually has a mix of investment and occupational properties and therefore their information management needs are similar. This means that their information requirements cross from estate management and rental billing through to facilities management and property maintenance. The AMP process has also addressed the issues of disabled access, environmentally friendly buildings and the energy use within the portfolio and these measures were given earlier emphasis than in other sectors.

The issue of outsourcing looms large in the public sector. Both residential holdings and operational commercial portfolios have been sold to the private sector alongside contracts for the authorities to use the property for long periods of time. These schemes can be on the Private Finance Initiative (PFI) or Public Private Partnership (PPP) schemes.

Divestment of properties in this way has a number of advantages.

1. The authority receives a large capital receipt for the properties it sells and this can be used in part against annual budgets.
2. The Government generally aims to reduce its asset base and by doing this is able to provide its services with fewer assets.
3. The properties are maintained by the public sector to a required minimum standard that should be more efficiently undertaken by private sector companies with national coverage rather than authorities with only local coverage. Rightly or wrongly, experience of and expertise in managing property is often perceived to be greater within the private sector.
4. Private sector companies have the flexibility to trade and raise finance on properties as long as the minimum service requirements are maintained.
5. The authority requires fewer direct staff to manage its affairs and the private sector company bears responsibility for all TUPE[8] requirements.

8 Transfer of Undertakings (Protection of Employment) Regulations 1981

6. This movement to outsourcing the provision of properties has, as mentioned above, been followed by the private sector and has lead to the emergence of new companies and consortiums of private sector companies who fund and manage these portfolios; the best known are Mapeley and LS Trillium.

These companies need to act like a property company in the way that they fund the purchase of large freehold portfolios but have to understand the intricacies of space management, help desks for maintenance and energy management. Consequently, their information requirements are the most complete and complex of all the sectors mentioned here.

Moving forward

Information about all aspects of property is extensive and varied. Traditionally, the companies that relied on property data above all else, the property companies, funds and agents, needed only to keep relatively small subsets of data. However, as cost cutting and business effectiveness initiatives continue their relentless pace in the public and private sectors, more information is needed – and on a regular and frequent basis.

Add to this the increasing demands from the expanding investment community and ever more statutory requirements, and it is easy to see why information requirements are uppermost in the minds of many property people.

The latest technology can significantly improve the management of information in the property world, yet often it fails to do so. How can we resolve this to allow property people to work more effectively and to take advantage of the business opportunities outlined in this chapter?

Let's start by looking at what individuals in the property industry have already achieved.

2 What IT is available and what are people using?

"OK, what should I buy?"

"Does it really matter which I system I choose?"

In the UK, there seems to be an extraordinarily large number of IT systems on the market for property professionals. At the Property Computer Show 2004 in London, there were more than 70 suppliers and Freeman's Property Service Providers directory lists more than 150 companies who supply the property software market. In the US there are more than 300 information system suppliers in the market.

These software companies cover a wide range of functionality and features but many property people remain convinced that the property software market only provides property management solutions.

Furthermore, property professionals are quick with criticisms that the property software suppliers fail to meet the needs of users and new entrants to market have frequently failed to achieve a substantial client base. This may be due to the quality of their product but, whether or not this is the case, the perception remains that property software is old-fashioned and even new solutions cannot be trusted.

This is obviously not a great position for the property software industry to be in. However, this is not all the fault of the software and good solutions have been implemented in many companies. As we will see later in this book, any effective implementation of a system relies on both the technology itself and a change in business processes.

Let's start, therefore, with the traditional property management sector and then expand our horizons to look at solutions in use in the most innovative property organisations.

Property management – the software landscape

We defined a number of terms for property management in Chapter 1: namely, Asset Management (AM), Estates Management (EM), Facilities Management (FM) and Fixed Asset Management (FAM). These are useful for structuring a look at property management systems.

The majority of traditional systems in the UK provide functionality for estates managers. This is typically lease management, diary functions and rent/service charge collection.

However, with the increased emphasis on management of corporate assets over the last 10 years, functionality of the larger systems has increased to cover areas that were not traditionally provided by EM systems. This in turn has allowed the EM systems to encroach on the markets of FM systems and, sometimes, FAM systems. The FM software suppliers have also sought to expand their functionality, as have the FAM suppliers.

This constant vying for market position among the property software providers is confused further by the large accounting software suppliers, particularly the enterprise systems, which have produced specific functionality for all these sectors.

We therefore have a multitude of systems[1] from differing backgrounds all providing overlapping functionality.

The resulting overlaps are shown in Figure 2.1. You will see that in this diagram, AM is replaced by accounting systems. The reason for this is that software support for financial asset management is ill defined and tends to be supported by specialist packages. In many cases development of accounting functionality to cover these requirements is common and hence, the adoption of accounting packages for this area produces a more coherent approach.

Clearly, this is not a complete and detailed analysis of the property software industry but it serves to illustrate the complexities of the question, "Which software is best for me?"

Often the drivers for choosing a particular type or brand of software derive from a combination of the following:

Current software

The type of software already in use in an organisation. Particularly in large organisations, there may be very good reasons for choosing to extend the functionality of an existing accounting package to cover the property team's requirements. Of paramount importance to many companies is integration of information from one department to another and this is exactly what many enterprise solutions promise.

Accounting Structure

There are companies, such as many managing agents and some corporate occupiers, who want completely separate accounting systems for their corporate and property

1 A list of systems with contact details can be found at www.itforpropertypeople.com

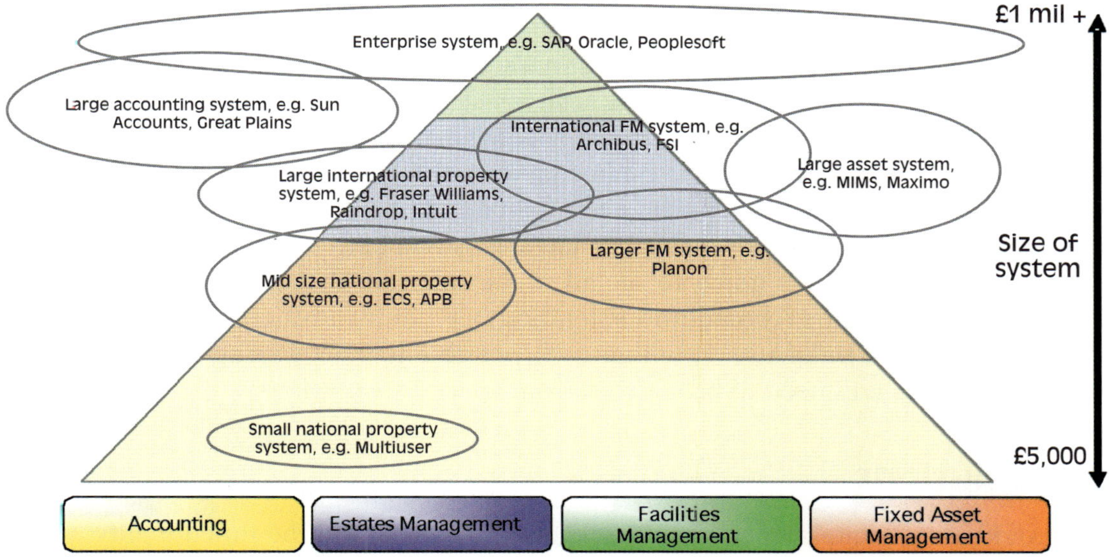

Figure 2.1 Property management software landscape

accounting. Others, property companies perhaps, will want a completely integrated system. A requirement based around property accounting requirements alone is likely to be satisfied by estates management software. However, corporate accounting support in the property packages is often patchy and will not match the generic accounting systems.

FM functions

The corporate occupiers in particular have a need to manage the maintenance and capital project requirements of a large portfolio. Facilities management often drives this set of requirements and, if the property accounting is run in the corporate accounting system, as is often the case, a facilities management system may be most appropriate. CADFM systems, with FM functionality based around a CAD package may also be useful.

FAM functions

If the management of all assets, not just real property is the objective, specific functionality and data fields to match property leases may be less important than being able to track the life cycle of plant and machinery. Utilities and transport are two areas where the pressure to invest in property systems is driven by a need to control all assets, not just real property.

Despite these differences in approach, most medium to large systems will be capable of being modified to provide, say, 50% of functionality across a wide range of requirements. Given that many organisations have traditionally relied on systems providing less than 40% fit with requirements[2], almost all new systems are capable of improving the business.

It is therefore often easier to predict the type of system which will be chosen by looking at the background and training of the estate manager, than by looking at the functionality.

Despite this, it is best at an early stage to retain an open mind in respect of the type of system required and then narrow the focus later. This will help to ensure that all possible solutions are considered. By going to see all of the software that might offer a solution, you will be able to develop a broad understanding of what features are generic and which specialist areas might be of use. It will also be possible to start getting an indication of which functionality will need to be sourced from specialist suppliers.

Other solutions

Many providers of estate management packages have increased the functionality offered by their packages to fill gaps in the market. Some have provided software to value and analyse property portfolios. Others have provided help desk solutions. Others still have concentrated on automating the accounting functions more effectively and integrating to electronic payment systems.

However, few have expanded effectively into areas such as agency or customer relationship management. Very few have looked at providing online collaboration tools or the infrastructure for knowledge management. Furthermore, the specialist applications for areas such as valuations and electronic payments are often more acceptable and more effective if ways can be found of integrating them into the company's property processes.

The range of property functions is vast. The possibility of choosing a system that only supports part of your business is just as great.

One of the mistakes that is often made is to allow the suppliers of packaged property management systems to drive the process of choosing IT support. It is important to start by looking at what is available to find new ideas; however, before specifying a solution, we need to look at what the business actually needs.

As we will see later, unyielding devotion to providing software for the specific requirements of the company can be expensive, time consuming and risky. However, many of the most successful companies using property software have taken a step back from what is provided by the market, decided what would provide the best return on their investment and concentrated on that specific functionality.

Achieving the right balance is difficult and there are as many companies who use packaged solutions as the base for their solution as those who build their own. The following case studies illustrate some of the solutions that have been successful.

2 REMIT Survey 1997, Ernst & Young

The case studies

There follows a selection of stories that illustrate how organisations, both large and small, have found solutions to property business problems.

Jones Lang LaSalle shows how to achieve adoption of new IT – not by imposing a near perfect system that has been developed behind the scenes, but by involving the users in the design of the answer.

Equity Office Properties shows what can be achieved when a program re-engineers processes first and then adds IT – rather than by getting IT to work with old processes.

British Land has set up an organisation structure that allows new ideas and innovation to be captured from the business, and provides the funding and controls to make things happen.

Broadgate Estates has developed an online community for their tenants, which improves tenant retention. They have developed the necessary software but have avoided becoming an IT company.

Peel Holdings has taken a standard property management system and have developed it themselves to provide a far greater range of functionality than would be available off-the-shelf.

As a much smaller company than Equity Office Properties or Jones Lang LaSalle, Mayfield Property Consultants does not have the resources to build and maintain new systems. It has used the implementation of their property management system as a basis to procure support for all their IT. This is provided as one, easy to manage package from a single supplier.

Here's how these companies did it.

CASE STUDY

Jones Lang LaSalle

Capital Markets Exchange

Jones Lang LaSalle is one of the largest global property advisors and their property investment advisory department, known as the Capital Markets team, is one of the largest of any property firm across Europe.

In the early days of the dot.com boom, 1997 to 1998, Richard Auterac, Director of Jones Lang LaSalle's auction team, had experimented with online property marketing, incorporating the automation of his team's processes. This early project was called REACH, the Real Estate Auction Channel, and it had achieved a considerable amount of success with his team and, usefully for Jones Lang LaSalle, coverage in the UK property press.

Richard persuaded his colleagues in the Capital Markets team to consider a similar type of approach to their work and this resulted in a facilitated workshop among 22 Capital Markets directors from across Europe.

At that moment, it would be fair to say that the Capital Markets team were aware of the impending threat of the internet but most had no idea how they could use it for their own benefit. Indeed, the early part of the workshop session simply concentrated on bringing everyone up to speed with developments in other industries.

What emerged from the workshop was agreement to start building an internet platform which would:

- automate the process of creating sales particulars both online and in brochure format
- centralise a sales contact database for the marketing of the particulars
- hold transaction details and documents and allow Jones Lang LaSalle and their client to track progress.

An in-house team of developers developed the project and Version 1 of the Capital Markets eXchange (CMX) was launched approximately nine months after the original workshop.

CMX

Version 1 of CMX allowed the users to input property details into a standard web browser screen. This automatically generates a web brochure and sends a summary of the details to the client for checking and, if necessary, to the brochure designer. The brochure designer sends back draft artwork for circulation in the next day or so.

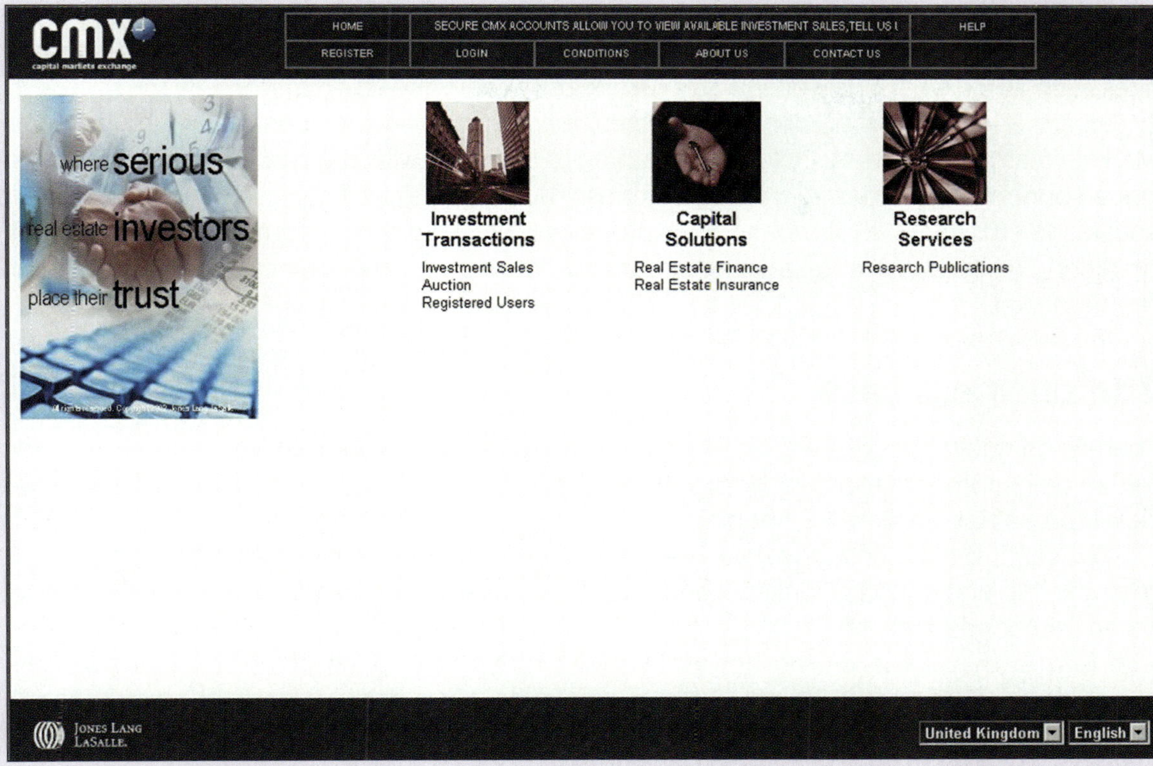

CMX Screenshot

As soon as the details and brochure are ready and authorised by the client, the mailing list is defined from those held in a central database. The centralisation of these records ensures that records are continually updated and, over time, the central database will become a fully comprehensive record of potential property investors registered with Jones Lang LaSalle.

The CMX application allows the agent to send out details electronically or by mail and then monitor responses. Interested parties can log on to the application to access the data they require on the property and request more details.

Version 2, launched a year later, provided more functionality, particularly around the ability to transact and monitor Buy-side investment deals.

This new functionality has re-affirmed that this is not a site which the market can just browse. CMX is a formal business-to-business site which is largely closed to the majority of casual enquiries. The central database now has over 7,000 registered investors and other agents need to be invited into CMX for particular transactions. If another agent's client withdraws from the purchase of an advertised property, CMX access can also be withdrawn from that agent.

Maintaining strict access controls to the site has allowed the site to develop as a tool for Jones Lang LaSalle rather than competing head-to-head with commercial marketing and listing sites such as UKPiP or Primepitch in the UK, or Loopnet in the US.

Richard Shepherd-Cross, one of the champions for CMX in the Jones Lang LaSalle Capital Markets team, comments, "Building something to compete with the commercial listing sites is not an option we considered. We wanted to use the processes we know well and improve their speed and efficiency. CMX is not simply a property listing service; it automates the elements of marketing real estate that take up time, but adds little to the advice we can provide as experts in the market."

The business case

There is no doubt that this was an extensive exercise for Jones Lang LaSalle to undertake. The initial development took four programmers nine months to complete and further development for Version 2 is ongoing.

How could this be cost effective when the Capital Markets team could more cheaply buy membership and subscriptions to commercially available online marketing solutions such as those mentioned above?

It is true that some of the benefits realised could have been achieved by regular and effective use of commercial services. For example, the time taken to produce a brochure and send it to the market has been reduced from an average of 31 days to just under six days. This represents an 80% saving in elapsed time but there are now web-based services for doing this.

Shepherd-Cross: "The difference in CMX is that it replicates the way in which Jones Lang LaSalle works. CMX allows us to provide the same quality as our traditional processes would achieve, only faster. CMX also controls a number of different functions that we would have had to buy separately and then integrate. I do not think that we would have been able to achieve the same use of the system by using a commercial service."

In one case the brochure was sent out in just 24 hours; in another, full details of a 10-building portfolio were presented through CMX to the market in just two weeks. The portfolio was under offer one month later.

The information on CMX was so comprehensive that the offered price was achieved without deductions following due diligence. Shepherd-Cross adds, "Jones Lang LaSalle has always prided itself that the information put out to the market at an early stage of marketing is comprehensive and accurate. One of the great things about CMX is that this accuracy is maintained despite the dramatic reductions in timescale. We don't get 'price chips' where the buyer finds negotiating points within an inaccurate data pack."

Additionally, the savings in investment marketing costs have been shown to average £10,000 per sale.

Further savings and opportunities have been realised through the use of a central database of contacts. Agents can now concentrate on the marketing message and whether to limit the number of mailings rather than worrying about how to put together the most accurate list.

This centralisation of data within the Capital Markets team has led to far greater efficiency in dealing with a contact list populated by up to 100 Capital Markets staff. Most of us have been in large organisations which have tried to formalise the contacts database and it soon becomes out of date. Here, the database is just one part of an effective tool to directly earn fees – it is kept up to date automatically.

The other aspect of the underlying database is the capture of property details in a way that can be re-used later. At last the purchase orders for new filing cabinets and the retrieval of archive boxes will begin to slow. Digitised property details from elsewhere in the company can be used to generate sales particulars even quicker than the standard process and this will add to the overall efficiency of the company. This linkage to other Jones Lang LaSalle systems is one great benefit of having their own application. The commercial offers will catch up, but they are not there yet.

The use of CMX to achieve real savings in marketing costs provides a key differentiator in promoting Jones Lang LaSalle's Capital Markets services. This has been picked up by the team especially among the more junior agents who find the benefits easy to sell.

The cost of marketing is not on its own going to influence a decision to appoint an agent. However, as a client, faced with two agents wanting to sell your building, and one offering a professional service plus a saving of £20,000, it is not hard to see how Jones Lang LaSalle are putting increased pressure on their competitors. Even where agents need to absorb the cost of marketing themselves, Jones Lang LaSalle are at an advantage; their lower costs will allow them to improve their profit margin.

By developing the system themselves, the agents had to become involved in its design and implementation. This process created buy-in from the team and within six months of the launch of Version 2, 80% of the team were using the software. This differs from a typical roll-out of an internet application in property organisations where take up can be patchy at best. There is often limited training and there is a reluctance to use a system in which few people from the organisation have had a say in development.

The Jones Lang LaSalle team started the process sceptical and largely ignorant of the potential for such a system. Now that CMX is embedded in the way they do business, it would be hard for them to return to the previous way of creating and circulating particulars. Thus, it matters less now which system they use: CMX or one which is commercially available.

However, the recent developments to this software have effectively locked them into CMX as a basis for their work. Many of the Jones Lang LaSalle agents use the other online services – they may need access to a particular type of contact or their client may insist on a particular service. However, by using CMX, the property data becomes part of the Jones Lang LaSalle database which they realise may reduce the time they spend on the next deal.

Alison Warburg, who is now in charge of developing the tool, comments, "The main difficulties with CMX were the same as any other new system; internal take up initially was poor. However, because we had spent time with key directors and managers and had accurately addressed their issues, we were able to show real life examples of how CMX would help the teams.

"We are really pleased with how well the project has been adopted. We have been in regular contact with offices in other countries to help them prepare for CMX and we are now converting the software for our leasing agency business."

Conclusion

Jones Lang LaSalle have taken a simple idea and tailored it to suit their own needs. It does not compete with listing sites; it improves the way Jones Lang LaSalle do business. Moreover, it has changed the way in which individual agents achieve success in marketing buildings and automatically captures the information they use. Real estate agents have traditionally not been effective at writing down the information for others to use and this system, with its benefits in saving the agent's time, achieves this goal unobtrusively.

Investment in commercial property has traditionally involved complex transactions and it is often said that these deals will not benefit from internet marketing. Importantly, this project focused on the automation of the time-consuming and mundane elements of marketing and CMX has therefore found acceptance.

An interesting by-product of this change in working practices is that, at the start of the project, no one could foresee lot sizes larger than £5m being part of the CMX system. It was seen as an adjunct to the auction process and for private investors. An indication of the success of this project is that within months, agents were using CMX for projects worth over £100m.

Jones Lang LaSalle's CMX provides a classic example of how new technology should be developed. The team looked at their processes to see what was time-consuming and mundane. They spent time with influential members of the team to inform them of the options and worked with them to develop the idea of automation. As a result the team wanted the change to occur and readily adopted the technology when it arrived.

This development works because the team designed it and they use it to sell their business. Despite alternatives being commercially available in the market to their competitors, it has put Jones Lang LaSalle ahead of the game. The trick now is to stay ahead.

CASE STUDY

Vicinitee

One of the great ideas of the dot.com era was the online community. The electronic bulletin boards of the IT industries evolved into online communities and offered the chance for all companies to communicate with their customers and clients over the Web.

By the year 2000 it was almost essential to start a community. Services sprang up overnight bringing together groups of people interested in everything from buying cars to discussing the latest technology.

In the real estate industry globally, many landlords looked at setting up communities for their tenants, providing:

- goods and services – enabling tenants to buy flowers, pizzas, travel, hire cars, etc
- local information and traffic news
- news feeds
- building services help desks – automated logging of repair and maintenance issues
- information libraries – easy access to building and contract-specific information.

The tenants gained access to relevant data and services. The landlords received the commission from sales that would fund the additional free services; or so the theory went.

Both sides benefit

The benefits were, and are, many. The landlord is able to provide additional services to the tenants, thus moving away from a simple "rent for property" business model. Both landlords and managing agents can show that they are adding value into the leasing contract. Tenants can use additional information provided to them at minimal cost and benefit from the online help desk.

The problem with the idea is the revenue model. Commission on goods and services pays pennies and most of the other information content either requires regular work to keep it up-to-date, extra salary costs, or must be bought from a supplier.

For many of the sites provided by service companies, this only became a real problem when the venture capitalists took their money away. The services that had been marketed on the basis that that they would cover their own costs have found it increasingly difficult to survive. In fact the majority have not survived and of the few that remain, some have adapted to different business models.

Services still in demand

There are still good reasons for the landlords and managing agents to provide the service. The landlord operators of these websites are finding that tenants often ask whether they can continue to use the services when they leave the estate.

Probably the best-known UK example of such a site is Broadgate Estate's Vicinitee. Vicinitee is the quintessential property idea. It was born over a drink in Cannes during the scrum of MIPIM. Like all the most technology-based ideas, its genesis lay not in technology itself, but in a desire to communicate.

Virtual representation

Vicinitee looks like an intranet system, somewhere between an electronic concierge and an online facilities management service. You could describe a building's Vicinitee system as a virtual representation of the building and its immediate environment, which the occupants can use to both increase the building's operational efficiency, and help employees enjoy their lives more.

How does it achieve this? Well, the site divides roughly into two separate sections. The first is the building management tools. This is, for the building owner, the real engine of the site. It's a central point for the management of everything from minor repairs to issuing licences for major building works. Even outside contractors can be given limited access to the site to allow them to check details of their work and upload reports.

The second, showier, part of the site is the occupier information service. On a prosaic level, this provides day-to-day property information needs, such as room-booking facilities or interfacing with the building management side of the website. Of more interest to most staff, and to the agents tempting occupiers into Vicinitee buildings, is the vast range of information about the local areas. This can include travel details (the Broadgate Vicinitee has a web-cam view of the departure boards at Liverpool Street station), events, shopping guides and special offers, and concierge services.

The secret of this is extensive research from a Vicinitee team to compile a comprehensive local shops and What's On-style guide to the area around each Vicinitee. It's this investment that can limit the site's use to other people. The time and money needed to assemble the database behind each Vicinitee restricts it to business parks or urban developments where there is a big enough critical mass of space to make it cost-effective. Of course, once that's done, adding another local building is not so costly.

The site was launched at Broadgate in 2001 and rolled out across the portfolio of buildings managed by Broadgate Estates. From 2003, Vicinitee has been available to third parties at what Vicinitee estimates to be "a few pence per employee per week". So far the concept has been spread to over 60 buildings in London, Blythe Valley Business Park in Birmingham and Allied London's' Skypark development in Glasgow. This gives a user base of more than 100,000 people in over 300 companies.

The Business Case

Antony Slumbers, founder and director of Vicinitee comments, "Vicinitee was founded on the precept that the levels of service provided to tenants by the property industry had to improve. In every other area of business the bar was constantly being raised in terms of value to the customer, but much of the property industry was stuck in a time warp of inefficiency and indifference towards their customers. To remain competitive, to increase the value of their "brand" and to differentiate themselves, forward thinking owners, developers and managers would demand the tools to improve customer service.

"At Vicinitee we looked closely at what services and products were required to stand apart from the crowd. We concentrated equally on systems and content: where did information bottlenecks exist, where could inefficient paper processes be removed, how do you build on and strengthen relationships with tenants? Critically, we aimed to allow Vicinitee users to greatly improve their customer service at minimal net cost.

"All product development has been based on real business need and Vicinitee now offers a wide range of modules that are simple to use, highly efficient and popular with occupiers, owners and managers alike."

Conclusion

This example raises two issues: first, and despite the high attrition rate in the early days, Vicinitee shows that communities can work for landlords and managing agents. Broadgate Estates and Vicinitee have concentrated on aspects of the community that will be attractive to tenants but they have not lost sight of what the community adds to their offering as building and portfolio managers. Ultimately, the role of Broadgate Estates is to improve the value of the estate: Vicinitee can help do this by retaining current tenants and forming an attractive additional feature to potential ones.

Broadgate Estate's investment has brought benefits from improved tenant relationships, lower costs and an enviable market-facing image. Against this, the site itself makes little profit and so may not function on a standalone basis. The benefit for Broadgate Estates has to be justified by the improvement in their business and the lowering of management costs.

The second point is that by partnering with Vicinitee, Broadgate Estates have mitigated the risks of setting up and running a software and services company. Broadgate Estates has provided input into the design and development of the services but has not allowed the development of Vicinitee to distract it from its core business of managing property. Broadgate's management style appears to be flexible enough to adapt to this but many traditional property companies and managers may struggle.

There are additional potential benefits to this structure. Broadgate Estates would be unlikely to develop the system and services for resale to other landlords on their own. However, with a partner such as Vicinitee taking care of support and maintenance, sales to third parties become a possibility – the benefits of which can be shared by Broadgate Estates. They also have control over how much of the functionality is sold on and may retain to the most-up-to-date features for itself.

Yet, given the uncertain overall revenue model, it will be interesting to see how these sites develop and whether they become a standard offering from the larger landlords in the next five years.

A last word from Antony Slumbers: "Quality costs money, and Vicinitee has made the required investment to create software and content of the highest quality. However the problems and issues Vicinitee addresses are common across the industry. Broadgate Estates and Vicinitee believe the market requires a dedicated, specialist supplier and by partnering with Vicinitee our clients receive a better, more professional and cost-effective solution than they could possibly achieve by going it alone."

Part of this case study was based on an article by Adam Tinworth first published in Estates Gazette.

CASE STUDY

Equity Office Properties

Business Process Transformation

Equity Office Properties Trust (NYSE:EOP) is the largest publicly traded office building investment trust (REIT) in the US. As of December 2003 the company owned and managed 684 office buildings in 27 US metropolitan markets[1].

It has achieved the position of being a Fortune Most Admired Company, and was the first real estate company to be named to the S&P 500.

Originally founded in 1976 when Sam Zell, the company's chairman, created an "integrated real estate management and acquisition organisation", EOP held its Initial Public Offering (IPO) in July 1997. Between 1997 and 2001 the company executed three of the largest mergers in the real estate industry and expanded its portfolio from 32.2 million square feet to 128.2 million square feet. At the end of the first quarter 2005 the company had a total market capitalisation of more than $27bn[2].

Managing this amount of property is a formidable achievement by any standards and EOP has implemented significant operating changes over the last three years.

EOP set out to build a platform for its business that focused on a portfolio level of management rather than a building level. Instead of the industry's traditional operating model that positions property managers as "jacks of all trades", EOP established dedicated teams to more efficiently manage process: everyday customer service requests, property accounting, procurement, parking, engineering, construction, telecommunications, security, tenant improvements and energy.

The company facilitated this new structure by centralising these functions – some at the regional level and some at the corporate level.

The new operating model streamlines the responsibilities of property managers, enabling them to get out from behind their desks, so they can focus on proactively serving customers and on cultivating relationships with them.

Using this approach, the company has also reduced the number of its vendors (HVAC, uniforms, janitorial services, etc), from 950 to 68, thus further streamlining both management and customer operating costs.

1 Equity Office Properties Trust 2003 Annual Report
2 Equity Office Properties Trust 2003 Annual Report

The use of technology

EOP's operations are underpinned by the effective use of information systems. Indeed, it would not be possible to manage such a vast portfolio across the US without an integrated technology platform. It is the combination of technology and the development of a new operating model that sets EOP apart from other real estate companies. EOP has fundamentally re-engineered the way in which it does business, and the company is using technology to automate and connect the new processes.

David Baruch is CIO of EOP. Formerly with Accenture, he has a background in assisting Fortune 500 companies develop and integrate large scale IT systems. David is concentrating on how EOP can apply best practices from other Fortune 500 companies and he says that combining technology with process change, "Business Integration" as he terms it, is the only way to implement robust change in a company. "It is a partnership", says Baruch, "and this partnership has to be strong. Technology without process changes brings no benefit. Technology enables the business to change the way it works."

Change in EOP was driven by a need to more fully leverage the company's unprecedented size and scale in real estate. Technology was seen as a vital tool in sharing information throughout the company, and with external stakeholders.

Behind the scenes, dealings with suppliers and consultants are also automated in the same way. Lawyers have access to systems so that they can more effectively deal with leasing and sales; suppliers have access to their account information.

Business process change

As EOP set out to change its operating model, it focused on improvements in the following areas:

- Customer service.
- Minimising costs.
- Maximising the sales channel.

EOP centralised its regional teams leading to a reduction from 169 to 48 offices. This allowed the company to share offices and regional functional teams, eg for accounting. Centralisation also facilitated the sharing of best practices and through proximity, strengthened the culture of the organisation. Finally, EOP achieved a cost reduction in headcount and was able to release its former office space.

Another part of the company's restructure was a shift to a portfolio-level management approach. For example, procurement and lease cycle times were both addressed with ambitious plans to drive out inefficient processes and to use web-based technology wherever possible.

In leasing, EOP significantly shortened its lease cycle time by simplifying its lease form and implementing a system with inherent transparency to prevent bottlenecks and back logs. EOP's revised lease form eliminated many of the more contentious clauses found in industry-standard leases and made the process easier for third party brokers representing tenants. The streamlined process saves customers time and money and helps them move into their office space more quickly.

Another area within EOP's new leasing and marketing strategy was a renewed focus on broker relations to maximise the company's sales channels; brokers represent 90% of the customers that sign leases with Equity Office. Among the company's new efforts are a revised broker commission policy, which now includes full commissions on all renewal and expansion leases, and full payment of commissions within 48 hours of lease signing.

Finally, EOP's new operating model reviewed technology. For example, wireless customer work orders and online systems were integrated into company processes. Changes were made to existing systems to allow them to link together around a common JD Edwards (now Oracle) system. Off-the-shelf systems were used where possible but bespoke work was done to the systems where necessary. The key factor was the improvement of processes and these were prioritised by the users, leading to greater buy-in and smoother change in working practices.

David Baruch, CIO, is addressing further upgrades to the systems, but is always in partnership with the internal business customers. For example, he says, "We are planning to consolidate the Accounts Receivable (AR) function and develop a Shared Service Centre (SSC) operation. The business changes, and estimates of the benefits, are being developed by the business teams themselves: we have to address the problem at the same time and develop solutions together.

"Similarly, we have new technologies to automate procurement but first, the business is spending time on re-engineering the way it works."

The business case

The objective of EOP's restructuring was to fully leverage this huge portfolio from the operations and sales perspectives. The re-organisation of the teams went a long way towards doing this but there is no doubt that web-based technology significantly helped the way that change was implemented.

The new model needed to deliver benefits in the areas of customer service, minimising costs and maximising the sales channel. Feedback from EOP's annual Voice of the Customer and Voice of the Broker surveys has shown a significant improvement.

For example, between 1998 and 2002, the company was averaging about a 45% retention rate. This increased in 2004 to roughly 60%. Moreover, in 2003, 70% of brokers surveyed said they were likely to do business with Equity Office, a significant increase from 59% in 2002. Given the size of the portfolio and the cost of commissions across that portfolio, the numbers here are significant.

These success stories support the business case for EOP's new operating platform, which is successful because of the alignment of the company's technology and business objectives.

Conclusion

EOP's approach to redefining the way it does business included changing underlying processes and using web technology to automate the platform. In doing so, EOP applied changes to the business first; the technology could then be applied where necessary.

Later in this book, we discuss in detail the case for identifying the critical issues in the business first and then addressing them with the most suitable technology. By combining the potential of technology with real change in the business processes undertaken, EOP have achieved considerable – and measurable – success.

Many of the changes could have been made without the new technology but their effect would not have been so pronounced. It is the combination of process change and the application of technology, which transformed the way EOP does business.

Thanks to David Baruch of EOP for providing the insights in this case study.

CASE STUDY

Peel Holdings

Developing packaged systems

Peel Holdings is a leading property and transport company in the UK with assets valued at over £2bn. Headquartered in The Trafford Centre, Manchester, the company has four divisions.

1. The Trafford Centre, an award winning regional shopping and leisure complex.
2. Peel Land & Property, owners of substantial property investment, development and land assets.
3. Peel Ports, operators of the ports of Clydeport and the Manchester Ship Canal.
4. Peel Airports, operators of airports at Liverpool, Durham Tees Valley, Robin Hood Doncaster Sheffield and Sheffield City.

Peel Land & Property (Peel) holds and manages general property investments, The Trafford Centre, and the ports and airports of the other group companies. Peel has a UK property investment and land portfolio consisting of five million sq ft of investment property and 14,000 acres of land. Overseas, Peel also has investments in Bermuda, The Bahamas and Spain. Peel chose Intuit MRI's property management solution to administer their property portfolios and this has been in place since 1997. Approximately 100 people have access to the system and this includes Peel's retained agents who have access to information to allow them to undertake rent reviews.

Beyond the basic system

Philip Doyle is responsible for developing the system at Peel. Philip is a property manager and it is this experience that has enabled him to effectively prioritise the system improvements that Peel has developed. Peel has heavily customised the basic Intuit MRI system that they originally installed. Straightforward amendments have included colour-coded screens and modifications that allow all leases and invoices to be scanned into the system.

They have also developed a system of "post-it" note flags that show up on the users' screens and are triggered by event dates logged in the system. Some of these adaptations have been engineered into the standard Intuit MRI offering over time but many remain unique to Peel.

More radically, Peel has developed functionality in the system that allows them to log and recharge water and telecoms costs at their properties. This functionality has allowed them to develop a position as landlords who can provide cost effective utilities to their tenants. Not only does this provide benefits for the tenants in terms of a one-stop service billed through their landlord, it is also a strong sales proposition to distinguish them from other landlords. In this way, Peel is achieving some of the benefits of tenant retention targeted by Broadgate[1] and Equity Office Properties[2].

Peel are enthusiastic members of the Intuit MRI user group which is held quarterly and this allows them to keep up to date with latest developments and feed back their own experiences. The knowledge gained from these sessions allows Philip to judge whether new developments to the system should be undertaken internally or whether there might be a solution developed for others that would fit their requirements.

Intuit MRI considers that Peel Holdings is ahead of many other users of their system because of the attention they pay to developing new functions and features. You might expect them to be disappointed that the system has been developed by the customer rather than by Intuit MRI's own software developers, but MRI are supportive because this shows how far customers can develop functionality around the basic package.

MRI encourages customers to use their ApplicationToolKit, a software tool that allows customers to change almost any part of the software and still retain that functionality when the software is upgraded. Philip underwent the training required to use the ApplicationToolKit and now has the flexibility to develop whatever changes they need. Hence Peel remains one of Intuit MRI's key references sites.

Benefits

The internal focus of prioritising and developing new functions means that once work is agreed, the developers can concentrate on delivering the new software; often this means it can be done faster than by using external developers and changes and teething troubles can be reviewed quickly.

Philip comments, "The usual problems of defining software for developers are overcome easily because the development team know the users. It is often more difficult to get the users to adopt the new ideas than to produce useful software."

Ideas raised, including mapping the portfolio to CAD drawings, have in the past been dropped because the users were as yet uninterested, despite Philip's estimates of time saving and added value through these features. On the whole, though, most new initiatives have been welcomed and it has become increasingly easy to rollout new functions.

Conclusion

Many property companies buy packaged software and, with effective implementation, it will usually work well. However, the best fit that most companies can expect of software "out of

1 See case study, page 41
2 See case study, page 45

the box" will be 60-70%. Peel has taken the route of developing the last 30% for themselves and has shown that this approach works for them.

As more companies develop functionality to, for example, improve their relationships with their tenants, more software vendors will develop this into their basic package. This should improve the fit of the software in more companies. However, as each property company seeks to differentiate itself in a competitive market, the number of differing types of software improvement is likely to increase. The bar is continually raised.

This creates further dilemmas of choice for the software vendors and may leave companies without the exact solution they need. Although Peel may suffer from being at the leading edge of development of new solutions, Philip Doyle's close relationship with the users should reduce the number of possible false starts and keep Peel ahead.

This example shows that a proactive approach can work and that it is often supported by software vendors. The continual development of new functionality by customers will not only push the vendors to improve their products, but will also provide useful feedback on what provides good return on investment for customers.

What would happen if Peel had no software development team? Peel may rely on Intuit MRI to provide programming resource and this is likely to increase the cost and reduce flexibility. However, the risks of resourcing the team itself might be lessened and, in theory, the new software development cost may be spread over more than one customer.

The message from this example is that software can, and should, be continually developed to support business initiatives; packaged software is a good starting point from which to build your own, and if necessary unique, information system.

CASE STUDY

Mayfield Property Consultants

Managed Service Provider

Mayfield Property Consultants is a 12-person property management company based in London. The company was founded in 1996 with three people and has grown over the last nine years to the point where it is now managing £800m of assets for a number of clients. In addition to the management team of 12 there are six on-site building managers; a subsidiary security company of some 150 staff; a building surveying/project management company and a contracting company.

The company chose Trace Solution's TRAMPS property management software at the company start-up to manage their portfolios and this has grown with the company to the point where it was upgraded to the newer version of TRAMPS in 2004.

The system is available to all the central London staff and also to the six remote staff via a terminal server connection.

IT support

In 1996, being a small company, Mayfield relied almost entirely on Trace to resolve IT issues and to start with Caron Jawed, the Accounts Manager, was able to keep the IT support issues to a manageable portion of her role. This included keeping the servers on site and support for all the other software the company needed.

Because Trace had provided all the software, including office applications and e-mail, they were able to advise as matters arose on an ad hoc basis. However, by 2002, the internal IT management role had increased to become a significant demand on Caron's time and the company decided to look for a better way of resourcing the function. While the role was not full time, it needed enough of her attention to distract Caron from her "day-job".

The set of demands for resolving the IT function is not unusual for this type of organisation The company needed to reassure itself that:

- an expert would be available to fix problems as they occur
- the function should take a minimal amount of time from key internal staff, allowing them to concentrate on maximising the core business
- the function should be resourced at minimum cost.

An additional issue was that they needed to find external resources for this and Mayfield, like most small companies, did not have a good knowledge of the IT support market; choosing a supplier from the IT market felt risky to them.

Solution

Coincidentally, Caron had been meeting with Trace that was eager to upgrade Mayfield to their new TRAMPS product. They understood that Mayfield had a bigger set of problems to resolve than simply upgrading to a new version of a property management system and they suggested that they structure an IT Facilities Management (FM) contract to deal with the IT support issues. Trace already had a good knowledge of Mayfield's IT background from the ad hoc support they provided and it was therefore straightforward to agree terms based on current usage.

Mayfield now rely on Trace for all their IT support and Trace, for example, organised all the IT elements of Mayfield's move to new office premises in 2004. All of the first-line help for any element of the IT systems is now taken care of by Trace's help desk and Trace's account manager usually visits the head office about once each quarter to ensure everything is going well.

Benefits

Tony McDonagh, Mayfield's Head of Management considers that the major benefit of the contract is as a type of insurance. "It is difficult to measure its value in day-to-day work because there is an absence of crisis; if it were not structured this way, who knows how many problems we would have experienced?

"We have had only one significant IT problem since the start of the contract. Although this took the system down, it was fixed quickly with very limited involvement from us; it would have been far more difficult without the contract in place."

Caron believes that the contract, for them, is in its early stages and they are happy to see how the arrangement develops. Because of their established relationship and mutual trust, the contracts was not tendered, nor are there complicated service levels agreed. "We accepted Trace's standard contract for this first agreement; we see the next stage of the contract as developing service level agreements now we understand more about the way the contract is running.

"We would also like to see Trace being more proactive and advising us how to start seeing new benefits from the way IT supports our business. There is a lot of potential for working closely with a supplier like this."

However, such change in the business is something Tony sees as an area in which potential issues may arise. "The contract ties all our IT support together and although this is convenient, our business will change and I would not like this support from one supplier to hinder our growth into new areas." Any new contract will therefore need to be flexible.

Conclusion

The property industry is predominantly made up of small and medium sized businesses with limited numbers of direct staff. The problem of how to achieve "big company" IT support in a small company is industry-wide. Here, Mayfield have leveraged an existing, trusted, business relationship to provide more complete IT cover. The FM contract has changed their internal roles away from IT fire fighting and back towards their core business; this in itself should result in both revenue and client service benefits.

Given Mayfield's focus on cost-effective support, it may at first seem strange that Mayfield were so trusting of Trace about pricing on the first contract. However, their focus on getting the service running and then reviewing the costs and benefits has allowed them to learn quickly.

This approach would not have been possible with an unknown provider; both Trace and Mayfield stand to benefit from enhancing their existing nine-year relationship.

Mayfield recognised that Trace would have been shortsighted to overcharge in this first year.

The current contract appears to work well and there are sufficient drivers for both parties to keep the relationship strong. Mayfield will benefit by regularising the contract against the market over time, perhaps by market testing in due course. Trace will have the opportunity to develop their services and the products they provide to help Mayfield grow and become more effective.

IT outsourcing in small companies often seems risky; letting important functions outside the business often seems to be relinquishing too much control. This is a useful example of how to take the first steps to outsource IT support without diving straight into the IT services market.

CASE STUDY

British Land

The Business Group

One of the difficulties facing all organisations is how to keep up with change. Fear of wasting money on failure is omnipresent and we saw how, in the frenzy of investment in e-business at the turn of the century, many property organisations invested in businesses that did not succeed.

How can we realistically select an investment to improve the business when outcomes are uncertain and technology fashions in particular can change direction with alarming speed and regularity? The company's core business is property, not technology, and even in related fields such as retailing and logistics, it is difficult to keep pace with innovation,

One response to this is to examine the way in which property owners invest in property. Very few large property companies invest in a single asset and then wait for it to produce an income. Rather, they collect a portfolio of different types of properties that produce different yields and which are likely to show different rental and capital growth characteristics. In this way they balance poor short-term performance in one property against high initial yields in another.

A similar approach is taken by venture capitalists when selecting their investments. In their case, one successful investment may pay for the development of 10 failures.

British Land (BL), one of the largest UK property companies, has taken a similar approach to dealing with innovation in their business. At the height of the dot.com boom they invested in many different ideas and, on the back of this experience, created the Business Group.

The threats to BL in not developing new initiatives are:

- that best use is not made of new management processes or systems and BL's costs of business exceed those of its competitors
- that competitors find more effective ways of producing non-property income from their portfolio.

Add to these threats the opportunity to take a step forward in management practices with successful initiatives, and the case for a separate team looks compelling.

The Business Group

BL created the Business Group as an internal team that would identify and co-ordinate opportunities to improve the business. The Group is intended to build on the strengths of BL across the whole company, particularly in its culture of innovation.

The principle objective of the Business Group is defined by the company as "to create, identify and develop commercial initiatives which enhance BL's core business and/or add value to the group."

This is not a part-time group who meet when possible to discuss trends: it is set up under a board director of the main company, Nick Ritblat, who acts as business sponsor. Justin Snoxall and Stephen Spooner, both directors of BL, manage the creation of business cases, and co-ordinate input of resources throughout the business.

The Group also includes directors of other departments on a part-time basis and thus the structure provides a mixture of innovation and general business management with in-depth property knowledge.

The key points about the structure and purpose of the Business Group can be summarised as follows.

- New initiatives relate to BL's principle businesses of property investment, development and management but are intended to create additional income or an enhancement in asset value.
- While responsible for managing a number of projects in its own right, the Business Group works closely with operational departments in BL.
- After initial development, any new projects not managed externally are ultimately to be managed within the Group's core business.
- Costs are controlled in the same way as they would be in the remainder of the BL Group companies.

New projects are proposed and discussed at the monthly Business Group meetings and each project has a named executive sponsor who takes responsibility for developing the initiative.

Example projects

The Business Group is not responsible for technology – that is the domain of the Information Systems (IS) department – but it does work with the IS team to initiate change brought through technology.

A key success for BL has been the introduction of The Accelerated Response Centre (The ARC) at Meadowhall shopping centre, near Sheffield in the UK. The ARC is a solution to the problem of retail tenants who would like to have more sales space but are confined to the existing size of the shopping centre units.

BL, through Meadowhall, have partnered with Excel Logistics to provide storage space for retail stock within walking distance of the centre. The benefits are manifold.

- Deliveries to The ARC can be more flexible than within the centre and also, more frequent replenishment of stock can be achieved at the retail unit for fast moving items.
- Pre-merchandising activity can be undertaken without losing sales staff to the back of the store.

- Retailers can use sophisticated stock management systems that may not be possible in a small unit stockroom.

More than 70 retailers have used The ARC and the following benefits have been found.

- One retailer has increased sales by 10% due to their use of the more flexible storage – they were able to hold a larger product range than they could with a single unit.
- Another tenant, USC, reduced shrinkage by 70% by using The ARC and their store beat target by 240%.

Many of the other individual initiatives are of comparatively small scale and it is the ability to co-ordinate the various teams involved which makes the Business Group approach successful. The Group's remit is wide ranging as can be seen from the following examples:

1 **Commercialisation at shopping centres and retail parks.** There is an opportunity to diversify the income from retail properties by increasing the number of directly controlled outlets. The Business Group has therefore set up a team with a third party to review how increased provision of vending machines, children's rides, posters, ATMs and car valet services could be used effectively.
2 **Building Information Modelling.** At 10 Exchange Square, a major office building in the Broadgate development, the Business Group has encouraged the development and use of a collaboration tool which has been used to create a 3D model to avoid clashes between pipe-work in the building's construction.
3 **Wireless Communications Group.** The Business Group, working with the IS department, are conducting some more creative, forward-looking ideas by considering the changes in wireless technology.

Importantly, though, the Group also uses its position as a central part of BL's structure to support and influence initiatives for the whole real estate industry. BL has been a founder member of cross-industry initiatives such as Asite (online construction procurement), High Speed Office (Broadband services to office tenants) and PISCES (Property Information System Common Exchange Standard).[1]

It is this last initiative, which seeks to set a standard data schema (data set) to enable property systems to swap data, that has formed the basis for much of BL's system development; the Business Group's sponsorship of the standard throughout BL and more widely in the UK and US property industries has helped bring about far greater understanding of the benefits of PISCES. It has also helped BL become an early adopter of leading practice in the way information flows through their business.

Stephen Spooner comments, "Since the Business Group was created, its focus has evolved and the proportion of projects undertaken internally has increased as we have learnt what projects need in order to be successful.

1 OSCRE (Open Standards Consortium for Real Estate) in the US.

"The important point about the group is that it builds on British Land's strengths and provides focus and support for ideas already being generated. The Group is not seen as an isolated think-tank and it is this integration with the business which is the key to its success."

Conclusion

BL has committed valuable resource to the Business Group and it has rewarded them with savings on existing construction projects, generation of untapped revenue, and better customer facing services.

These are projects that are unlikely to have been started without the intervention of a dedicated group. In most businesses, apparently straightforward projects are often left on one side through time pressures in day-to-day work and this example shows an effective mechanism for releasing value.

Furthermore, adoption of new techniques and technology often languishes unless an initial pilot is forced through. Here is a way of freeing logjams and introducing change from within the business.

Lastly, the process of developing new projects has been formalised and that gives comfort to the Board that their investment in risky new ventures is managed and can be audited.

In Chapter 9, I suggest ways of reducing or outsourcing the IT department in a property organisation and these departments often possess substantial business knowledge and understanding. Perhaps the creation of a Business Group from the "old" IT team would be an effective way of promoting and managing changes to the business.

3 How to make sense of it all

It is always difficult to know where to start. It is even more difficult to get a project started if your starting point is not a clean sheet. Most companies have inherited work practices and IT from previous generations that have taken a particular path. It may be difficult to see how to adopt latest thinking and IT from where you are at present.

There is an old joke about a motorist, completely lost, who asks a farmer how to get to a town about 20 miles away. "If I was you sir," drawls the farmer, "I wouldn't be starting from here at all." Hardly much use if your "destination" is a better set of working practices and you are "lost" with the wrong starting point for the new systems.

Whatever your previous ventures into systems, they will inevitably seem to be pointing you in the wrong direction. Deciding on a new direction and how best to turn around is only the start of your problems. Seeing the options clearly is the first step and this chapter looks at some tools to bring some clarity to the decision process.

We have seen how companies have grasped the opportunity to use new technology and change the way they do business. However, real life isn't always like that. The larger the organisation you work in, the more there will be internal meetings that seem to get in the way of doing real work.

If there *are* opportunities to improve the way you work, they compete with many other priorities that are already being discussed at internal meetings. The thought of creating more heat at meetings by suggesting yet more changes fills most people with dread.

It is also difficult to find the person responsible for authorising changes. Should the head of IT be involved, or the head of department? Should you seek out the sponsor of the last successful change project or should you go straight to the executive board?

So, large companies find change difficult. Yet, in small businesses, it is even more difficult to find time to consider improvements to the way the company works. Fewer people to help run day-to-day tasks usually means fewer hours to think strategically.

The problem is one of priority. The first priority is to keep the core business running, whether that is buying properties, managing portfolios or developing new buildings. Improvements in core business at best come in second place. But assuming that you can create enough time to consider new ideas, we discover the great barrier made up of those two letters; **IT**.

At this point most businessmen, let alone property professionals, go back to what they were working on before the subject came up. The letters IT conjure up images of daily PC problems, internet access headaches, that new piece of software which "just won't work", and failed IT projects.

The problems of choice

We often know enough to recognise broadly what IT could do for us if it were installed correctly. We have seen how Microsoft Office with its Word, Excel and PowerPoint applications works more often than not and allow us to dispense with highly skilled secretarial staff for most day-to-day needs.

It is this vision of how much easier our day-to-day life would be that drives most IT projects and without this vision, few people buy into the technology required for change. We deal with business cases and creating a shared desire for change in later chapters. However, the difference between office applications and business IT is that much of the benefit is dependent on many variables; when it comes to business IT, life becomes so much more confusing.

For example, a managing director (MD) I spoke to told me that his problem was simple; his plans were to double the size of the company in the next three years and he knew that he would need a new telephone system. Which should he choose? Oh, and he would also need to increase the capabilities of his accounting system in the same time period. Should he choose an enterprise system that could take over the property management team's requirements as well? Which system would do all that?

The conversation went on to cover mobile working, hosted solutions, flexible working, and came back to the telephone system.

Our MD had seen so many good ideas from so many different suppliers that paralysis had set in. Individually all the solutions seemed simple but how would they work together and, if he settled on one solution, would it be the best solution in all areas or just a compromise?

This problem of choice is deep-rooted and exists in all walks of life, not just in IT. It may be difficult to choose between Bluetooth™, Wifi or 3G as the company's mobile technology solution because of a lack of knowledge about the implications of each technology. But, even at a more basic level, many people have difficulty in knowing what to select and buy even in their local supermarket.

If we can look at the basic human problems of managing choices before examining technology, we can make the selection process much simpler.

Professor Barry Schwartz recently discussed this issue in his book, *The Paradox of Choice*[1]. He discusses the situation faced by many consumers when they must choose between maybe 20 brands of jam. Many consumers simply give up and defer their purchase. His research shows that a consumer faced with only six brands of jam is far more likely to make a selection. That might be useful to improve sales in a supermarket but where is the link to business IT?

Schwartz analysed the difficulties surrounding choice in great detail and suggests that consumers can be subdivided into two types.

Those who demand the absolute best and who agonise over their decision are called "Maximisers". The agonies of this type of consumer will be well known to anyone who has visited a high-end hi-fi shop. The consumer is faced with dozens, possibly hundreds, of solutions that will all satisfy the basic need to reproduce good quality sound. However, the maximiser will only be happy when he has the very best combination from the subtly different selections.

The other type of consumer will accept a solution that adequately does the job. This person Professor Schwartz calls a "Satisficer". This type of consumer can happily make his choice and move on, knowing that what he has chosen will "do the job".

You will be able to imagine the arguments that could ensue between maximisers and satisficers. Maximisers often think of satisficers as lazy or as compromisers. Satificers cannot bear the thought of the delay caused by the extreme analysis of options and the constant review of choices.

What can be even more frustrating is when several maximisers work together on a selection. The chance of them agreeing the criteria is remote and each will insist that their needs must be met in full before granting their assent. In my experience, professionals are often maximisers and this causes some of the greatest bottlenecks in choosing new technology.

A maximiser will argue that by "making do", nothing of worth will be achieved and will point to any number of examples of perfection being achieved through attention to detail. However, this is often a hidden excuse for taking no action.

One senior property industry figure with whom I once worked is famous for his attention to detail, and the properties with which he and his company have been involved are some of the finest in the UK. However, the motto he ingrained on our project was "80% is good enough". He wanted us to achieve 80% of what is possible and then move on.

In reality, 80% was far in excess of what the competition could achieve and by moving the project forward, it was implemented on time. It became reality whereas ultimate loyalty to perfection would have produced failure.

1 *The Paradox of Choice: Why More Is Less by Barry Schwartz*, 2005 – HarperCollins

Further justification for this approach comes from research carried out at Ernst & Young in 1997 and in the year 2000[2]. Two surveys were undertaken to find out how companies managed the information about their property holdings. The survey was completed by the Times Top 1000 companies in 1997 and by similar companies across 13 countries in Europe in 1999. One set of findings related to the use of the property management systems operated by the respondents. In both surveys, the use of the systems employed amounted to only 30–40% of their functionality. Any company that can achieve 80% of their requirement through effective implementation will therefore double the ability of their system compared with the competition.

The difficulty in achieving 100% is one of the main reasons that many software developers have taken to adopting Rapid Application Development (RAD) methods over the last few years.

The problem that RAD tries to solve is this: a traditional, or waterfall, development approach takes each element of the project in turn. In simplistic terms, the business analysis is completed to everyone's satisfaction, the design stage for the whole application is signed off, and the development team builds all aspects of the system together.

In a RAD approach, all functional areas of the project are split up into small parts and each function is analysed, designed, built, tested and rolled out. Delays in the early stages of one functional element are not allowed to delay milestones for the whole system. In this way the majority of the system is completed on time and the "last 20%" can be re-prioritised.

Our maximisers may not approve of this outcome but the majority of system users will appreciate that they will be able to get started on a more limited, but functional, system. Most of a system delivered today is usually better than the whole system delivered next year.

Clearly there are situations when the approach of a maximiser is essential. I suspect that there have been no winners of a Nobel Prize who settled for 80% and the health or aeronautics industries could not function without close to perfect performances. There will also be property organisations that can expect and impose perfection through strong leadership or culture.

Getting the balance right is essential but it is also important to recognise the difference in accepting 80% of the functionality as a compromise and achieving the implementation of that functionality on time and on budget. These elements are not exclusive and this differentiation allows us to see where companies can impose strong management disciplines (such as Six Sigma, where there is almost no compromise on quality) and define a functional level that achieves business goals but is not driven by absolute perfection. Furthermore, once the initial implementation has achieved these goals, the processes and systems can be refined in further phases as the business benefits of further development become clearer.

2 REMIT 1997 and Real Estate Management IT 2000, Ernst & Young

An increasing number of companies have accepted the challenge of Six Sigma, and having worked with Six Sigma teams in a consulting capacity, I know that it is effective. To achieve Six Sigma, a process must not produce more than 3.4 defects per million opportunities. This requires a complete change in the way projects are approached and reaps large benefits on major projects.

Even without Six Sigma, defining the functionality should involve a pragmatic set of decisions based on what is possible and this will form a firm basis for implementation.

The first thing to realise when trying to realise improvements in business is therefore "learn to love 80%". The term "satisficer" may not be an attractive one, but it often represents a pragmatic and realistic approach to dealing with IT.

Business applications, office applications and infrastructure

We have started to deal with the problems of choice through managing expectations and the next step is to start narrowing the range of options to deal with. The pragmatic approach to achieving the right result allows us to dismiss thoughts of achieving the nth degree of perfection in a new system. We can therefore start thinking about what improvement opportunities there are.

Therefore, the second stage of understanding where to start is to clearly establish which areas of technology a business manager can influence. The blocking letters "IT" provide a blanket over all things technological. As such, most business managers glaze over even if they have sufficient time to address the issue.

Typical excuses are:

- we have an IT department which will deal with all this
- it is bound to cost too much money and we have no budget this year
- why should we waste time and money? We did this before and had to replace the whole system within five years
- we won't be able to get the systems to talk to each other
- well, that's fine for my team but Mike's team will never change.

Part of the problem is that each participant in the discussion will have a different view of what is required. The IT manager has plenty of solutions but neither the budget nor the sponsorship to undertake them. Often, no one has explained clearly what they want, or why they want it. It is therefore convenient to blame the IT manager when the new systems fail to deliver.

Different departments will look at the same problem in different ways. For example, the property management team may require a new IT system which retains their ability to bill and reconcile monies due from tenants, but improves their reporting and the flow of documents around their team.

This new property management system could help the agency team access details of properties in preparation for sale or allow the investment team to run forecasting scenarios on the portfolio. However they all require different subsets of the information.

- The agency team will need basic data about the property that will reduce the time they take to prepare sales particulars.
- The investment team will need to add market trend data and comparable property details to the system.
- The management team will need to be able to calculate debtor days across the portfolio.

Additionally, none of the business managers will know if it is possible to link the information in the departments.

The IT manager will know that this is all possible at a price but how can he decide if that cost is reasonable in light of the perceived business benefits?

On top of this, there are other stakeholders and other types of IT in the organisation that require new investment. The bank of servers created by the IT department appears to "eat money" and the secretaries constantly insist that their copies of Word and PowerPoint do not link with newer versions in the business. The website, often the responsibility of the marketing department, has become unintelligible to most clients and nobody has been able to pick up their e-mails when they are away from the office since last week. In corporate occupier teams, their requirements need to compete with other business-critical requirements that don't even relate to property.

The simple answer given every time in this situation is that we need a strategy. It is the IT manager who gets given the opportunity to prove his worth by setting up a strategy to present to the board.

Inevitably, approval for the strategy and release of the necessary funds falls at the first hurdle when the cost for infrastructure is discussed. The response from the Board is, "Why do we need such heavy investment in IT? All we need is to connect a few bits of software."

It is this lack of understanding of the infrastructure of IT that needs to be stripped out of any discussion. The business must first discuss the real benefits available from implementing the right business solutions before deciding if the infrastructure is sufficient.

To over-use a common analogy, if you need a vehicle to take you two miles to the shops everyday, it is unlikely that you will choose a Formula One racing car. Your mechanics might enjoy the challenge of working on the latest thoroughbred engine but it will be entirely inappropriate and will break down when you need it most. However, a moped may not be your first choice if you need to regularly commute between London and Birmingham.

In the same way, it is worth spending some time discussing with the business managers where most of the value in their work is created or lost. To do this, the detailed technology is almost irrelevant. True, we may need to ask if Blackberry e-mail devices are the way forward for those people not in the office all day; however, it would be better ask "How do I access my e-mail when I am away from my desk?" The answer may be a Blackberry or it might be a different solution – perhaps, in the extreme, even through allowing you to work from a fixed desk for more of the day. The first stage of prioritising this is therefore to strip out areas of IT that are irrelevant to, or not understood by, the business managers.

An easy way of identifying where to spend most time in defining the new applications is to use the diagram below.

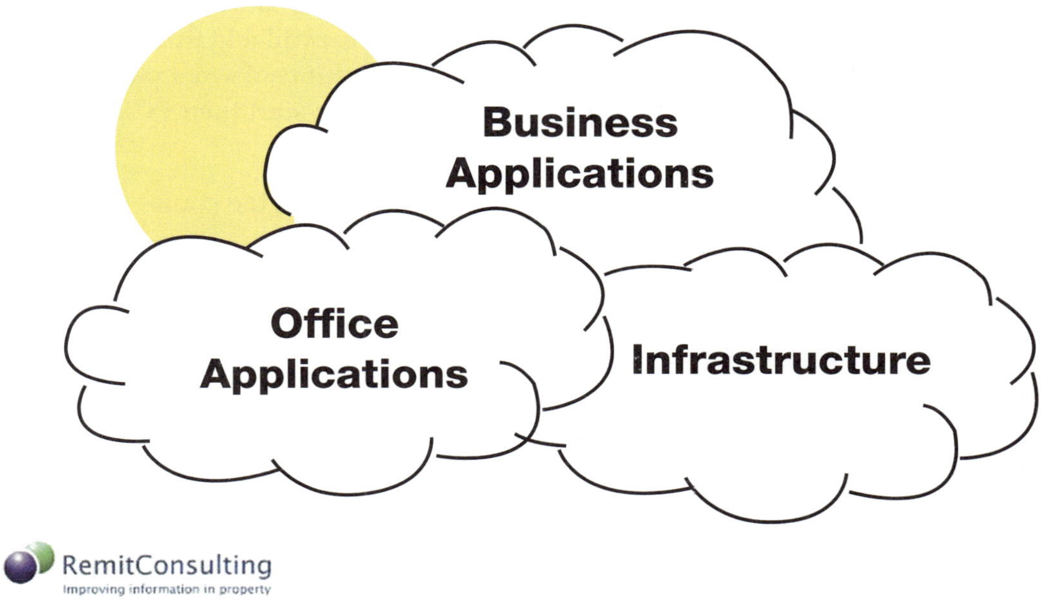

Figure 3.1 Three Clouds Analysis

The areas in the diagram above are the very simplest ways of breaking down all the aspects covered by IT in an organisation. As such, there will be debate over where particular solutions fit and this is useful. Without discussion of where to categorise individual items, it will be impossible to gain an understanding of the relative importance of solutions.

Office Applications

The best place to start is to define what is included within office applications. These applications in their simplest form comprise the usual suite of word processor, spreadsheet and presentation tools. This will usually be one of the versions of Microsoft Office but could be provided by Lotus, Ability Office or many others like Openoffice from a growing list built to work on Linux.

Also included in this section could be databases such as Microsoft Access, project management tools like MS Project, or design tools such as MS Visio. The Microsoft applications are most commonly used and are therefore useful to describe the types of tools in this section. However, many non-Microsoft tools are available in these categories and are often less expensive.

The property team typically uses all these applications every day. They are easy to deploy widely, often requiring little training, and user help is available through the Web or embedded in the application. They are the standard minimum software packages that property managers and their assistants expect to see when they start their PC or laptop.

Work required to maintain these packages is usually limited to:

- ensuring that sufficient licences are held by the company for all the copies of software in use
- buying additional software licences for new joiners
- arranging training on advanced features
- co-ordinating upgrades to the next release of the software.

The IT department need not do these tasks. They can be co-ordinated by one of the support staff and this is probably the defining factor of these software tools – they do not require detailed technical knowledge in order to get the best from them. A little training here will go a long way to reducing the demands on the IT function in the business. We will not always eliminate the need for the IT team support, however, this approach moves the responsibility for a number of straightforward applications to those who use them regularly and who know the issues which arise.

On that basis, it may be possible to include other IT applications. Maintenance of the website is often given to the marketing team for similar reasons to those above. This can also be covered in this group. Often, the intranet can similarly be taken out of the discussions about more complex IT, although as an enabler of more advanced project communications, this may remain within business applications, below.

In all these cases you may wish to centralise purchasing through the IT team and first line and technical support will probably still be provided through the help desk. However, the responsibility for making sure this type of software is available needs no detailed IT knowledge.

Infrastructure

Now we have excluded office applications, we need to do something about infrastructure. This section of the diagram includes all the software and hardware that needs to be dealt with behind the scenes and it is this group of IT that was probably the cause of hiring your first IT manager. No surveyor or businessman I have ever met in property has claimed to know anything about IT infrastructure and many IT managers have only a passing acquaintance with the more technical aspects of servers and networks. This is a subject of which I usually steer well clear and leave to the experts.

Typical requirements that need to be covered here are:

- Operations
  - Installation and Configuration
  - Performance management
  - Capacity Management
- Control
  - Standards
  - Network Architecture
  - Asset Management
  - Business Continuity Planning and Security
- User Support
  - Help desk
  - Applications support
  - Break fix

This is to name but a few of the areas which should be the responsibility of the IT team or whoever is appointed to manage the IT infrastructure[3].

A discussion at this level of detail among the owners and managers of the company is pointless. It is complex and requires an understanding of why the particular configuration for the current network was chosen.

Most business managers would understand that any decision made to, say, change the operating system from MS Windows to Linux, should be taken in full knowledge of the effect that this will have on the whole system. Likewise, the applications strategy for the company may have an effect on any business change. A new Voice over IP (VoIP) telephone system or the purchase of an enterprise accounting solution will need to be fitted to an existing infrastructure and this is best left to the technical team.

The aim with this group of requirements is to be able to provide a sufficiently clear understanding of the business needs so that the technical team can assess the impact on the existing system and define a plan to implement those requirements. Often the business managers will have come into the meeting to discuss a solution recommended to them by a third party or by someone they know of from a previous job. The result ultimately agreed at the meeting may not use exactly the technology suggested by these business managers, but it must provide the functionality required in an effective and flexible manner.

3 For more detail on this subject see Chapter 9

Except on grounds of cost, the means for providing new functionality, as opposed to infrastructure, should not be an opportunity for conflict between business and IT. If it is a source of conflict, the most usual cause is that the business requirements have not been defined clearly enough.

We should not underestimate the difficulties in justifying the cost of the infrastructure itself and this may prevent some improvements to functionality. However, at this stage of the discussion, we are concentrating on the decision process for new software applications; this analysis is intended to move the discussion away from areas about which the management have little direct knowledge.

The responsibility for providing infrastructure may be within the company if you have an IT team or, increasingly, it may be outsourced to a specialist provider. Regardless, keeping discussion about infrastructure to a minimum allows the business managers to decide which areas of the business are capable of significant improvement.

This leads us neatly to the last requirement area.

Business Applications

Business applications are all those items that are not covered above. They are the generic and specific software applications that have been bought to support the core activities of the business. They may cover requirements in accounting, property management, valuations or agency. They might manage lists of client details within a Customer Relationship Management (CRM) system or provide essential property market information through any one of a number of subscription services.

Despite having excluded two large areas of IT, the breadth of systems available is huge and it is this area where business managers can most effectively compete for scarce funds. Now that we have excluded infrastructure from the discussions, the decision process is much easier because, whatever application is chosen by the business managers, they will hand the decision to the IT team for validation and implementation.

This enables the business managers to concentrate on what is needed to grow the business or earn greater profits. Hence, discussions about the IT strategy can be related much more closely to the drivers of the business as a whole, rather than the constraints of the IT infrastructure.

Earlier, we discussed a managing director who asked how to upgrade his telephone system. Using the process of elimination outlined here he encouraged his directors to prioritise just two ways to improve the business for that year.

The first was to improve the flow of invoices around the business. They decided to review the process of authorising invoices and passing them for payment and by scanning all invoices as they arrived at the office they removed nearly a working month of labour from the process. The quick calculations they made based on wages and opportunity costs, estimated that savings of nearly £1m pa would arise from this improvement alone.

The second requirement they defined was to improve their management of client information by joining up client records across the firm. Again, significant process change would be required but they estimated that this should result in a 10-20% increase in business.

This shows the benefit of separating the various aspects of IT and concentrating on the business applications. The directors were comfortable discussing the aspects of the business they knew well and were well able to estimate the benefits that would accrue from the proposals. The IT manager was able to take away the ideas which had approval and then structure an approach to solving the requirement together with options and costings. Budgets can be fixed, timescales agreed.

The directors had defined the brief and the IT director could be left to deliver, taking into account the infrastructure and applications already in existence. Often, existing applications can be developed to deal with new functionality and, if this is the case, the IT manager is free to put a strong case for not using that new solution which may have come to the attention of a director.

Interestingly, the team in our example made no mention of the telephone system that had been the reason for the initial call. Since they had prioritised the drivers for the business, the directors asked that the IT manager put together a strategy for the next few years which addressed all their concerns and many more. A new telephone system was relegated to its proper place in the infrastructure plan and would be addressed in good time for its replacement. In the meantime, money would be saved from the business priorities.

Software support – Business functions

At a very high level, our property business has made a break with its past, concentrated on defining the areas of the business which will drive growth, and has given a list of priorities to the IT department. The IT team can make a start on defining a strategy and knows which new applications are needed and when. They also know the level of return the business needs on any new investment and therefore can estimate the budget they have with which to make changes.

If, as is often the case, it is not immediately clear where business priorities lie, the directors may need some more help in deciding what is possible and how they might develop their business. To do this, we can subdivide the business applications group in a number of ways and the most useful next step is to look at the different ways in which IT solutions could help the business.

Software solutions tend to be quite generic in their approach so that they can be sold to as many different businesses as possible. However, early property software packages tended to be developed for one particular client and suffered with their development as a result. Decisions on functionality often had to be unpicked when implemented by other property teams.

Over the past few years' things have changed and the property software market has now reached a balance between functionality that is property specific and the ability to apply general principles to an implementation.

This has meant that although a few companies still build their software from scratch, most business buy applications off-the-shelf from suppliers and occasionally use software from other industries. As a result it can be confusing to see solutions from both property and non-property suppliers, and they are all likely to use different terminology for the same function, or, more often, the same terminology for different functions.

Once again, in order to better understand the choices available, it is useful to divide the market into smaller pieces. The following exercise helps to gain agreement and understanding about which functional areas should be covered in a new soft ware solution.

The diagram below sets out the basic functions of different types of systems and this can be used to identify the strong areas of a software application or define some of the team's requirements.

RemitConsulting
Improving information in property

Figure 3.2 Five Globes Diagram

The titles on the diagram relate to the following functions:

Transactions

This type of software deals with the process of buying or selling. The items to be bought can range from paper clips to office buildings but all transactions involve a similar style of process.

The process can be supported online over the internet or offline in an accounts department. Alternatively, it might involve producing marketing brochures in an agency department or managing the sales process.

Communities

This section relates to the management of information about a selection of contacts with whom you want to or need to keep in touch. The community could be your tenants or your clients and this function tends to involve keeping a large number of people informed with regular small items of information.

Collaboration

In contrast to the small items of information in communities, Collaboration involves keeping large items of information centrally available for a few or a few dozen people. This functionality is often used in the construction industry and in corporate finance where a large number of important documents can be kept centrally and accessed by those with the appropriate security level.

Increasingly, collaboration tools are used in investment agency to manage a central "deal room" or "project office".

Information and Knowledge

It is often said that the assets of a professional services firm walk out of the front door at 5.30pm. In property firms, the time is more likely to be 6.30-7pm but the principle is the same. Professional service firms the world over are therefore attempting to capture as much of their staff's knowledge as possible so that it can be re-used by others in the firm.

This type of knowledge management has barely touched the property world but as relationships change between the firms and their clients, more attention will be paid to this aspect of technology and culture change within the firms.

Finance & Operations

This section of the diagram includes the majority of back-office applications. These could be accounting systems, property management systems and even CRM systems.

Clearly there is some overlap in all of these groupings. For example, procurement of offices relies on lists of information and knowledge of the market. Where, the property market supplies information solutions for this an overlap between procurement, and knowledge and information is inevitable. Conveniently, if solutions are plotted on the diagram, this overlap of functions helps to differentiate the placing of the solutions on the diagram.

Figure 3.3 shows how solutions can be placed on the Five Globes diagram to help position their relative strengths. The next chapter discusses how this diagram is used in more detail but the early discussions about where solutions fit sets the scene for more detail later.

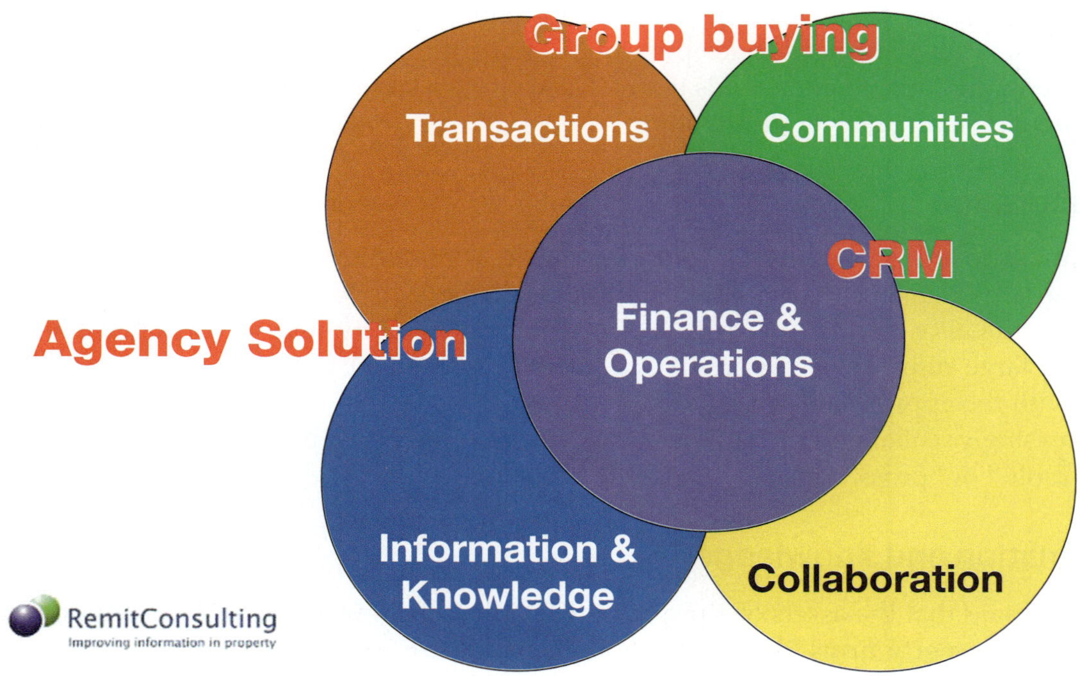

Figure 3.3

In this way a discussion can be held with the business managers to establish the types of software available and what types of functionality are offered in each case.

Very few software applications are equally strong in all areas and through discussion and further investigation a stronger understanding of the different types of software available can be achieved.

This model's main use is to aid discussion among users so as to define more clearly what is needed. As each model takes the discussion to a new level of detail, key points will emerge which will help shape the agreed requirement. Other points and ideas will be discarded along the way and through the discussion an overall consensus can be reached.

There is an added benefit that this levels the playing field for software applications at this early stage. Particular favourites that are put forward can be seen to be competitive or relatively unique and all suggested solutions are dealt with on equal terms.

This analysis can be taken a stage further to differentiate potential solutions. The four outer globes tend to be areas that provide opportunities for a company to differentiate itself from the competition. Finance and operations, on the other hand, is largely unseen by clients and business partners. It is usually assumed (not always correctly) that major companies have cast iron back-office processes and this discussion will soon identify if finance and operations need improvement as a first priority.

We will come back to this later in more detail when determining an IT strategy but this can be a useful way of prioritising limited investment budget. Is it more important to show openly how far ahead your company is compared with the competition or will basic functions need to be addressed to compete at all?

Down into the detail

At this point we have taken the view that a new system will not be perfect – if it achieves 80% it will still be better than the one we have and it will probably be better than that of our competitor.

We have dismissed technical IT considerations from our discussion so that we can concentrate on what business opportunities there are. We have also prioritised a group of solutions into manageable areas that relate roughly to available software. Many of the initial ideas have fallen by the wayside or will be considered in Phase 2.

During the process of prioritisation an assessment of potential savings and/or increased sales will have been made to support arguments over priorities; these can be used to develop a rudimentary business case to support the selections.

We are now at the stage where we have defined the business area we should address first and we need to understand how the business works in more depth. To do this we need to look at the component parts of the business in more detail.

This is the point where we can start getting into the detail of the processes that need to be improved. At first site this can be a daunting task. What are the chances of really getting to grips with Margaret's role in Accounts? She has worked the same way for the last nine years and even if you could identify a better way of working, establishing a change to her routine seems unattainable.

The first step is to look at the current state of the processes we are trying to review and for this we will need a template of typical processes in the relevant functional area.

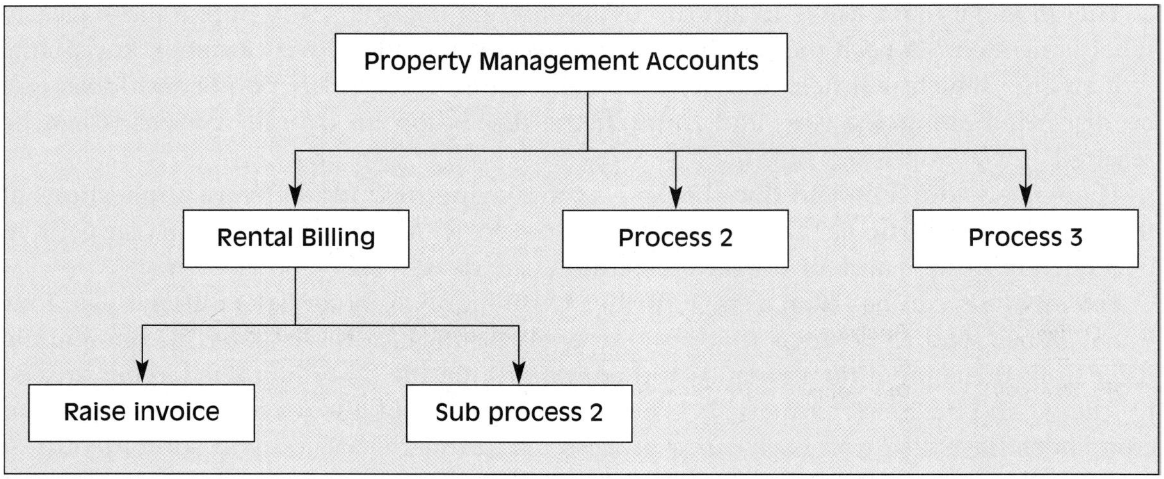

Figure 3.4 Rental Billing process decomposition

We use an approach we call the RPM (Remit Process Model). This sets out four or five basic areas of business functions and then divides and subdivides these areas until a simple process can be determined. For example, the functional area of property management accounts can be "de-composed" down to the level of raising a rental invoice and the steps might be as follows:

At the lowest level there will be a process diagram that will detail each step in the process of producing a rental invoice. I do not propose to go into the detail of process mapping because there are far more detailed textbooks available on this subject. However, this model allows the user to manage the volume of information generated by a process review and structure it in a format that can be directly compared with those of similar estates teams.

The RPM structures all of these processes for a property organisation into a manageable diagram. A typical top-level RPM from property management is shown below.

At the first level (purple) are the mega processes of Set Strategy, Implement Strategy, Support, Manage Estate and Maintain Estate. The five major processes set out under each of these use more familiar terminology and beneath each major process there will be between three and six sub-processes. There may be further levels before reaching process diagrams.

The usefulness in the RPM approach is that each sub-process has a catalogued position and, once a few reviews have been undertaken, each can be compared against industry leading practice.

Critical Processes

Depending on the number of sub-process levels, there are typically between 125 and 300 processes in a typical property management company or estates department. This is too

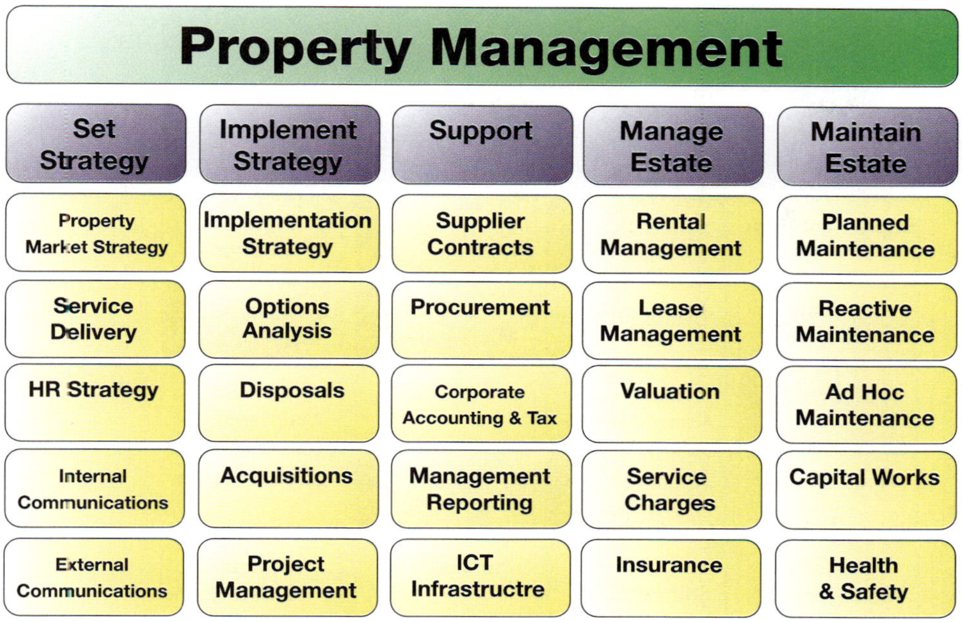

Figure 3.5 Typical Top level Property Management RPM

RemitConsulting
Improving information in property

many to deal with in detail at one time and the prioritisation started in the Five Globes exercise can be continued with the business managers and their team to identify the critical processes in a business.

The critical processes are those that add most value to a business or those that have to improve in order to address serious weakness in current processes. How you define the critical processes will depend on whether you intend to buy or build a new solution. An RPM showing typical critical processes (shown in red) in the estates team of a corporate occupier might be as per Figure 3.6.

All process mapping is extremely time-consuming and if we can avoid detailing every process, we should take the opportunity to save some resource and time. This is where early identification of the critical processes proves its worth. Typically we can reduce the number of major processes (yellow boxes) that need further analysis to between six and 10.

At the level below the yellow boxes, we normally expect between 20 and 30 critical sub-processes within Phase 1 of a project. This is manageable and allows closer definition of the business case for the project and better chance of a successful outcome.

Detailed analysis of the current state critical processes may still not be necessary. If you are likely to buy a new system, it may not be necessary at this stage to develop the future state of the processes because much will depend on the solution which will be chosen. If

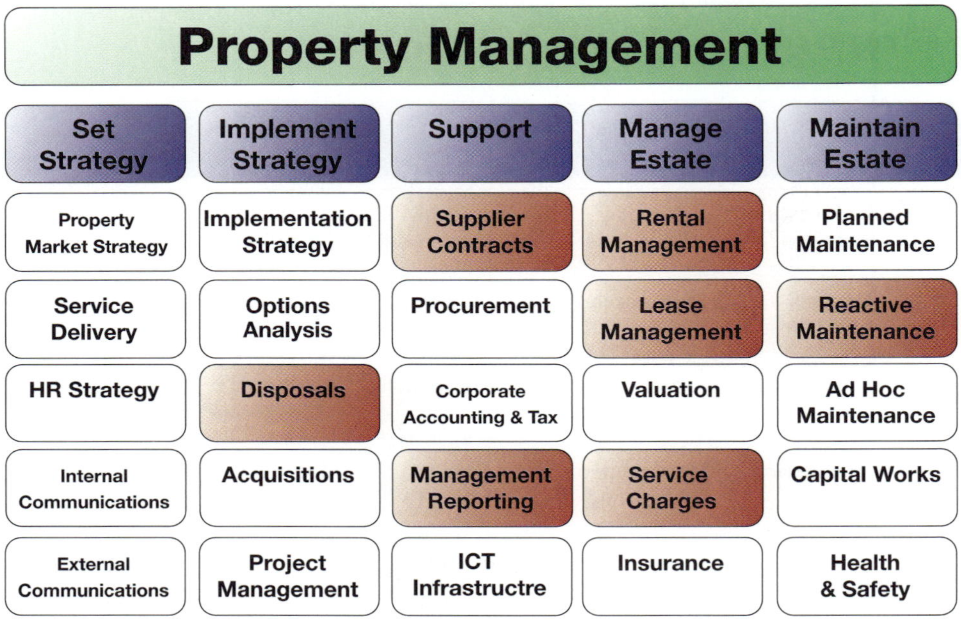

Figure 3.6 Estate team RPM showing typical critical processes

RemitConsulting
Improving information in property

the chosen new system is very prescriptive in its approach, the detailed development of a future state will have wasted valuable time.

However, the documentation of current failings and ideas for improvement will be useful in determining a specification for a system and essential if you wish to improve your current systems.

An added benefit of the RPM approach is that any functionality that is left for Phase 2 is structured in a way that remains relevant even after the six-nine months of a typical Phase 1 project. Phase 2 can be picked up where it was left, reviewed and added to the now completed Phase 1.

By now we will have a good idea of where the main improvements will arise and the style of IT solution that will be appropriate.

We started this exercise with too much choice about how we can improve the business and either a vague idea that IT could help or too many solutions competing for resources. We are now at the point where, in many cases, it would be easy to argue that no off-the-shelf software will be able to satisfy our requirements. This is why we need to keep hold of the idea that an 80% solution will be sufficient.

The next few chapters will take the tools introduced in this chapter and use them to select and implement a new solution.

4 Narrowing the Selection

The approaches discussed in the previous chapter bring some clarity to the process of selecting a new system. Our overall objective is to develop a series of projects that will improve the way the business works but, without a positive outcome from the first project, further projects will not be sanctioned.

Therefore, the focus for this first initiative will be to choose a project that has the greatest chance of success in the least possible time. Phase 2, or the next project, will rely on success being recognised within the first project.

In real life, companies usually come to a decision that they need new software through one of the following two routes.

1. A senior individual or central team decides to improve the way that the business works generally by applying new technology. This route implies that there has been, or will be, debate and agreement over a planned development of new systems.
2. There is a pressing need in a department for a replacement system because the current one is out dated, inefficient or not working.

Often it is the latter which drives the timetable, even if there is a central plan to improve the business. The urgency of the issues in one department tends towards self-selection of the first project. In other words, the area of greatest business need becomes the centre of the new IT project and others wait their turn. This, in turn, increases the risk: difficulties with mission-critical projects can rarely be buried and even small problems can seem catastrophic.

There is an argument to say that selecting a single point solution to a problem in one department is an inefficient way to implement new systems which should ultimately form part of an integrated whole. However, for many organisations, simple economics and business timescales dictate that he who shouts loudest gets his new system first.

Given that we live in reality rather than Utopia, we need an approach that will allow the selection of a single application but also provides the flexibility to upgrade to a full strategy after the first system is live, or in parallel.

First steps

Whether we are defining a strategy or selecting a point solution, we need to understand where the new system requirement fits within the company and within the market for software.

Going back to the steps outlined in Chapter 3, we must first identify which applications and responsibilities fall within each part of the Three Clouds diagram.

Areas where precise responsibilities become disputed are usually within the following areas:

- **Website** – Is this an office application? It is probably neither the responsibility of the technical team, nor the business managers. Perhaps the roles of the website can be split so that marketing is responsible for content and IT is responsible for development. In smaller organisations, a senior PA often takes responsibility for the website and this can sit alongside responsibility for other office applications.

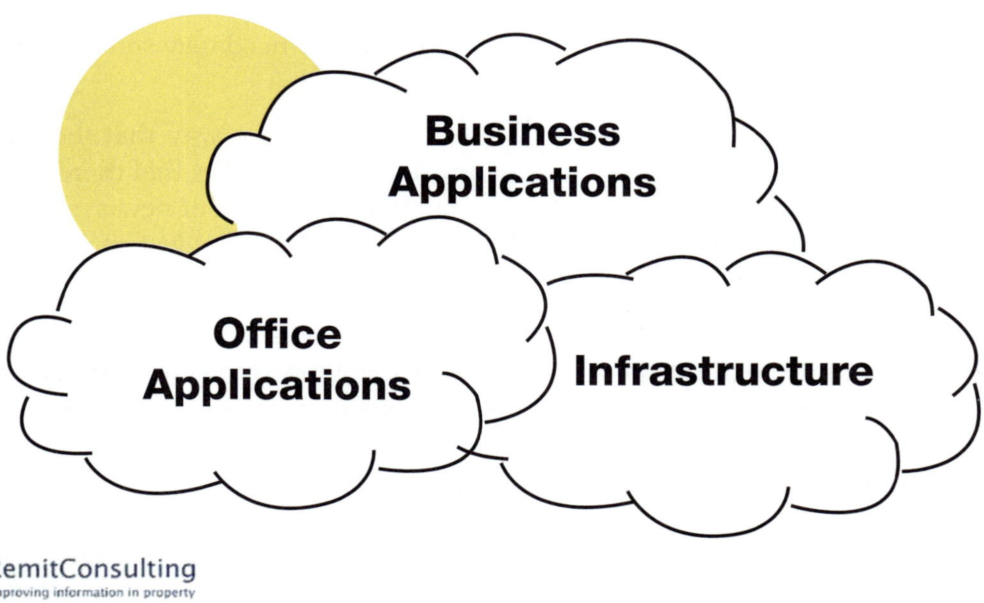

Figure 4.1 Three Clouds Analysis

- **Client Relationship Management (CRM)** – This is probably a business application but there are circumstances where responsibility for all office applications is given to support departments and management of this area may include CRM. Likewise, time accounting systems may fall within office applications if the business is structured in this way.
- **E-mail** – E-mail applications are often considered to be infrastructure because they provide a communications foundation for the business and are increasingly linked to telecoms through technology such as VoIP (internet telephony).
- **Electronic Document Management (EDM)** – There are arguments that the software required to manage electronic documents should be dealt with in the same way as e-mail applications. There is little that business managers wish to add to the running of such a system. However, for those businesses without EDM, the lack of it is often a business application problem. The structure of the system and how it is used will affect the efficiency of the business and managers will be fully involved in its design and implementation. Some organisations leave EDM in business applications until it is running effectively, then it becomes "invisible" in the same way as e-mail and is turned over to infrastructure.
- **Market Information** – Many of the news feeds and general market knowledge portals are as unobtrusive as the internet or e-mail and therefore a case may be made for them to be located within office applications. Others will be business critical. Different applications may be the responsibility of different teams.

Regardless of where your organisation chooses to put responsibility for different applications, it is the exercise of agreeing the completion of the Three Clouds diagram that lays the foundation for the project. Without agreement at this basic level, it will be difficult to establish sponsorship or ownership of the new solutions that have to be delivered.

Having carried out this exercise, there will be a better understanding of where responsibility for the new point solution falls and, if the obvious sponsor for that area is unwilling to take full responsibility, perhaps an alternative solution should be selected as the first project.

The framework provided by this exercise also sets the foundation for a strategic IT plan because it identifies broad areas of responsibility within which individuals can research requirements and start to put together cases for improvement. As such the framework can be used to validate and define a point solution or start with a blank sheet of paper.

On the assumption that we are looking at a point solution, we can identify the areas of responsibility and take the analysis to the next, more detailed, level.

The Five Globes in operation

We shall assume that the business need for a new system has arisen in business applications, and, depending on the type of property organisation, the likely priorities for new systems will differ. For example, a property company that employs managing agents to look after its portfolio will need different software to a corporate occupier that manages its own premises.

There are two levels of analysis that need to be undertaken. The first, using the Five Globes identifies which types of software solutions will improve the focus of the organisation on the business strategy. The second, at a more detailed level allows the company to identify which processes are impacted by the proposed system.

To give a flavour of the type of results we might see, let us apply the Five Globes diagram to different types of property business and, using the assumptions from Chapter 1, show how the likely priority areas for each relates to the diagram. This analysis takes the business needs for each sector and identifies the type(s) of solution most likely to benefit that type of company.

Property companies

This sector of the industry is driven by the need to increase capital value and improve revenue. Traditionally property companies' revenue came from tenants who held long inflexible leases and, except at lease-end every 25 years, the landlords could largely ignore customer relations.

The change in market characteristics and a greater attention to corporate and social responsibility has more recently enlarged the number of areas in which a property company would like to become more efficient and these areas tend to be as follows:

- **Transactions** – Efficient procurement of goods and services will reduce their costs and minimise the time taken to deal with administration. Streamlining the disposal and acquisition processes will, in addition, reduce costs further and will make the company more efficient by reducing the costs of purchase and sale. Being able to buy properties more quickly when in a competitive situation will make the company more effective.
- **Collaboration** – When the company develops, sells or acquires property, its teams may benefit from using collaboration tools to co-ordinate the many documents.
- **Community** – Increasing emphasis on maintaining the tenant base has led some landlords to develop community websites for their tenants, as we have seen with Broadgate Estate's Vicinitee[1].
- **Knowledge** – Increasing fees from advisors are leading many companies to try and establish knowledge bases of best practice so that they are less reliant on basic information when they need advice. Market knowledge is also now easier to buy on a subscription basis and this needs to be managed as part of an overall solution.

1 Case Study, page 41

- **Finance and Operations** – The back-office systems that underpin the company will probably include rent accounting because this directly affects their profitability but service charge management is often outsourced. Corporate accounting systems will often be tied directly to the rent accounting systems. Improvements in reporting often significantly improve the efficiency of managing these functional areas.

This gives a requirement in every part of the Five Globes and therefore further prioritisation is required.

Typically, an established property company will already have accounting systems that serve their purposes. However, there may be a need to integrate information from their managing agents more effectively.

If their managing agents deal with the majority of the tenants, there may not be an immediate need for the property company to build a community website for its tenants.

Dealing with property transactions and construction teams needs an effective method of allowing teams to collaborate and an online system for sharing documents in a single repository brings savings and efficiency.

A lower priority, but a long-term need, will be to increase the amount of knowledge used within the various processes in the business. Although there is often a strong

RemitConsulting
Improving information in property

Figure 4.2 Property Company Priorities

business case for this element of new systems, the disruption to established methods and the investment in culture change often militates against this solution.

The diagram above plots the possible priorities for a property company on the Five Globes diagram. The use of this diagram allows us to start differentiating the requirements of property companies from other organisations and, if software exists which matches this profile, it will be more readily apparent.

Institutions

Unlike property companies, institutional fund managers tend to appoint agents to manage the properties while they concentrate on the investment strategy and cash management. Their priorities will be to their investors and information and transparent reporting is becoming increasingly important.

Their priorities in each globe are therefore likely to be as follows:

- **Finance and Operations** – Key to institutions' systems will be effective financial management. The core systems will usually be well established but increasing demands on the visible management of cash flows and controls on tax structures often require additional systems.
- **Communities** – Fund managers increasingly wish to interact more openly with investors and provide detailed summaries of investments and performance measures on a dynamic website. Creating a community of investors could therefore be attractive.
- **Collaboration** – Collaboration tools will allow the investment managers to monitor and contribute to acquisition and disposal projects with their project team. This is an easy solution to delegate to agents or to solicitors. However, for reasons of control, fund managers may consider setting up their own system.
- **Information and Knowledge** – Information and knowledge solutions will contribute to setting strategies and monitoring performance against market activity. Coordinating and integrating the various sources of information, especially across non-property investment fields, may be hard work; however, this could reduce an individual fund manager's work considerably.

Plotting these requirements on the Five Globes in Figure 4.3 shows that institutions would usually require a much narrower grouping of solutions reflecting the fact that much of the management work is contracted to agents.

Property agents and consultants

This group of companies have many and wide ranging requirements from systems although, traditionally, much of the investment in systems has been in property management. However, most teams will now require some degree of automation and agents should be examining solutions in all of the globes.

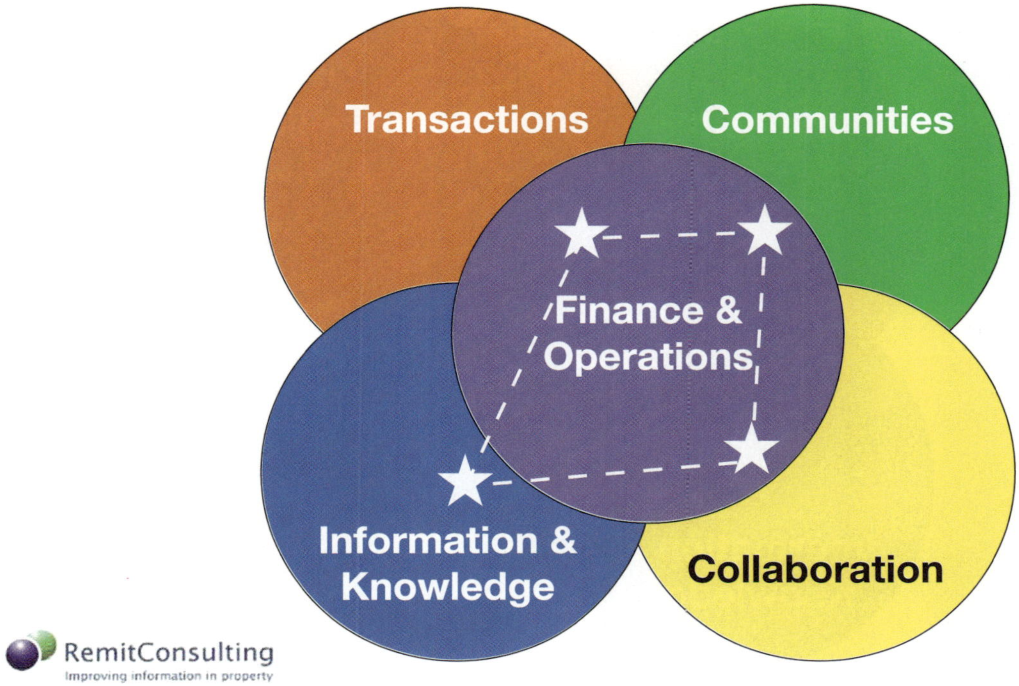

Figure 4.3 Institution Priorities

- **Transactions** – The agency teams can use online portals and new services to speed the production of brochures. The property management teams will be able to use their purchasing power to benefit all their clients, thus reducing the costs of property management and reducing the time and paperwork in procuring goods and services.
- **Collaboration** – Agencies are often central in the flow of information in transactions and collaboration tools are becoming widely established in the agency of larger property deals. Clients are increasingly coming to expect these systems to be provided by their advisors and this represents an opportunity for the advisor to become more central in the control of the information around a deal.
- **Communities** – Agencies have at least two communities that they can manage – their clients and the tenants within the portfolios they manage. Nearly all agents are having difficulties implementing CRM systems but most are persevering because of the possible value of this to their long-term business.

Additionally, few agencies are exploiting the potential of tying their tenants to their services through community portals; this represents a straightforward opportunity to differentiate their service in what is becoming viewed as a commodity service by clients.

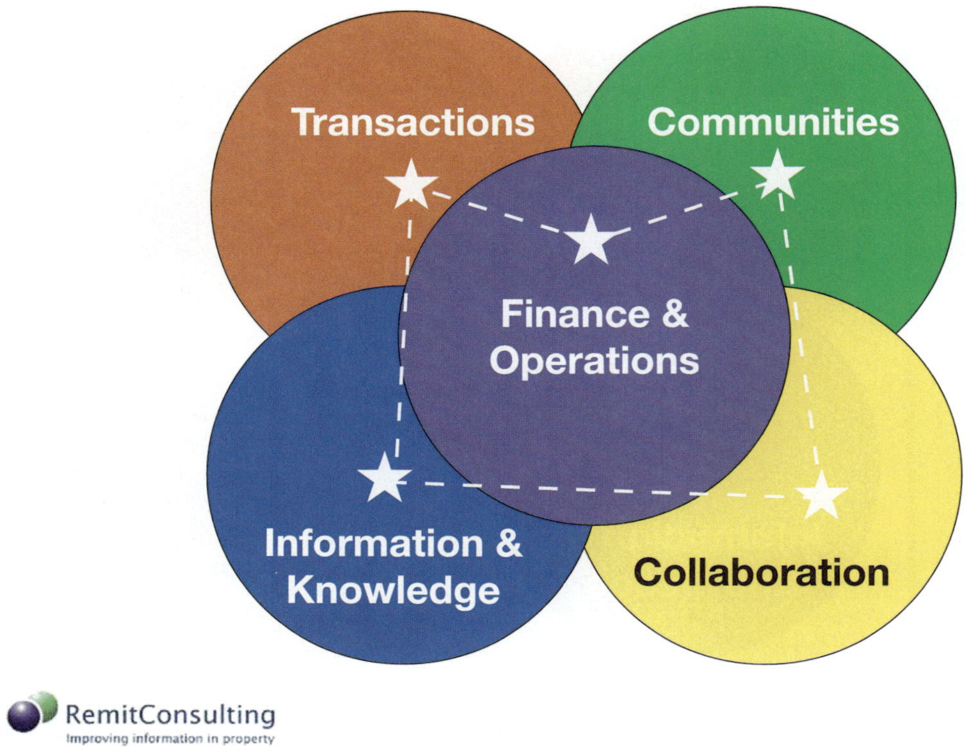

Figure 4.4 Property Agents Priorities

- **Information and Knowledge** – The biggest challenge of the next few years for professional services firms will be to capture the knowledge from their staff without debasing the value of the knowledge held by individual agents and valuers. This area will require a change in culture in most organisations and systems will be only a foundation for improvements in this area.
- **Finance and Operations** – Most agencies will have their own internal accounting systems but improvements in possible systems to serve clients are occurring rapidly and this provides opportunities to make processes more efficient and save cost.

Agencies, with possible solutions in all areas, will probably have the most difficult choices to make in prioritising their systems investment; however, they have the advantage that they will already have individuals responsible for different business areas and these managers will prepare their own business cases for the most important changes. The competitive environment that this fosters should make the best of whatever resources are available.

Corporate occupiers

Most estates teams within corporate occupiers will be required to use the company's internal accounting systems but may need to augment this with specific property functionality in order to manage rental and service charge payments. The degree of adoption of corporate systems will vary from one company to the next.

- **Transactions** – The key areas for corporates will be to minimise the costs of the estate. Because of most lease requirements on tenants to maintain the property, much of the estates team's solution requirements will be in respect of managing the procurement of services, be they for maintenance and repair or new works.

This requirement may drive the search for a solution towards FM rather than EM functionality and this will become clearer as the RPM is analysed in the next stage.

- **Collaboration** – Occupiers will often rely on their agents or lawyers to provide collaboration tools for deals and for capital works. Few estates teams set up their own but where they do, these can be used internally as well as for external teams.
- **Communities** – There is an opportunity to provide better management of consultants and contractors through online portals but this is not often a high priority. Internally, building managers and retail store managers can be considered to be an important community and this could be a useful focus of a community solution.

Bill Gates wrote about the fact that the most popular pages on the Microsoft intranet are those where the estates teams have set out the floor plans of all the Microsoft buildings[2]. The users of property are interested in where they work. The estates team can exploit this interest to foster a community that makes their use of property more effective.

- **Information and Knowledge** – the management of costs in the estate is core to this group's business and therefore the property terrier/database will be at the heart of the systems.

As property services outsourcing becomes more widespread, it is important to digitally capture as much knowledge about the portfolio as possible, thus reducing the risk of transferring all that knowledge to a third party provider in the heads of the outsourced team.

- **Finance and Operations** – The reporting of information on the estate will require the database to be linked to the financial systems and it is this combination that will support the majority of the management in the estates team.

2 *Business @ the Speed of Thought,* Bill Gates 1999, Penguin Books Limited

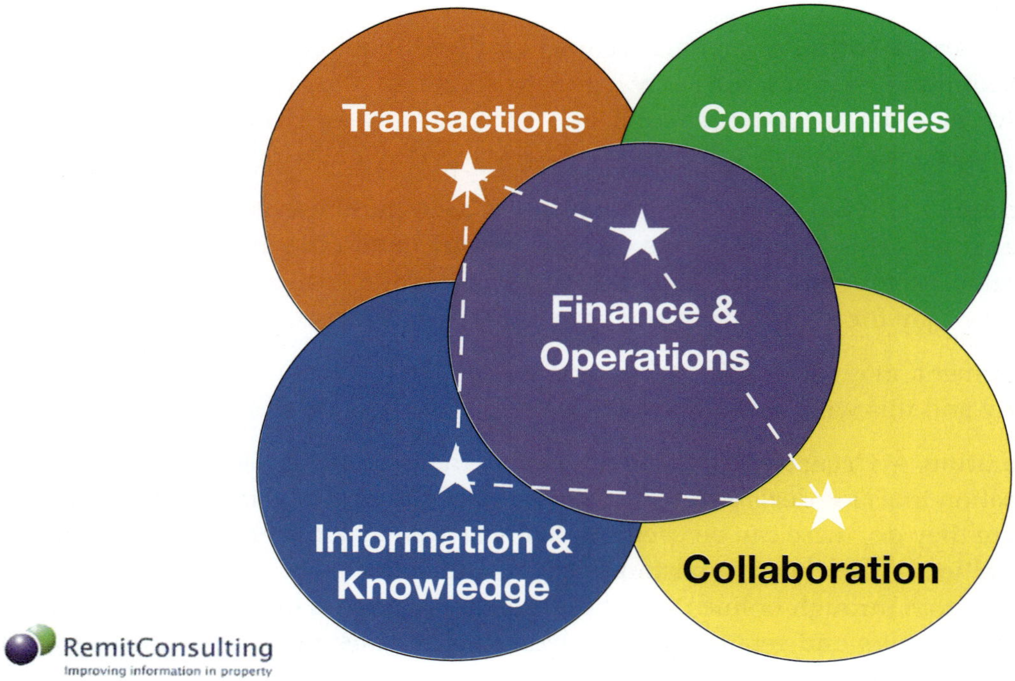

Figure 4.5 Corporate Occupier and government priorities

Government

Central and local government estates teams have similar requirements to those of corporate occupiers but also often act as landlords. The pattern of requirement within the Five Globes diagram is therefore very similar to that of corporate occupiers.

If anything, knowledge of leading practice methodologies in managing public sector property is often given a higher priority than in the private sector and, as with corporate property, outsourcing key parts of the provision of property services is a significant issue; knowledge management will therefore be a high priority.

Comparisons

The different shaped requirements in this model serve to show how differently various sectors of the property industry treat requirements for new systems. It is often thought that in property systems one size fits all. However, customers are increasingly aware of their different requirements and more packages are catering to specific markets.

Examples of this, at the time of writing,[3] are:

- Concept FSI or Archibus for facilities management
- Trace Bluebox for investors, Trace Tramps for managing agents
- Intuit MRI or SAP Real Estate for international investors and occupiers.

It is possible to plot the functionality of each software package across the requirements for each sector but at this level, the large amount of work to do this, coupled with ever changing software specifications, makes this exercise a low priority.

It is better to use the Five Globes analysis to gain:

- an understanding of the wide range of technology options available to property teams
- identification of key areas of functional need
- agreement on the importance of each area.

If a point solution has been proposed by an individual or team, this process will expand the vision of the group proposing the solution and allow the identification of functionality which may not be part of the solution as originally expected. This should improve the fit of the solution to the business and improve the business case.

In the case of developing a strategy, this is the first step to defining what type of solution will be developed first and the next section describes the process of narrowing down the available options.

Priorities – Next steps

The resources required for these new initiatives will need funding and it is therefore essential to keep the bigger picture in mind. The more closely the request for funds matches the organisation's priorities, the easier it will be to gain approval. It is therefore worth looking at how the initiatives fit within the company's overall position.

GE Capital and Ernst & Young developed a model for describing how different companies should view the advent of the internet and how they might prepare initiatives to grow the business.

A version of the model is set out in Figure 4.6.

In my experience, there are three generic strategic steps.

1. **Protect the Core** – eg ensure that you are at least able to sustain your current competitive position and that the opportunities for efficiency are being fully utilised – that you are "up with the pack".
2. **Change the Game** – by becoming more effective through doing all the right things (eg in the way the business responds to customer needs remember Porter said "it is more important to do the right things than to do things right").

3 More comparisons can be found at www.itforproperty.com

3. **Step Change** – create a completely new business from scratch to exploit different market opportunities that are emerging.

As Figure 4.6 shows, the steps can be defined in terms of threats and opportunities. The lower steps are taken merely to prevent your competitive advantage being eroded. Once these steps have been addressed, the business can look at breaking away from the pack and develop new initiatives that will be more profitable.

Examples at each step tend to be similar in every industry and in the property industry. Protecting the core tends to involve the automation of back-office processes. This allows the property management team to process invoices more effectively or the agency team to manage their contact records efficiently.

Change the game initiatives tend to be more focused on the client, customer or tenant. Examples of this include collaboration tools that allow clients to access the details in a large transaction or creation of a community of interest for tenants or suppliers. Often the defining feature of change the game initiatives is that they are quite straightforward to set up and there is little reason why competitors cannot do the same. This means that within six-12 months, these initiatives are often copied by competitors and the innovation involved becomes commonplace. In fact, it is worse than that; without that initiative, clients and customers perceive your business as lacking the level of services required.

In the construction industry it is now essential to have access to a collaboration tool if you, as a contractor, are bidding for a large project. Many large law practices have also introduced these online tools and have thus attracted some clients who become tied into processes within those tools. It is a compelling argument to start using one of these tools, especially if it is offered for free: the client reduces time spent, wasted costs and confusion. Once a client has used the collaboration tool, they are comfortable with its layout and the natural human tendency with IT towards inertia may deter them from switching to a system offered by a competitor.

The third step, step change, relates to completely new business and this is the rarest to be achieved. The key point about step change is that it takes your business model so far ahead of the competition that it is difficult for them to catch up. The type of initiative that this covers is a revolution in the way a company does business or changes the way in which customers expect to do business with that sector.

Although rare, a good example is that of YHD.com. The company (YHD stands for Your Home Direct) launched its online estate agency service in New Jersey in the year 2000 having received venture capital at the height of the dot.com boom. Over the course of the next two years it merged with Foxtons, the London based estate agency, and achieved 300% annual revenue growth. It did this while charging 50% of the industry standard fee basis. Along the way the company won the coveted Business Week Ebiz25 award.

YHD.com was smart in that it kept the traditional values of the estate agency business; it is a service business and relies on its customers, employees and suppliers. However, its philosophy was to be technology driven with rigorously controlled automated processes.

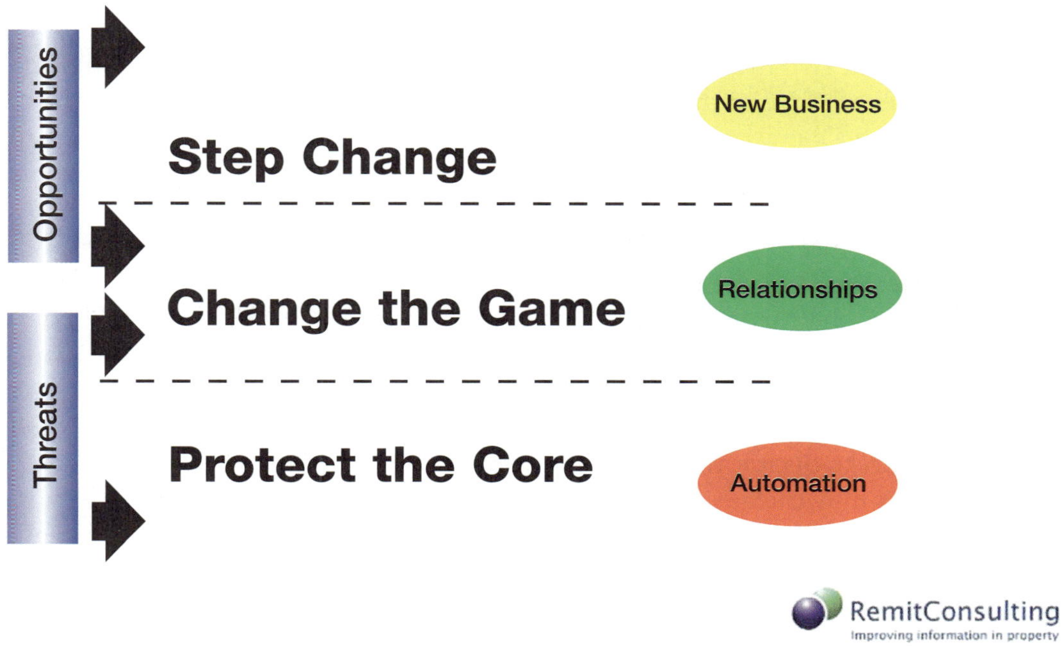

Figure 4.6 Business Opportunity Framework

The structure of the company was organised around activities and thus they developed specialists in all the aspects of estate agency. They had few offices and the agents themselves were mobile workers. Customers accessed property details over the internet and after two years had saved an estimated total of $30m in fees.

What emerged was a company with immensely scaleable processes and a low cost base. Hence the fee basis they worked with was profitable without compromising service.

Foxtons have incorporated a lot of what they learnt from YHD.com into their London operations but it is very difficult to compete with this approach if you are an incumbent operator in the market. This new business had no legacy of buildings, branches and outdated equipment – let alone a large number of staff needing to be retrained.

This is where the new business model goes full circle. It is these start-up businesses that often pose the greatest threat to the traditional market leaders and force them into the "protect the core" step.

Likewise, it is insufficient to carry out a single "change the game" project and relax. Business will continue to evolve and it is this pressure that will drive innovation. The opportunity framework eloquently shows why there is a recurrent and frequent need for companies to develop innovation. There is very little step change in business because others can quickly replicate most new ideas. Companies are therefore forced to innovate on a regular basis to stay ahead; if your company fails to produce at least one new proposition each year, it will be consistently playing catch-up.

Relating the Opportunity Framework to Five Globes

The overlap in these two models shows up when one compares the types of initiative that are produced by each area of the Five Globes. As shown in the diagram below, the central globe, Finance and Operations, tends towards initiatives that are back-office functions – the basic requirements in a business. They tend not to be client-facing systems and are therefore usually protect the core initiatives.

The outer globes are change the game initiatives and these tend therefore to be more focused on customers and clients. They are therefore opportunities to raise the company's position relative to their competition.

By matching the opportunity framework to the Five Globes, we begin to differentiate solutions such as property management and accounting systems from collaboration tools and community websites. Now that these groups of systems are distinguished, the company can start to decide what to implement first.

Market drivers may dictate that the company's core systems are not effective enough to compete and it is therefore a straightforward decision to invest in core basic systems that will raise the company effectiveness to the minimum market level.

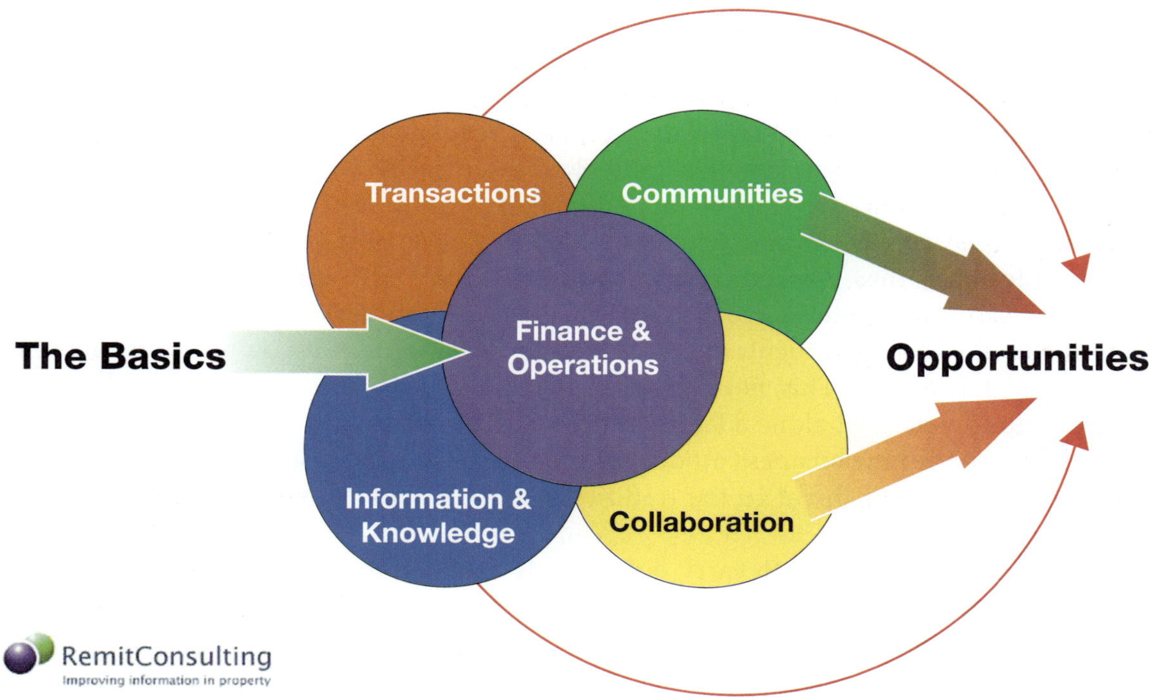

Figure 4.7 Five Globes – types of innovation

However, if most of the basic systems are in place and operate reasonably effectively, the company can start to look at systems that change the game. Such initiatives are likely to be numerous and some have been described in the sector-by-sector analysis earlier in this chapter. Each sector will adopt solutions in a different order and at a different rate because of their own priorities.

For example, implementing a collaboration tool for property transactions in a property company may not be necessary because the company can use tools provided by their lawyers. However, the development team in the same company might seek a consistent approach across all their advisors and build their own project office tool. British Land's approach to evaluating new ideas through their Business Group[4] shows an intelligent approach to this type of prioritisation.

Occasionally, all companies will have the opportunity to create step change. This is by its very nature more risky, and, even if they have the opportunity, many companies will turn this down.

Many of these types of idea surfaced during the dot.com boom. Some prospered and changed the way many people work or shop: Amazon, lastminute.com and Freeserve are three non-property examples that come to mind. Many more, eg PrimePitch, Propex and UKPiP (all in the UK), have attracted client bases and make money but have not yet, after three years, transformed their industry.

Although good businesses in their own right, these step change initiatives show why existing companies may shy away from this type of investment. All these examples share the fact that they developed independently or away from their parent's main business. They are more resource intensive, more risky, and ultimately distract management from the current core focus of the company. Although there are still good arguments to encourage companies to challenge their core business, refining and improving an existing service or product often comes more easily.

In our quest to improve the company we have stated that we should seek early success in order to justify further investment in systems initiatives. For this reason, we are likely to stay within the change the game step.

Revenue Distance

It is clearly important to introduce the concept of Return on Investment (ROI) during this process and many software companies have spent significant amounts of time developing ROI calculations to support the purchase of their software. For example, Microsoft developed a concept called Revenue Distance. This proposes that ROI is higher in new systems, the closer the system is applied to the customer.

4 Case Study, page 55.

The theory goes that it is more effective to invest funds on systems that enhance the customer's experience. If we look at YHD.com, the experience of buying or selling a house is made easier for the customer. The seller need not visit an inconvenient branch office. They simply use the telephone or the internet to arrange a valuation.

Buyers of property have access to frequently updated details of properties and other value added services can be added quickly and easily. It reduces the time spent by buyers and sellers and the benefits are self-apparent.

Taking this concept further, this approach suggests that back office and basic systems are unlikely to produce as high a ROI as customer facing systems. However, this is debatable and will depend on your business drivers. Professional services firms may benefit from improving their client relationships but companies with large-scale logistics operations will view this type of measure differently.

Relating this to real estate, back-office systems minimise cost rather than creating new revenue. However, if basic systems such as those for accounting or asset management do not work, an upgraded client interface will expose the weaknesses and drive clients away. If basic systems must be upgraded to compete effectively, these must take priority. Once these systems are effective, the company can look at customer facing systems and continue to "Change the Game".

The risk in using ROI measures is that they are used either to justify investment or find a case not to invest. Rather than providing independent validation, they are just one tool to use to establish the priority of a proposal. However, if none of the ROI measures commonly used justify the project, it is probably worth investing in a different initiative.

The Business Case

We started this chapter with two assumptions.

1. That there were either many calls on scarce resources and we needed to clarify what solution would benefit the business the most in the short term, or;
2. That a single department needed a new system and that this would need to be provided regardless of how the overall strategy for building integrated systems would be progressed in the short term.

The approach we have taken has either brought us to recognise the area that would most benefit from a system or has refined the team's thinking on their replacement system to a point where the detailed specification can be defined.

In either case, we now need to put together a formal business case to attract the necessary funding to proceed with the project. What we need to produce is a well-reasoned argument that covers:

- details of the business need and sponsorship
- an estimate of the savings or revenue enhancement which will be brought about by the solution

- an estimate of resources required and costs
- an estimate of the timescale for the overall project and, in particular, the first phase of the project
- measures of success.

All organisations have their own style of business case that needs to be submitted but most cover these basic elements. At this stage of the project it is impossible to know every detail because the discussions so far have necessarily been at a high-level. However, if the project is approved at this stage, even in part, it will help justify the time to gather more detail in the next phase. It will also inform the fund-holders of the benefits and gather useful feedback that will guide the project through the next stages,

Let's look at each part of the case in more detail to see what is possible and how much detail should be included.

Business Need and Sponsorship

This is perhaps the easiest part of the business case because we have spent time with the users to define the need and in the course of this we will have identified the key sponsor. This section gives us the chance to set out some of the background and set expectations about what the project needs to achieve.

The question of sponsorship is paramount since it is the choice of sponsor that will usually make or break the project. The sponsor will not only have to set out the case for investment but will have to clear the various blockages which will appear during the course of the project. Without the right senior level sponsor who can make decisions and follow through on promises of support, it will be best to review whether to put the project forward at all.

This is another advantage of building the business case at this stage because lack of a sponsor might turn you towards an alternative project.

Savings or new revenue

Having prioritised the projects on the basis of "Protect the Core" and "Change the Game", and further rationalised the choice through looking at ROI, this section becomes much easier to write. At this stage it is unrealistic to claim precise accuracy of the figures put forward but, after discussions with the users, it should be possible to reach some sort of consensus; this should provide a monetary figure over a period of time which can be used to justify the investment.

If the figures are accepted by the Board as being realistic estimates of what could be saved or produced in extra revenue, the majority of the case will have been made. The Board will have a better understanding of the business costs and opportunities than the IT costs, and if the business justification is there, more than half the battle is won.

Resources required and costs

This will probably be the most difficult section to complete. It is unlikely that any decent specification has been developed to the point where suppliers can estimate costs. There are, however, a number of ways in which to gain an understanding of likely costs.

- Seek advice from peers and contacts in other companies who have undertaken similar projects.
- Develop a Request for Information (RFI) that you can send to a few suppliers for their advice. This is a simplified specification that asks suppliers to set out their approach to this type of project with a list of issues that need to be addressed and a range of likely costs based on broad assumptions.
- You might ask a specialist consultant to advise on typical costs but beware that they may just take you through the process of an RFI, adding little knowledge themselves.

Whatever the result of your enquiries, add at least a further 20% for contingency before seeking approval. Furthermore, it is always useful to bear in mind that a typical cost ratio for larger systems is:

Two parts software: one part hardware: two-four parts change management consultancy

Take this ratio into account when assessing results from the RFI and the resulting cost may seem horrific; however, it is better to dismiss the project now for lack of funds, than to get half-way through and explain to the sponsor and the Board that you now need twice as much cash for the same business benefit.

Depending on the policies in your organisation, you may need to account for internal costs on top of the above. Do not forget that you will need a full-time project manager and I recommend that you do not skimp on this role.

Timescale

The research done among peers and the RFI should give an indication of the timescale you will need. This may be driven by the needs of the project itself and do not accept unrealistic timescales which cannot be achieved. It is best to re-scope the project into several phases if there is a risk that the timescale is too short. Being firm on what will be in scope at this stage is one of the most important roles for the project management at this early stage.

It is just as dangerous to estimate the timescale to be too long. Work fills the time allotted and the easiest way to blow the budget is to over-specify the timescale.

Again, take soundings from others and talk to suppliers.

Project measures

The Board will take comfort from a well thought out set of project measures. These will help frame the context of the project and provide benchmarks that can be easily assessed.

If the initiative is to provide a collaboration tool that will reduce the stationery used in a large project and reduce the number of meetings, you will already have stated some of the cash benefits to accrue from the solution. When you propose Phase 2 (or the next initiative), you will want to use these measures to show how beneficial this first project was to the company; therefore, a realistic set of indices, which can be easily measured and which are relevant to the original objectives, should be set out.

Writing the Business Case

The business case should be as short as possible but contain sufficient detail to give comfort that the bold statements therein can be justified. Most of the skill in writing a business case is the same as in writing any other report and I can do no better than to point you towards *Pyramid Principle* by Barbara Minto which describes how to write business reports in a logical and accessible style[5].

In essence, *Pyramid Principle* suggests a pyramid structure for reports with the key question at the apex of the pyramid and then logical arguments set out below. The report takes the following form.

- Situation – what we are addressing.
- Complication – what has happened which changes the situation and what the implications are.
- Question – What question is being answered here?

The support for the answer to the question, and any new questions arising, are laid out in pyramids below the main question and this provides a formal, but readable, structure for the report.

With the content suggested above, laid out in a concise, logical fashion, it will be clear whether the business case is supportable for this first project, and with this approach it should be possible to gain authority to proceed to detailed specification of the solution.

Narrowing the selection

We have now reached a point where the detailed requirements will need to be defined. Using the Five Globes initial research into the priority area can be undertaken and a selection of solutions broadly fitting the requirements will be found.

5 *Pyramid Principle*, Barbara Minto, 1987, Prentice Hall/FT

How do we find a list of suitable solutions? The most common routes are listed below.

- Conduct an internet search through one of the search engines such as Google or Yahoo![6].
- Contact your friends and peers. They will almost certainly have come across systems that will solve some of the requirements and, using the Five Globes, it will be easy to test each solution against your requirement.
- Visit the industry shows. In the UK, PCS-Expo is the obvious choice to see most property systems but others, including the IPD and OPD conferences, Corenet Global and the Henry Stewart Occupier Symposium all focus on systems from time to time.
- In Europe MIPIM in Cannes, France is an obvious focus point and in the US, Canada and Asia Realcomm is the major IT focused annual conference for real estate.
- The main directories of property systems suppliers are the PCS property suppliers directory, available at the PCS-Expo, and Freemans Directory of Property Service Providers, available online or in print.
- Journals – From time to time both the Estates Gazette and Property Week run articles about property systems and the Property Systems Review specialises in this area and is available quarterly.

If you have not done so when developing an RFI, it is worthwhile attending as many demonstrations of available systems as possible because all will have a slightly different approach to similar problems. None of the systems will cover all of the possible requirements but seeing a broad selection of systems will give the opportunity to start prioritising some of the detailed functionality.

A further advantage of meeting the software suppliers is that you will be able to judge the style and manner of the staff at each supplier. Whether you are comfortable with the supplier's staff is often more important than the software itself. Most suppliers regularly improve their software, and features unavailable in one solution are likely to become available in due course.

The software therefore will improve. It is unlikely though that your relationship with a supplier will and with luck you will not be changing the software for 10 years. The relationship at the start of the contract is therefore of critical importance. If you fail to see eye to eye with the supplier when he is trying to sell to you, it will be far worse when you are in dispute over poor delivery or maintenance.

It is therefore perfectly acceptable to discount software from your list on the basis of the team they put forward at the demonstration. If the software appears to be a realistic choice and the options are narrow, it may be worth seeking an alternative team from the supplier but the warning signs will already be there.

6 More solutions can be found at www.itforpropertypeople

The result of this set of exercises will be that you have a good idea of the list of software suppliers that could satisfy your requirement. These demonstrations have not been to select the software you will use but to gain an understanding of the vast number of different approaches available to improve the chosen area of your business.

Where are we?

By this point we should have project sponsorship, agreement on at least initial funding, key project objectives and measures in place and a list of suppliers who might be considered.

The next stage deals with the detail and this is the least attractive part of selecting new solutions. It is the stage often skipped but it is essential for reasons that will become clear through the next few chapters. This is the part of the project where you will again ignore the software vendors – you already know roughly what they can provide. You need to define precisely what the software will actually achieve and this means that we need to return to the users and work through their processes in detail.

Take the phone off the hook to the suppliers and concentrate on internal processes for the next couple of months.

5 System specifications

Developing a specification

You have the authorisation you need to proceed. You will by now also have suppliers pushing you to become involved in a tender process, or offering yet more demonstrations so that your final specification starts to take on the appearance of their product.

The suppliers will be asking for a detailed functional specification so that they can start to put together quotations. They will have their own standard ideas of what each type of company might require but it will only be possible to estimate the costs in detail when the functional specification has been designed.

With reassurance from the suppliers and an increasing internal workload, it is easy to be drawn into a hurried tender process and leave the process analysis until later. As we will see later in this chapter, there is a logical argument for leaving much of the process review until after the software is selected. However, there is good reason to get to grips with current processes now. Let's see what problems we can avoid by spending more time with the internal team at this stage and how much work is required.

Traditional Approach

Everyone claims to know what a software tender looks like. This knowledge has been passed down from one selection to the next over many years and over time each set of additions has made it more complex.

The approach to a traditional tender document involves a workshop where all the users list their requirements. The discussion in the workshop focuses on delivering all of these requirements and they are all added to the specification.

What is typically produced over the next month is a thick A4 document which comprises 200–300 pages with 20 pages of introduction and many pages for the supplier to complete. A typical layout is shown in Figure 5.1.

		System Response				
Section	Process description/Feature	A	B	C	D	E
5	Rental billing					
5a	Must bill monthly and quarterly	X				
5b						

Figure 5.1

Each page to be completed has a wide column taking up two-thirds of the page on the left and this describes the requirement in as much detail as possible. There are a number of columns on the right for suppliers to grade the suitability of their solution.

The grading against each requirement can be 1-5 or A-E and reflects how well the product matches the specification. For example, a typical set of grades would be as follows:

A – Solution provides function as stated.

B – Solution provides function as stated with some modification required – up to one day's integration work.

C – Solution provides function as stated with some modification required –one to five days' integration work.

D – Solution does not provide function in this release but will be catered for in the next release.

E – Solution does not provide function in this or next release.

If the specification is completed properly and all grades applied accurately, the resulting set of grading can be compared in a spreadsheet showing the responses of all suppliers. Weightings can be applied to the importance of the functionality and the suppliers will gain differing scores. The winner will go forward to the next stage of the tender.

This is all very logical and you will, by now, be expecting a "but". The approach appears simple and, of course, it is too simple – it works well for neither the suppliers nor the customer.

The problems

The customer has spent months preparing the specification. Businesses change constantly and rapidly. Requirements will have changed in this time and urgent fixes will have been applied to areas of the business. Other parts of the organisation will have implemented new systems and these will impact the needs of the subject requirement. The specification will often be out of date by the time it is sent out.

Some areas of functionality will inevitably be ill described and most of the specification will be based on existing practices. There is limited scope for the supplier to suggest leading practice solutions because any deviation from the answers in the specification will either make the bid non-compliant or destroy the marking system.

The supplier's delight at being selected for the tender is quashed by the sight of the weighty tome that prints from the e-mail. (It can be argued that traditional specifications have become even larger since e-mail because the customer neither pays for the paper used to print out the document nor for shipping costs). The supplier will therefore often take longer to analyse and complete the tender, adding to the delay on the project.

The supplier is faced with a straightforward choice of A-E; each answer "E" represents probable failure in the tender and each answer "A" represents the opportunity to demonstrate their system to the customer and apply additional personal charm.

Unless the requirement is very unusual and the supplier knows that no other competitive system could support that need, there is obviously a great temptation to complete every box as "A". Indeed, some suppliers have in the past privately boasted about completing tenders in this way.

I know of one system selection that was completed using this selection method; the three top-scoring systems were unable to complete the functionality as stated in the specification, despite filling in the tender as if they could. The fourth system was found to be the most suitable despite having scored lower marks in the specification. Luckily, in this case, further pilot tests weeded out the non-compliant systems before implementation. However, the project was put back a further three months, and other systems are often implemented even though they cannot provide all the requested functionality.

In summary, this approach suits no one: the supplier is forced into a situation where they need to be economical with the truth to stay in the tender, the customer cannot compare similar functions in systems. The specifications often mix inappropriately intense detail with vague system requirements and they involve too much work on the part of both the customer and the supplier.

A better specification

In every industry, there will be software solutions developed which provide broadly similar functionality. In the property industry, the main systems for estate management have had up to 20 years experience of working with property users and, in the main, they perform adequately. They will have been adapted to work for most types of property organisation and although often the adaptation may not be elegant, most systems will provide the basic functionality.

It therefore follows that all UK estate management systems should recognise basic UK specific requirements such as quarter days and the legal requirements around rent reviews and lease ends. That means that filling endless pages of specification with standard features simply prolongs the process and wastes the time of all concerned.

The exception to this generalisation is the international systems that may have been localised to the UK requirements relatively recently and more attention to basic functionality is usually required. Some of this additional work can be dealt with through reference site interviews but this still needs to be managed carefully.

All users' requirements are different and many of their detailed requests may not make the first phase of implementation. The process we have followed to prioritise these needs will already have shaped a specification for a solution and this does not need to cover every aspect of the user's work.

For example, health and safety functionality may have been excluded from the scope on this phase of the project and, in the same way, many lower level processes can also be left for future phases.

The specification should concentrate on those functional areas that comprise the critical processes. What we aim for is approximately a dozen processes which can be described in detail to form test scripts for the demonstration of the solution and against which all systems can be judged. This will allow flexibility for suppliers to propose radical improvements to the process and will provide a level playing field against which to score how well each system performs. It will also be easier to judge how flexible and accommodating are the supplier team and how well the customer is likely to work with them.

Using this approach, the suppliers need to do more work. They cannot simply parade their standard demonstration and answer questions. They need to use a subset of the customer's data to generate the scenarios set out in the scripts and it is therefore important to take this route with a small short list so that the supplier perceives a good chance of success if they put in the additional work.

Set against this extra work, of course, is the fact that they need not work through a 200-page specification and that they explicitly get to understand what the customer is trying to achieve.

Unfortunately, we will not completely dispense with the specification checklist because there will be standard elements of the system, not tested by the script which will require confirmation that they exist. However, the decision to proceed will be based on the scripts that test the critical processes. The checklist will be a manageable part of the process for both sides.

This therefore represents the tender model at which we are aiming; how we develop this type of specification is discussed below.

Functional requirement – Current State Analysis

When we get to discuss the tender itself, there will be alternative routes to selecting systems. Among these options, it is possible to analyse the abilities of a short list of, say, three systems, or select a single, preferred supplier with whom you will work with to produce a solution. The pros and cons of each approach are discussed in Chapter 6 but, regardless of the approach, in each case it is important to define the functionality of your requirement in detail.

Some suppliers may offer to do this for you and this can be effective, especially since the supplier will already be aware of the work-arounds needed for certain functions. If you know and trust the supplier, perhaps through working with them previously, this is a valid way of shortening the selection process. There is still a need for a specification but the tender process is limited to the time taken for the supplier to cost the solution and for negotiation of contracts.

The supplier's knowledge of what works and where the difficulties arise will save time. However, there are two reasons why you might reject this approach.

1 It will be more difficult to test the price offered against the market and you will need to feel confident of your relationship with the supplier to be comfortable with this. There is no easy way round this; other suppliers will be loathe to give even ballpark figures without producing their own tender and it is therefore difficult to market test the price.
2 You will also probably find that by controlling this element of the project yourself, your team will understand the process better, buy-in will be greater, and you will feel more in control. You will therefore be better able to distinguish a good work-around to a major problem from a simple reassurance designed to ensure that the software sale is completed.

If you have selected a single preferred supplier it is important that he is aware of, and possibly present at, each stage of the definition of the functional requirement. His early involvement will allow him to guide the specification towards the achievable and start to inform his implementation team of the issues which need to be solved for the solution to be successful.

Because most property solutions for estate management cover very similar functionality it is the implementation that will make the difference in the final system, not the basic software. The most critical stages of the implementation are therefore before the implementation is started, ie in preparation, and the basic element of this is the functional requirement.

Whether you choose a single preferred supplier or wish to conduct a tender, it is now time to conduct a review of the processes to be covered by the new system. This will form the basis of the specification and defining the detail at this stage has many benefits.

1 It is a great opportunity to refine the way in which you work. Many of the improvements are likely to be possible without new software and some may be possible with

existing software. This process will identify the scope of the requirement and whether a new system is required at all.

2 As each process is identified, and refined, much of the business case for selecting a new system will also be defined. It will be possible to estimate the man-hours saved by improving a process and the exercise may show gaps in existing processes where further savings can be achieved.

3 The team will get to understand the improvements that can be made and will prioritise the most important changes. This will clarify the requirement to the supplier and provide a clear definition of what a successful solution will look like.

4 Because they will need to work through the processes together, your whole team will know what to expect of the new software and will eagerly anticipate the new solution. This is important in reducing the common problem of teams not accepting new IT or not adopting new working practices.

5 The process review will give a detailed understanding of the objectives and the team can therefore choose an internal project manager rather than rely on a contractor or consultant. An internal project manager who understands what the supplier has promised and knows the business needs should be able to recognise where the project falls short and take remedial action with the supplier. This will save the cost of an external project manager and again ensure that the solution directly relates to the needs of the team.

6 The functional specification will give you a series of check boxes to review the outcome of the solution and judge how successful was the implementation.

I described the approach to business process analysis using the RPM in Chapter 2. We have already identified where most business benefit will be achieved by using the Five Globes and the opportunity framework models. The RPM takes the analysis to much lower levels and provides a structure for holding information about individual processes. It allows you to build a map of the whole business within which certain areas can be automated and then, as Phase 2, other areas can be addressed without losing track of the overall strategy.

Whether at the level of a team, department or company, over time, the RPM will knit together with detailed process maps for every part of the structure. This can provide additional clarity and benefits when planning roles and responsibilities and also in providing documentation for Quality Assurance (QA) programs.

For now, we will look at how the RPM can be used to define the first, critical, processes to be automated.

The RPM

As described in Chapter 3, the RPM is a framework for defining common process areas in a business. The diagram in Figure 3.5 showed the top level of the property management

RPM and it is likely that through the prioritisation processes in Chapter 4, certain functional areas of the RPM will already have been defined as critical.

A typical RPM at this stage of the process is shown in Figure 5.2 where the red blocks indicate the critical processes.

The critical processes are initially identified through your own knowledge of the work the team undertakes or through discussion with the team. It will be clear from existing systems which areas are covered wholly or partly and it will become clear very quickly which areas produce the major headaches in dealing with day-to-day work.

There are two basic questions underpin the identification of critical areas.

1 Which areas provide the most problems, or would provide the most problems if not effectively supported by a system? Are there paper-flow issues or does this part of the process take a particularly long time? Do clients or other parts of the company frequently complain about the lateness of reports in this area or their lack of accuracy or consistency?
2 Which areas generate profit for the business? For a property company, it is most important to recover rent. For an occupier, it is most important to minimise costs. Try to analyse the functional areas that achieve these aims.

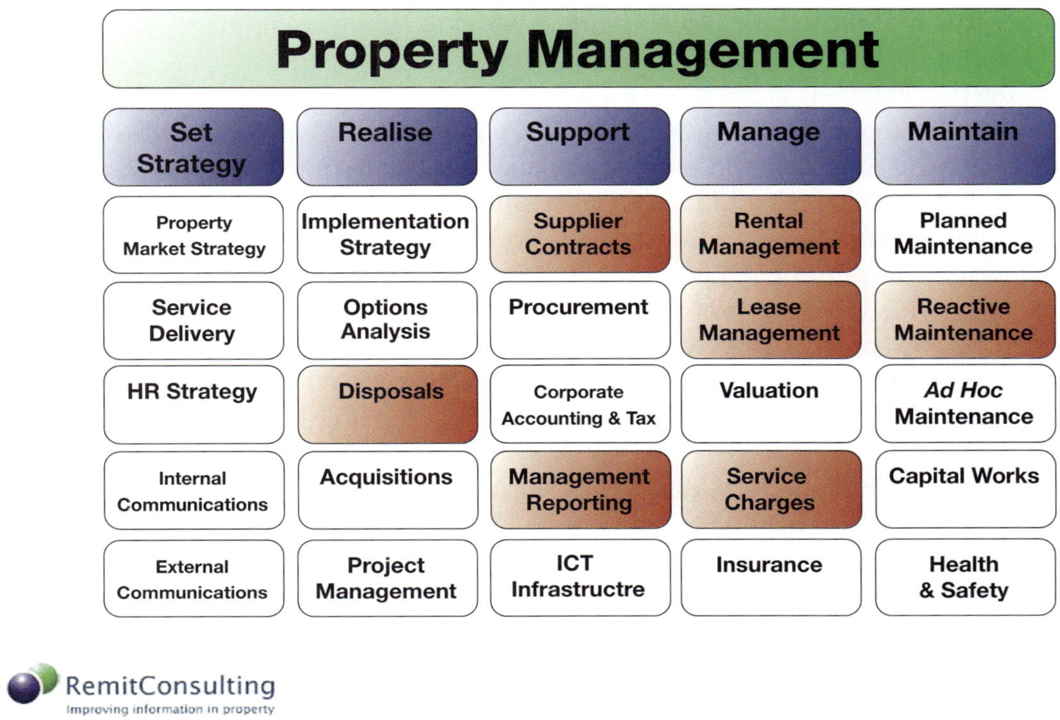

Figure 5.2 Property Management RPM showing critical process areas

In the selection of a new system, it is the critical processes which will make the most difference to the success of the new system and it is with these that you may wish to be most prescriptive. Other processes are important but you may be willing to adapt your workflow to a more generic solution.

Some processes may be unique to your organisation or may be particularly problematic. For example in corporate occupier teams links to finance and insurance teams will usually rely on the processes already in place in those departments. Identification of these processes at this stage will allow discussion about how to minimise any complications for a new system. It may be possible to eliminate complexity at this stage through discussion with the relevant department or team; if not, these process areas might be included in the critical process list.

In Figure 5.2, using these questions we have reduced the focus of the project from 25 possible areas to the seven that will make the most difference to the team. The other areas are not ignored; they will be part of any full estate management system and will need to be included in the specification in due course. However, it is the red process areas that are driving the business case for a new solution and these are the processes against which the system should be tested.

For simplicity I have not coloured the other parts of the diagram but typically other areas will be coloured yellow to show that the functional areas are performed adequately, or green to show that the areas need no work at present. Yellow areas are often identified as being suitable for review within Phase 2.

Each of the process areas in the diagram contains a significant number of sub-processes and most suffer from ambiguous titles. Even if the internal team agrees on the definition of an area, software suppliers will more than likely use different terminology and so it is important to define each area and its sub-processes.

Furthermore, the software supplier is likely to have drawn his process boundaries at different points – important if you want to minimise the integration issues, and key functionality is spread over several software modules.

In more complex process reviews, the definitions of each process can be logged on Process Description Sheets (PDS), an example of which is shown later in this chapter.[1] The PDS forms a set of reference notes that will form part of the basis for process documentation and review.

The next level down of the RPM diagram is shown in Figure 5.3. The diagram combines a number of different Level 1 functional areas and becomes much more closely tailored to the individual organisation. Each functional area by itself can be compared with leading practice in other companies but the way in which it interacts with other areas can be unique.

Figure 5.3 shows a RPM diagram that is typical for a property management accounting team, and, as such, represents only a portion of the processes highlighted in Figure 5.2 as critical.

1 Example PDS at page 112

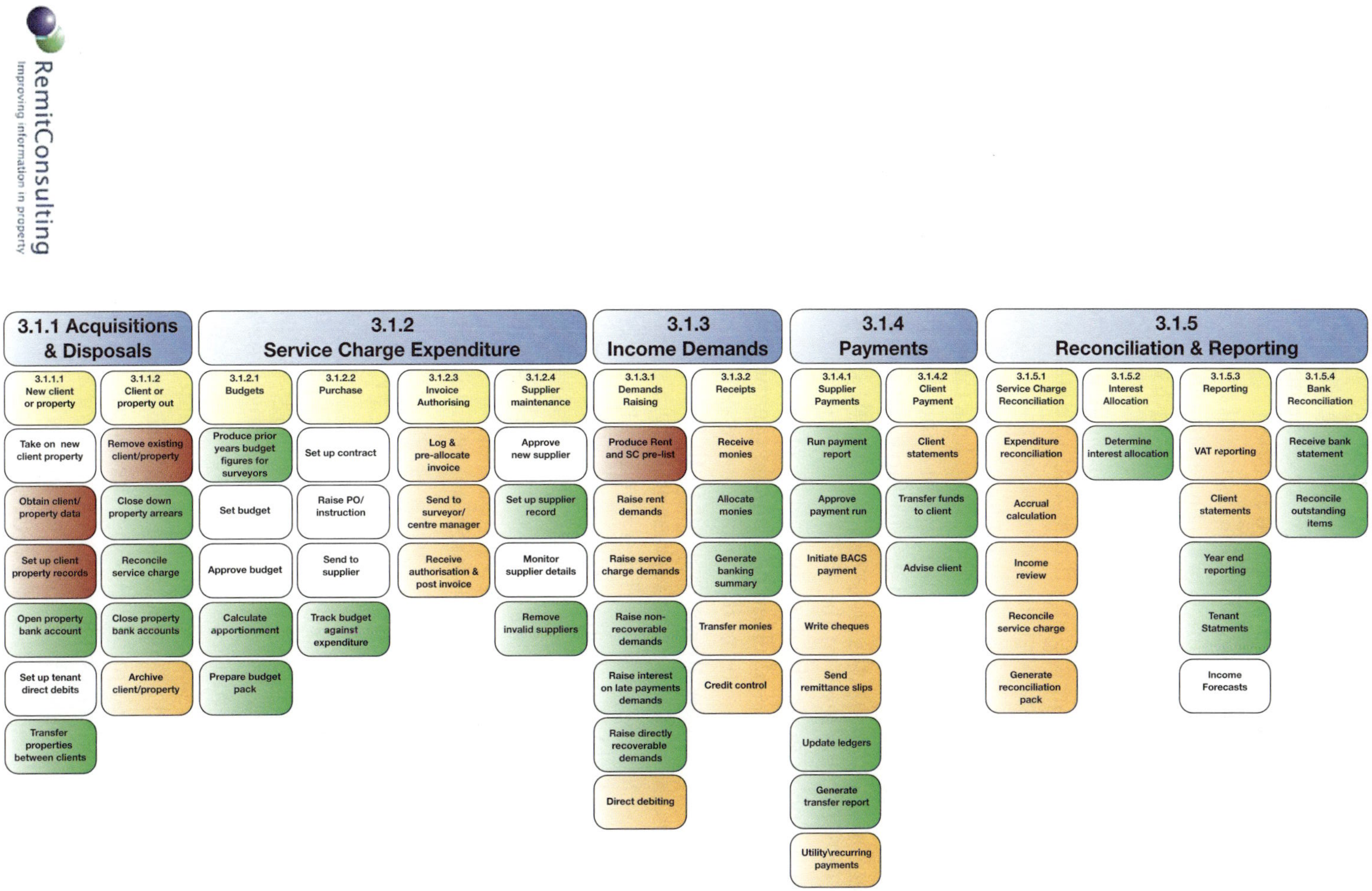

Figure 5.3 Property Management RPM Level 2 showing critical process areas

The large number of boxes in Figure 5.3 clearly demonstrates why we need to identify the critical processes. It would be too time-consuming to do this for every process in the top level RPM; if we tried to analyse every process the benefits of this detailed approach would be lost and the project would never be finished.

This level is significantly more detailed and some of the RPM decomposition begins to give a rough idea of how each process works. For example, in Figure 5.3, the process boxes under 3.1.1.1, "New Client or Property", give a distinct chronological order and a high-level workflow. Contrast this with the lack of workflow indicated under 3.1.5.3, "Reporting", where there is no indication of chronological order.

In each case, once we look at the functional area in detail, it is easy to see that much of the useful detail is still missing and the process of prioritising the critical areas needs to be undertaken again.

To judge how areas are prioritised for inclusion, let's take disposals as an example. The management department of an agency firm might hand the disposal to their agency team. The management department does not need to carry out the disposal work but may need to keep notes of the progress of the disposal. The needs of the management team can be detailed in the PDS for this level of the RPM diagram and if automation or workflow is necessary, it can be included in the system specification.

If the process is simply passed elsewhere in the organisation and the estates management team makes little revenue from it, nor do they waste much time on it, this process is not "Critical". Automation may therefore wait until Phase 2.

Often the next level of detail can be represented by a process map drawn with a software package such as Microsoft Visio. The same can be done in packages like Microsoft PowerPoint and Excel, but Visio is often more convenient for this type of exercise. It is also useful to buy a package that converts files to a PDF as used by Adobe Acrobat. This will enable you to share the results of the process mapping with colleagues and suppliers who do not have the same drawing package.

The process map in Figure 5.4 shows the flow of information through the budgeting process. There are different streams, or "swim lanes" to show the departments or roles involved in the process and the different shaped boxes represent different types of information flow, such as paper documents or databases.

The combination of notes within the PDS and the process chart gives a very good understanding of the detail of each process and, importantly, shows obvious points of difficulty or problems within the process. Identifying where the problems are is the starting point for improvement ideas and this detailed understanding will identify the types of savings that could be achieved if the problem or difficulty were solved.

For example, if a paper trail of signatures to authorise a transaction takes five days and involves two hours of staff time in tracking the paper, it is easy to judge how much resource/cost would be saved by changing, scrapping or automating this process through, for example, e-mail. By adding the various savings together across all the mapped processes, a set of savings figures can be achieved.

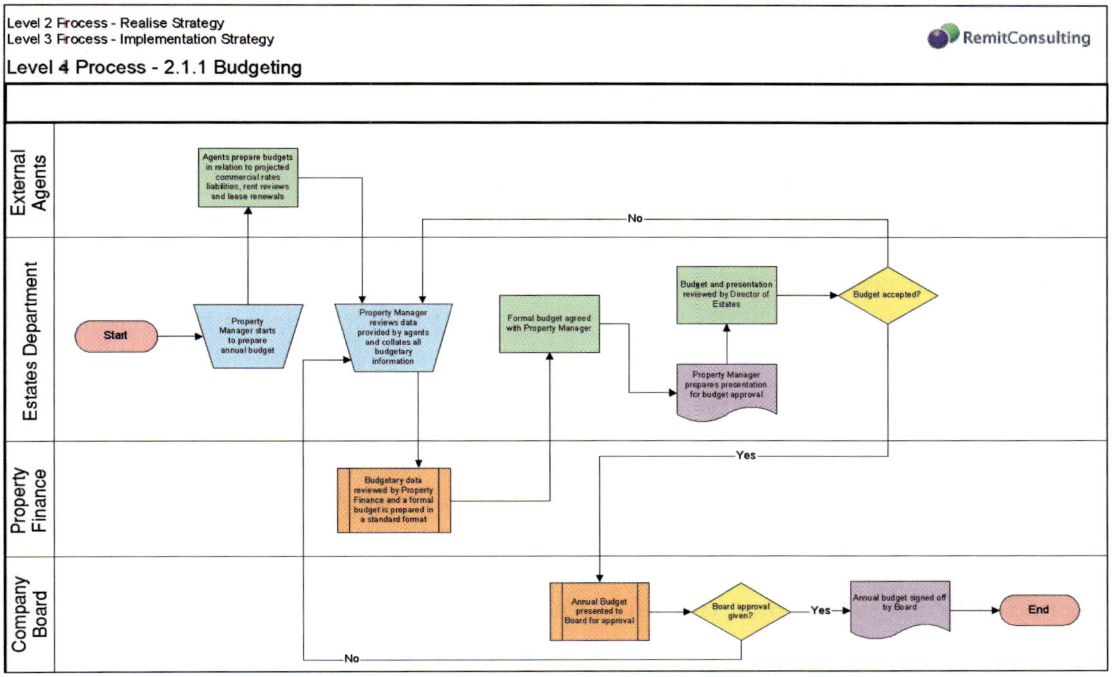

Figure 5.4 Typical process map

Additionally, many of the savings are likely to be achievable without a new system. Often this process identifies improvements that can be implemented immediately with no new system and these will be quick wins that will help to justify a new system.

Following the current state analysis, it is useful to look back at the business case and adjust the measures because this exercise will have added more detail and produced more realistic estimates.

Future State Analysis

The identification of quick wins is the first stage of designing the future state of the processes. The approach chosen for the future state analysis depends on several factors.

1. If a preferred supplier has already been chosen it is worth considering a jointly developed future state with that supplier. This will shorten the design phase and allow the supplier to influence the workflow agreed with the users.
2. If you intend to set up a tender, you will need to design generic future state processes which can be adapted to fit most systems.
3. If you have abandoned the idea of packaged software and intend to build a bespoke solution, the next exercise will be only the start of the specification stage.

A typical generic future state process is shown in Figure 5.5. The main process steps are shown but the particular aspects of the process that are unique to each implementation are not shown.

For example, the flow of the information between departments is not shown because this will depend on whether the system is stand alone or integrated across several teams. When reviewing the process flow from this basic level, authorisation points and inputs from each department can be added and challenged as the process is designed around the new system.

Notes can be added to the diagram showing which reports are necessary at each process step and this will then complement the reports analysis described later in this chapter[2].

The advantage of the generic diagram is that the suppliers have the opportunity to redesign the process to take account of the level of integration between departments and roles in their system.

In all cases, the intention of the generic future state diagram is to act as a baseline case so that different systems can be compared effectively: apples and apples, rather than apples and pears. This approach also saves time for the supplier who has less need to carry out business analysis at this early stage with you.

Armed with the future state diagrams for all the critical processes, we can define the test scripts.

Test Scripts

A test script has to demonstrate that the proposed solution will work in a certain way and produce the required result. But what do we mean by a test script?

One type of test script is always used by software developers to check that the software behaves as expected. For example, if a screen requires the input of numbers that can be calculated to produce a result in a valuation, the role of a tester is to work through each step of the process of inputting data and pressing the calculation button. In this way bugs and malfunctions will be found early on in the software development and fed back to the programmers for amendment.

We are all used to international software from large companies such as Microsoft and Adobe that normally work perfectly straight out of the packaging. It will not usually matter in which order the keys are pressed; the program will help you out and there are ways of recovering lost data if the worst happens. Even on the Web, most websites that are produced by large organisations have been thoroughly tested and will not crash or hang.

2 Reports Analysis, page 119

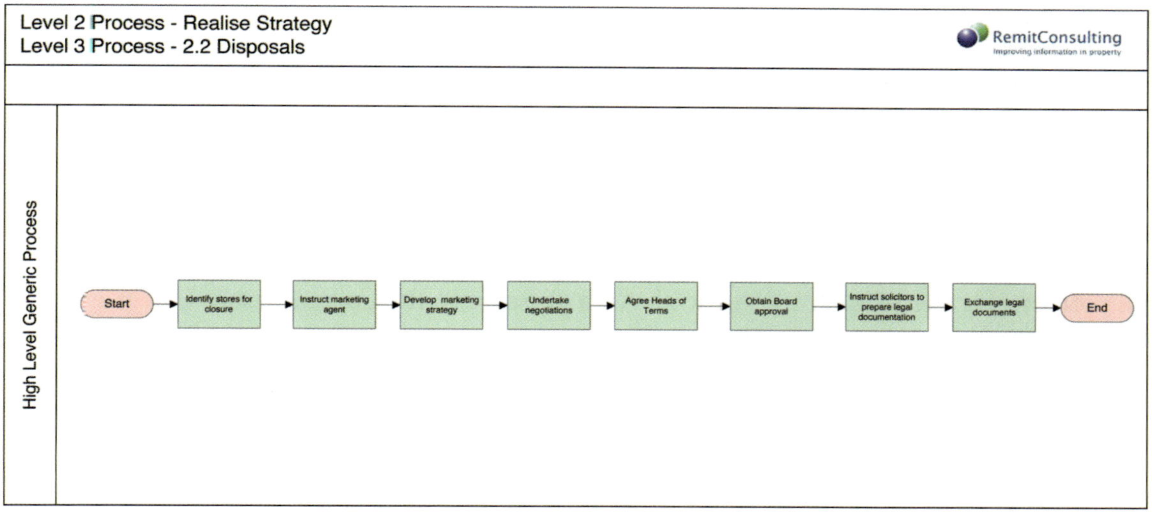

Figure 5.5 Generic Future State Process

The same process occurs when property software companies develop software. The software will be tested to ensure that in the normal course of events a user will not get into too much trouble. The budgets in the property software industry are smaller than those in the global companies but the software should do what it says on the box.

Typically, a tester in a software development team will have been briefed by a user and/or business analyst and he will know which key-presses are relevant to each operation in the application. Individual areas of the software will be tested to destruction so that pressing strange keys in the middle of the operation will not result in a system failure.

Further, the software company's business analyst and other users will have provided typical scenarios for the tester to work through to show typical usage. These too can usually be relied upon to work.

However, despite the long history of property management through the ages, and the establishment of property management teams dealing with properties across the world, most property managers employ a wide variety of approaches to lower level processes. The route of an invoice from the post room to the payment of a cheque can be short or tortuous, depending on the organisation.

At one company I worked with they allowed their staff to carry out the same process six different ways across different client teams. Obviously this was not a conscious decision but as the number of teams had grown, with new people joining from other organisations, all the teams had developed their own approach to management. Consequently, the software they used supported no one effectively.

Advances in the use of software and better understanding of property management have helped standardise some of these processes, but it is likely that a great proportion of processes within a company will differ from those designed by the software company.

Thus, despite the efforts of the software company to test the software before it leaves their premises, it will seldom work with the processes in place in your company.

This, in itself, is not a problem. Most software implementation plans will adapt the software to work with the customer's processes or change the processes in the customer's team to match those of the software. However, the basic rule is to change the process, not the software. If the software does not have a close fit to the current processes, it is better to find software with a closer fit or change the processes than change the software.

It is by testing at an early stage that the customer can do the most to ensure that the system will actually improve the way in which the team works. Furthermore, the testing needs to be at a level of detail appropriate to what needs to be tested.

Designing the scripts

As discussed above, the basic testing of the system carried out by the software development team will have ensured that the solution will work in one or even a number of situations and will be stable. The testing, which now needs to be carried out, is to discover how different the customer's view is of how their critical processes should be undertaken from that of the supplier. In other words, how much will the system need to be changed if the system is implemented or, alternatively, how much will the customer have to change the working practices of their team?

We can usually expect the software to have been written to match the majority of processes that we have selected and we have, through the exercises in the preceding chapters, narrowed the selection to just those processes that are critical. We therefore have approximately half a dozen processes mapped to a level which, with the PDS, describes the input and output, the individual elements of the process, the roles and responsibilities, and any processes to which it links.

The aim of developing test scripts at this stage is to give the supplier enough information so that they can demonstrate the software in a situation that is relevant to the customer's current requirements. This is the first point at which the supplier has been encouraged to deviate from their pre-planned and well-honed demonstration. This is essential because the chances of the standard demonstration processes fitting your organisation out of the box are very low.

The information within the critical process analysis is needed to develop test scripts that allow the supplier to "walk through" the *customer's* critical process, showing how the software supports each step. It will not fit exactly but this procedure will show up obvious flaws and encourage discussion of how to solve the problems that become apparent.

The script will detail the start of a process, the actions to carry it out and the expected end result. As an example let us take the process of rent collection. We would usually

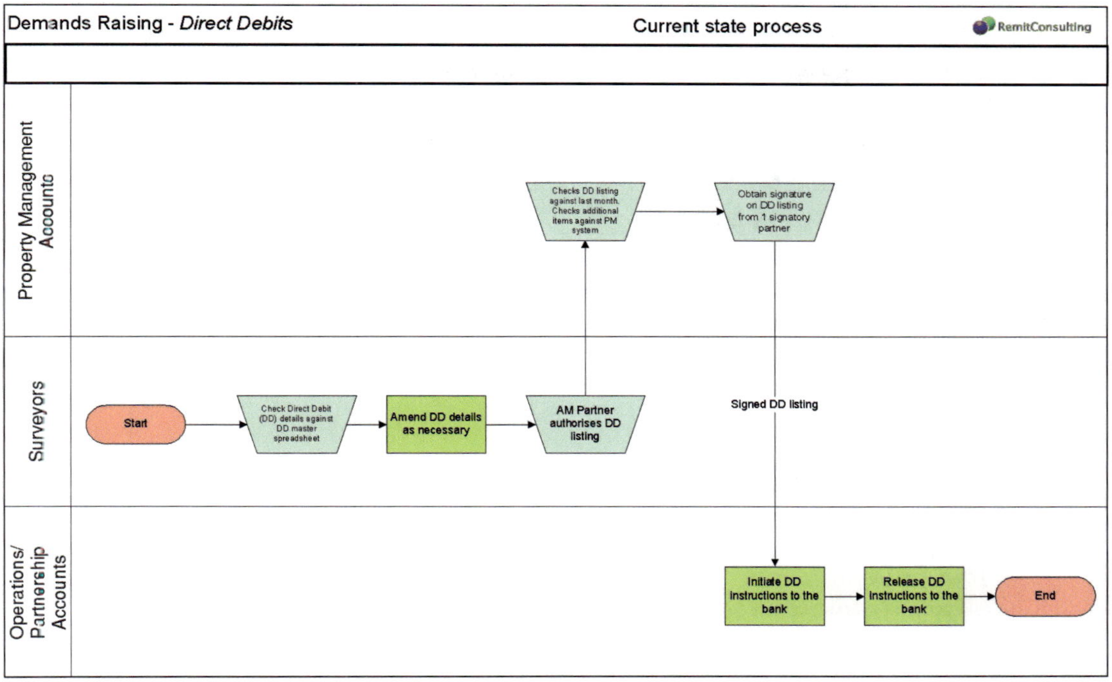

Figure 5.6

expect several different processes for raising demands depending on whether the demands are periodic (eg monthly or quarterly), raised *ad hoc* or demanded by direct debit. For simplicity, the diagram above (Figure 5.6) shows the process in place (current state) for direct debits although the other related processes will usually be more complex.

The PDS for demands raising, of which the diagram in Figure 5.6 is a part, is shown in Figure 5.7.

The test script will therefore comprise the following elements.

- Scenario.
- Test Data.
- Actions.
- Expected result.

The software supplier will be required to enter the test data in their system and show how the software can be used in the manner set out in the script. If the software deals with this set of actions in a different way from that expected, it will be very obvious. Likewise, if the software has not been configured to carry out this process, the test will show this up.

RemitConsulting
Improving information in property

Supplemental Process Descriptions

MEGA PROCESS: INCOME DEMANDS
Major Process: Demands raising
Purpose
Raise income (rent, service charge, insurance, interest) demands and send invoices to tenants for the properties managed on behalf of clients.
Inputs
Schedule for regular demands. Request from surveyor to raise a demand. Demands pre-list from last run (for Asset Managers review process). Direct debit master spreadsheet.
Outputs
Demands pre-list report. Expenditure report for directly recoverable properties. Summary directly recoverable spreadsheet. Rent review diary report. Lease expiry diary report. Interest on late payments report. Aged debtors report. Posting period charge report. Tenant Invoice. Information to tenants to accompany invoices (depending on situation e.g. SC budget). Updated direct debit information in bank system. Direct debit instructions to bank.
Other Notes
Sub-process: Generate rent and service charge pre-list
Investment Management (IM) receives a much more comprehensive set of reports than Asset Management (AM). Property Management Accounts (PMA) sends the Rent Pre-List to AM for authorisation one week before the demands are run. AM visually compares this month's pre-list report with last month's, and then checks any differences on Retrieve. AM finds this a laborious, unwelcome task which occasionally does not get done. Rent Pre-List provided to IM on a quarterly basis for most of their portfolio. This is a key control for the IM / PMA interface. System does not have audit reports that might be used to highlight changes since the last demand run.

PDS Demands raising.doc Page 1 of 1

Figure 5.7

It is not necessarily a problem that the software undertakes the process differently from the client's current state processes. It may be that the software company has actually implemented current market leading practice and this will be a good opportunity for the client to improve their processes. Once again this becomes immediately apparent from running through the scripts.

The example below is based on the rent collection process. This is a critical process for many real estate businesses and the system needs to show full functionality in this area.

Step 1 – The data

Generally for testing the purchaser would use real data, enabling the outcome generated by the system being tested to be matched to reality. However, if the purchaser is anticipating an increase in complexity in the estate, it may be advantageous to add in some "dummy" data. Data should be used for testing that is a reasonable reflection of the major part of the estate's value.

For this example we will use a property company called Duke Holdings that owns a mixed industrial and commercial estate in England and Scotland. Rent and service charge collection is carried out in-house. The estate has been built up over many years and there is no uniformity of service charge years or bases. Duke Holdings has two property managers and one service charge manager

Property 1

Unit 5b, White Way Industrial Park, Silverbridge, Barsetshire BA1 3AT

Rent – £24,500 pa payable quarterly in advance, usual quarter days

Lease for 15 years from 1 June 2000

Rateable Value – £13,000, Rateable value of whole business park – £198,000

Service charge – based on a proportion of rateable value

Service charge year – 1 Nov–31 Oct

Five yearly upward only reviews. Next review 1 June 2005

Tenant – Slo-fit Exhausts

Property Manager – P Finn

Service Charge Manager – L Standish

Property 2

1st Floor Offices, Matching House, Palliser Road, St Bungay, Edinburgh ED2 1PP

Rent – £17,875 pa payable quarterly in advance, Scottish quarter days

Lease for 20 years from 1 February 1996

GIA – 1,700 sq ft, Square footage of whole building 17,364 sq ft

Service charge – based on square footage

Service charge year – 1 Jan–31 Dec

Five yearly reviews. Next review due 1 Feb 2006

Tenant – Glencora Recruitment Consultants

Property Manager – E Eustace

Service Charge Manager – L Standish

Property 3

3rd and 4th Floor Offices, Proudie House, Grantly Way, Barchester,

Rent – 3rd Floor £4,500, 4th Floor £3,200

Lease of 3rd Floor for 20 years from 1 September 1990

Lease of 4th Floor for 17 and a quarter years from 1 June 1993

GIA of 3rd Floor 2,700 sq ft, GIA of 4th Floor 1,800 sq ft, Square footage of whole building 12,000 sq ft

Service charge – based on square footage

Service charge year – 1 March–28 Feb

Five yearly rent review on both. Due on 3rd Floor 1 Sept 2005 and on 4th Floor on 1 June 2008

Tenant – Omnium Holdings

Property Manager – M Grex

Service Charge Manager – L Standish

There is one quarter's rent arrears on 3rd Floor – (£1,150)

Step 2 – The tests.

This should be a typical scenario that system users would expect to encounter regularly. It will be easier to grade the system if the business process is stated clearly. The actual instructions should be stated in simple terms and broken down into the appropriate sub-processes. The expected outcomes should also be defined.

Scoring the Tests

The aim is to make grading as objective as possible. It is probably best done on a numeric scale, eg one–five rather than a simple yes or no. In theory, if you are making a comparison between more than one system it may be useful to weight the scores, however as we are concentrating on critical processes they will all have similar weights.

Mega Process – Manage Estate	Expected Outcome	Weighting	Grade	Comment
Major Process – Rent Collection				
Rent Collection				
Sub Process – Preparing the Rent Roll				
Information It is 15th December 2003.				
Requirement Run a report showing the rents due on 25th December	Sample Report 1			
Sub Process – Account for Rent				
Information It is 28th December 2003. A direct debit for £4468.75 has been received from Slo-fit Exhausts. A cheque has been received for £1,300 from Omnium Holdings with the code pertaining to 4th Floor. This is an overpayment of £500. No rent has been received for 3rd Floor.				
Requirement Show how the various sums will be entered into the system Show automatic generation of notice to M Grex of rent arrears Run post quarter day rent report.	Easy navigation round the screens; Automatic calculation of VAT; Rent outstanding amount should clear from Unit 5b. Depending on the business process of Duke Holdings, the incorrect rent received from 4th Floor should be returned with a request for an updated cheque. Alternatively the sum may be entered and should show a credit balance. A second failure to pay for 3rd Floor should escalate to action – automatic generation of a reminder to the property manager and automatic generation of letter to the tenant.			

A useful additional test is to abandon a transaction part way through, delete a property that is being updated elsewhere on the system, or turn off the PC to test that the basics software is robust.

The scripts should be demonstrated with as many members of your team present as possible. This is important because they have defined much of the work done to date and their presence at the demonstrations will allow them to voice any detailed concerns and seek reassurance from the suppliers.

Each member of the team should have an agenda for the demonstration session and a score sheet that can be discussed afterwards at a debriefing once the supplier has left.

It is through defining the test scripts that it also becomes clear whether there is a real understanding of how work is done within the team. If there are doubts as to how to detail a script, it is likely that there is disagreement among team members about the best way to carry out the work; a useful indicator that more time should be spent reaching agreement within the internal team.

Reports Analysis

The last area of functional requirement I cover here is "Reporting". This may be a good place to start the analysis of current processes but it is also a good safety check at the end of the exercises.

The theory behind the reports analysis is that your organisation will need a number of regular reports, be they daily, weekly, monthly, quarterly, etc. There will also be an occasional demand for *ad hoc* reports.

Many functional requirements describe their need for reporting as "very flexible, with the ability for all staff to easily create bespoke reports". Suppliers have responded accordingly with their marketing literature and sales demonstrations and there is a vast and well-established part of the software industry providing both simple and complex reporting software.

Why is there a need for this? Most reporting required from real estate systems is regular and repeated. Certainly, many people would like slightly different reports from time to time but the vast majority of regular reports should not change from month to month or year to year. If they need to, it implies that there was some woolly thinking going on when the report was first designed.

And yet, defining clearly what reports are required from the system tells so much about what the system does; it distils the essence of the problem and often points to the solution. If the board need to know only that capital receipts from disposals are in line with expectations, the system will need a link to the finance system; and in particular the area of the finance system where capital receipts are logged. If reporting is left as an afterthought, what chance is there of implementing a system which will pick up all the required detail? In my experience, not much.

This makes the reports analysis essential as both a starting point for the functional requirement and as a checklist before a tender is sent out. It is time-consuming and will, again, involve the system users compromising on layouts and styles. Hence, it is often left until last. There are ways to gain consensus from different views, some of which are discussed in Chapter 7, and this should not be a barrier on its own.

Reports analysis

In any organisation, there will be a wide range of reports that can be aligned by the level of the organisation to which they are relevant and by the time period between them. Figure 5.8 shows how they might be spread across both these axes in a typical organisation. Orange ovals represent the type of the report and their positioning shows roughly how often the reports are needed and the relative level of the organisation to which each is relevant.

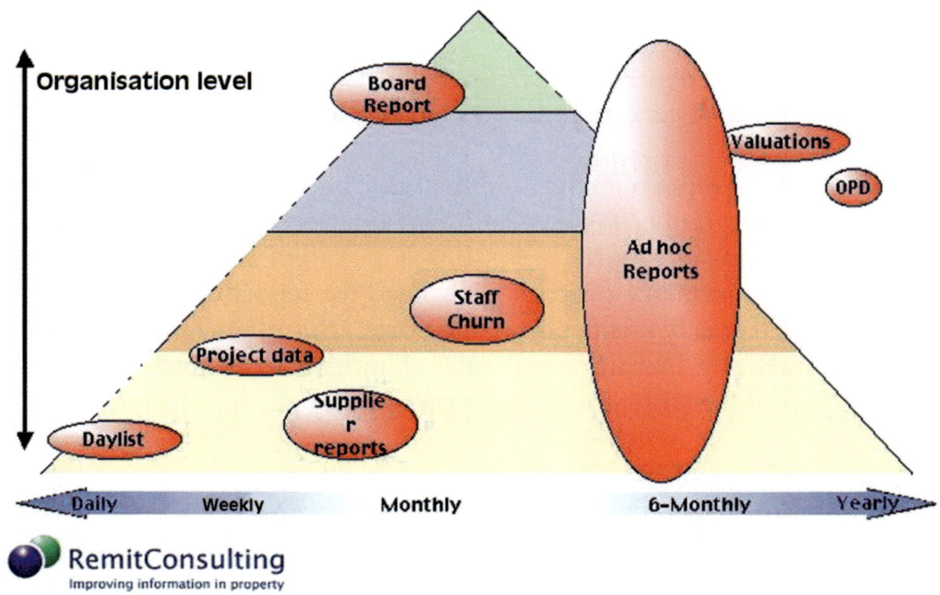

Figure 5.8 Reports analysis

Using this approach, each report can be logged in a table as shown in Figure 5.9 and this can be used as the basis for defining each report in turn. The advantage of using this technique is that discussions can be facilitated to ensure that any overlaps between similar reports are assessed; the output for each report can be agreed and validated.

A good starting point is always the existing set of reports in a company. It is amazing how many of these reports have been produced for years without review. Once a structured review is undertaken the number of reports in circulation reduces dramatically. This in itself helps to keep the reporting exercise within manageable limits. It is also useful to identify key improvement targets that can be used to focus the review.

An example of this could be to attempt to produce a single page report showing all key indicators for the Board. This has been achieved in the property fund sector where a single page report is the benchmark for reporting all the relevant performance figures for a fund. Each sector will have its own objectives and this exercise will, in itself, help the estates team to improve the way it interacts with other parts of the company. By examining the level of information provided to others and checking for relevance and consistency, the team should be able to provide concise data on the portfolio in a format which is useful – and thus improve the recognition of the team in the organisation.

Example Reports

Data	Monthly	Yearly	Ad hoc
• Outstanding rent reviews	• Board report	• Annual Valuation	• Merger/ acquisition reports
• Transaction status – e.g. Disposals	• Project updates	• Insurance revals	• Corporate strategy reviews
• Task list – Outlook	• Budget review	• Board summary	• Cost reduction exercises
	• Resourcing status	• Contract renewals	
	• Supplier contracts	• Yearly disposal list	
	• Benchmarking	• Rent review list	
	• Productivity		
	• Staff churn		

RemitConsulting
Improving information in property

Figure 5.9 Reports Analysis – Table Format

Some of the information required in the reports will be held in systems outside the control of the estate management team. This will open out the discussion to assess whether it is realistic to gather this data on a regular basis and if the system specification needs to include links to other systems.

Importantly, it will also show where the information enters the organisation and how it is managed once it is in the business. The worst situation is for data to arrive in the business in, say, paper format in more than one department. If it is keyed into two different systems with the hope that it is reconciled later, the chances of at least one department using bad information is quite high. The information may never be reconciled with predictable consequences as these errors build up over time.

Much of the information in the reports will be expected to be provided by the new system and this can now be clearly stated and rationalised against the functional requirement. For example, if there is information produced by the critical processes that is not used in a report, is the process really that critical? If it is critical, should information from that process be reported more effectively?

There may be information that is collected outside the scope of the critical processes and this exercise gives the opportunity to add or remove critical processes as a final check before the functional requirement is complete.

Data map

At the end of the reports analysis we will have a list of reports that have been defined in detail so that the objective of the report is clear. They will also have been at least roughly designed to show preferred layout and to check clarity.

In order to make this analysis truly useful to a system supplier, it is necessary to plot where the information on the reports is held on the various systems that have been identified above.

The format is relatively straightforward; there will be a single point at which the information enters the organisation. This might be the lease details from the lawyer to the estate manager, or a supplier invoice to the finance team.

At this point, the data entered into the system will become the point of reference and as this data flows through other systems it will remain the primary source of this piece of data. A typical data map is shown in Figure 5.10.

Functional Requirement – Summary

We have looked at the constituent parts of the functional requirement for a packaged system selection. We have defined the following.

- Process areas within scope.
- Critical processes and generic process maps (and process descriptions, where necessary).

- Test scripts and test data.
- Reporting analysis and data map.

These elements will be used in the tender described in the next document and will help the supplier to understand the requirement and tailor their response to your needs. More importantly, your team will have been a part of the definition process and your key team members will have defined exactly what they expect the system to achieve once it is implemented.

It is this last point that will make the difference in implementing your new solution. You are no longer relying on the supplier to sell you a system which he thinks will help your business; you know exactly what you expect, how you expect the software to achieve its goal and how to measure the project's success.

Large systems and integration

The majority of property systems in use in the UK and US are packages designed for the real estate market but an increasing number of companies are implementing real estate modules from the enterprise system suppliers such as SAP and Peoplesoft. Even in

Data	Source	Primary store (Parent)	Secondary store (Child)
Rent	Agent/Lawyer?	Property system	Finance system
Supplier invoice	Supplier	Finance System	Tax system
			FM system
			Property system

RemitConsulting
Improving information in property

Figure 5.10 Example Data map

smaller implementations, real estate systems often have to integrate with generic accounting systems. Many of these systems cannot be tested on the assumption that they will carry out most of the functionality as standard.

Indeed, many of the integration situations will not be testable until the system has been built. It is worthwhile knowing how differently these companies will approach this type of project and adapting accordingly.

Enterprise systems

Most very large systems that cover many different areas of an organisation are developed as a series of modules that can be linked to provide a match to the functionality required. They are like a large box of play bricks that are put together in a different way at each implementation.

This means that they are usually adapted to suit a company's required functionality within a set of parameters, and it is not possible to ask the supplier to demonstrate an exact solution to your critical processes.

In these cases, it is important to see the track record of the supplier/implementer. In most cases the software company (SAP, etc.) will not actually implement the system themselves – the solution will be sold and implemented by one of their partners, eg Accenture, IBM, CapGemini or one of many others.

The reference visits and due diligence become more important and it is vital that the client knows exactly what to expect. This is where the same approach to process mapping becomes invaluable – if the client does not know (and document) exactly what a process is expected to do, there is little chance that the implementer will provide a system which works as expected.

Integration

Even using a packaged real estate system solution, integration with accounting systems usually needs to be checked separately and sufficient time and budget allowed to take care of the unexpected.

Many real estate suppliers will have already provided links to the main accounting systems for previous clients but check which versions of the respective packages were integrated before believing that this will be straightforward; there are sometimes significant differences in the way that different versions integrate with other software.

Again, understanding the information flows across the integrated software in detail is essential and you will need to develop these process maps and performance metrics for these in addition to the critical processes.

Buying IT 6

Back in Chapter 5, I said that traditional approaches to IT tenders are based upon a thick document of 200 pages that is submitted to a number of suppliers. By following the approach in Chapter 5 we now appear to have created a similarly thick document to be issued to suppliers. What's the difference?

Well, the traditional tender would by now include a long list of every possible feature that the teams could think they might need in a new system. The system requirement in a traditional process would have grown from fixing just the original problem to fixing every conceivable problem. The traditional tender checks the specification of the system. Our tender explains the problem that needs to be fixed.

Our approach has probably reduced the breadth of the requirement by focusing on just the requirements that will make a difference and provide a solution. Many of the team's needs will have been deferred to Phase 2 or 3. The tender document details the requirements in a way that a system supplier can understand. It also provides a method of testing whether the software will resolve the key problems and involves the whole team in checking the system against the requirement.

However, we have now come to the stage when we can go to suppliers to tender the requirement and, before we do this, we need to work out what type of suppliers will be approached. This is not straightforward because we need not only approach providers of relevant software. Let me explain.

Shall we drive or fly?

Let's imagine that I live 30 miles from my new job and I have decided to buy a car to get there every day. If you are like me, it is impossible to decide sensibly on the type of new car because I can easily make a strong case for the most impractical form of transport if I really want it.

I can almost hear myself saying, "Of course we can get away with a two-seater for a family of five. It will persuade us only to use the car for the most important trips and we will help save the planet when we walk everywhere else".

I am unlikely to win that argument but from that point, the discussion will cover the advantages of 4x4 vehicles against estate cars against MPVs; the discussion is unlikely to return to the beginning where the initial question should not have been "What type of car should we buy?", but "How do I get to work when my job is 30 miles away". What I need is regular, cheap, comfortable, transport. Buying a car is only one way of achieving a solution and has various problems and risks associated with it, eg where to park it, the cost of insurance and servicing, and the risk it will break down and strand me on my way to work.

Depending on circumstances, there are a number of ways that would achieve a daily commute without me having to buy a car. I could:

- take the train
- take the bus
- arrange for a regular taxi ride
- hire a car only on the days I need to make the trip to the office
- commute with a work colleague who already drives to work.

Many of these solutions will be cheaper or more reliable than buying a car. None are likely to satisfy my desire for a shiny new car, nor will they answer other problems I may have, such as how I get the children to school each day. However, to solve my most pressing problem, I do not have to buy a car with all its associated costs and risks.

Similarly, the need to improve, say, the paying of invoices by your accounts team may not need the purchase and installation of new software. The problem in this instance is the poor performance of paying invoices. The symptoms are that invoices are left outstanding for weeks, suppliers are less willing to deal with your company, and surcharges and fines are imposed on the company for late payments.

New software may not be the answer and may make things worse. Perhaps sufficiently well qualified and experienced personnel are unavailable or invoices are sent to one site and dealt with at another. Whatever the underlying cause, it is likely that there is a problem with the process of dealing with invoices as well as a potential need for software.

Because by now we have prioritised the critical processes in the company, we already know how much of the problem is due to the old IT system and how much can be dealt with by agreeing and formalising new working processes. If the majority of the benefit will be achieved through acquiring a new system, we can investigate a number of IT solutions. These are typically as follows.

1. Buy and implement a traditional system that is set up on a server within your organisation. Your IT team will be responsible for maintaining the system subject to any upgrades that are applied to the solution over time. Your company is responsible for the data backup, hardware and network infrastructure that supports the software.
2. Alternatively, an increasing number of systems can now be accessed through a standard web browser, such as Microsoft Internet Explorer or Netscape.

3 If it is necessary to access your system remotely, say from another office or from home, it is possible to set this up. There are two underlying technologies that make this possible which are described in more detail below.

The Spin on Web Access

These days we are all used to using the internet from many different locations. We take for granted the flexibility it provides to access what we need, from wherever we are, using whatever PC happens to be available. This might be in our own or someone else's office, at home or even an internet café.

So if you are thinking about selecting a new system, one of your key considerations is bound to be whether or not you will be able to access the system from a variety of locations, either over the public internet or some form of private network or intranet.

Ask the property software suppliers if their products can be accessed over the internet and their answer will almost certainly be "yes". But how do they achieve this?

Broadly, there are two different ways that a system is likely to be provided to users over the internet.

1 The software supplier may have specifically "web-enabled" their product. The property system will be designed to operate as an interactive website and you will be able to read and input property information through a standard web browser. It may look something like Amazon or any other business website, or it may have been designed to look something like a normal Windows system. Behind the browser will be a web server and behind that an application server. All you as a user will need is a PC or laptop with something like Internet Explorer, plus an appropriate internet or intranet connection and security rights.

2 Alternatively, "thin-client" software may be employed. You will see the same screens that you are used to in the office and they will not necessarily look like a website. The standard property system will run as normal on its application server, and thin-client software "translates" the screens you use from your server across the internet and onto your remote computer. The thin client software actually sets up and manages a separate "session" for each user on the server. You will need to load the thin-client software on the PC or laptop you want to use and, once loaded, you can access the "session" over the internet or intranet. The concept is similar to that of an old-fashioned dumb terminal to mainframe connection.

The most common thin-client software available is supplied by Citrix, and this sits on top of, and enhances, Microsoft's own Windows Terminal Services thin-client. There are other cheaper products, for instance from Tarantella, but these are less well established. Thin-client software may even be an integral part of the system environment the property package supplier ships with their product.

Does it matter to you which method the supplier has chosen? In theory it does not but you might wish to consider the following points as a minimum.

The thin-client method normally relies on an extra element of software on the PC you want to use. This small piece of software is delivered to whichever PC you are using and automatically installed before you can start working.

While this installation is relatively simple to achieve, you might want to use a PC where it is not available or installation is not permitted, eg in an internet café or at a client. This is not an issue you are likely to encounter with web-enabled software requiring only a standard browser.

Thin-client software potentially adds some additional overheads. Citrix licence costs are not cheap but this may soon change because of new competition in the market following Tarantella's acquisition of Citrix rival, New Moon Systems. On the other hand, if the thin-client software is an integral part of the property system it may represent no extra cost. You will also need to consider the costs of a probably complex initial set-up, and any extra ongoing support overhead.

Your organisation may have already implemented a thin-client infrastructure for other systems, and this will certainly be a factor to take into account since you may already have the necessary software licences, infrastructure and expertise available. Thin-client technology often brings additional features such as centralised password management for all your systems and this can represent a cost-effective way of implementing this extra security.

You may also be thinking about remote access to specific functions on devices other than normal PCs or laptops, for instance on PDAs or tablet PCs. This is clearly a developing trend, and whichever option you choose there are a similar range of considerations with both solutions.

Property systems suppliers often make use of third party reporting tools (Business Objects, COGNOS, etc) to create and print reports as part of their offering. Whether web-enabled or thin-client, consider carefully how these fit into the overall solution.

There may be technical issues; there may be licence issues. Some thin-client solutions in the past have been less than perfect when it comes to properly directing reports from the server to your local printer. And remember that a 200-page report is 200 pages worth of data that has to be transferred over the internet or network whatever the chosen access method. Make sure your connection bandwidth can cope.

You will also want to ensure that the level of security you require can be provided (and it almost certainly can be whichever method is employed), particularly if you are accessing your system across the public internet.

Different property system suppliers have taken different approaches.

- A minority have fully web-enabled their products; that it is only a few is not surprising since it takes a significant development investment to reengineer to this extent.
- Some suppliers have assumed that core system functions, particularly data entry screens, will only be used centrally and not over an internet or intranet connection. Consequently, they have developed specific web-enabled functions, but often enquiry only and sometimes to provide only summary and management information.
- Other suppliers rely completely on thin-client technology to deliver their standard systems.

There is another interesting option for access to a system over the internet. Software such as GoToMyPc enables you to access your office PC desktop from any location connected to the internet through a web browser. Once connected, you can use any of your systems as though you are sitting in the office at your PC, even sending reports to a printer if you have one close by. Like all "remote-control" solutions, performance will depend on the speed of the internet connections, but if you are looking for an easy way to get secure remote access up and running from any location over the internet, this is an option worth investigating. For a small number of licences, the software is available on a subscription basis, and there is no other extra infrastructure required.

In conclusion, you will need to decide what are your specific needs and question in detail what the property systems suppliers tell you. It is impossible to tell which of these technologies is truly "future proof" and which may require replacement in five years time. However, all the approaches outlined above work and suppliers will be able to direct you to reference sites that function well.

As ever, good preparation and planning are the keys to selection. Work out how you use remote access now and make a plan for future use based on your actual needs. Once you have established these needs, it will be easier to validate each approach, and each supplier's proposal against your needs. In this way you can take control of the selection process, implement a solution, and move on to your next business requirement.

This section is taken from an article by Mark Jones of Remit Consulting that first appeared in Property Systems Review.

If you wish to buy the system and control it yourself, there are a number of issues to decide.

- Do I wish to buy and maintain the hardware and software involved in this solution?
- Do I wish to access the system remotely? If so, would I prefer to access it over the Web through a plain internet browser, or should I rely on proprietary software such as Citrix to enable remote working?

Get rid of your hardware

Taking this discussion one step further, if you would rather not buy and maintain the servers and infrastructure to support the software, it is possible to use the technology described above to purchase software as a service. What does this mean and how does it work?

Many people now access their bank accounts on the internet. They use an internet browser to access a software application that is calculating, monitoring and changing the amounts of money in your bank account. In this example, all the financial software being used in the process of paying a bill online is on the bank's servers and is maintained by their IT staff. Depending on the terms of your contract with the bank, you, as an individual, need not pay anything for the software at the bank and only need a PC to access it. If you log in from an internet café, you need not even invest in buying a PC – you can hire one for the length of time it takes to conduct a transaction.

In the same way, companies who develop property software are beginning to offer a service whereby they provide access to their software over the internet. If you wanted to run your property management business from an internet café, you would simply log into a secure website provided by the software company and conduct any transactions or maintenance to the property accounts online.

All of the software program and the data would be stored at the site of the software company. It would not matter if you accessed it from your office, from your study or wirelessly from the beach.

The type of company that can provide this type of arrangement is known as an Application Service Provider (ASP). The beauty of this arrangement is that it absolves the user from knowing anything about the IT hardware necessary to run the application.

It should spread the overall cost of buying IT systems over a longer period than if you were to buy and set up the system yourself. There may also be savings because the costs and risks can be spread over a large number of user companies. However, despite the improved affordability, like car leasing, the extra costs of finance and margins make the service more expensive in the long run.

The benefits are that the user need not hire IT staff to deal with the new applications and the software will be upgraded more frequently. The potential for this type of software procurement is discussed in more detail in Chapter 9.

Outsourcing by stealth

Unfortunately, it is never quite that simple. If you select this approach, you are in effect outsourcing the IT support for your critical business processes. In the previous chapters we have already prioritised the processes that make the most difference to your business and it is these for which we are currently seeking external support.

This therefore needs careful consideration and it is easy to underestimate the process of outsourcing this aspect of the contract. I deal with outsourcing later in this chapter but in respect of ASPs, it is often better to consider the software you need, the supplier of the hosted service, and the supplier of the IT infrastructure as separate items, even if you buy a package of these from your supplier.

You will see that the services provided by companies to run your IT could, in theory, be increased to support the processes for which you have bought the software. If the supplier provides the software to run your accounts payable, he could also provide the staff to

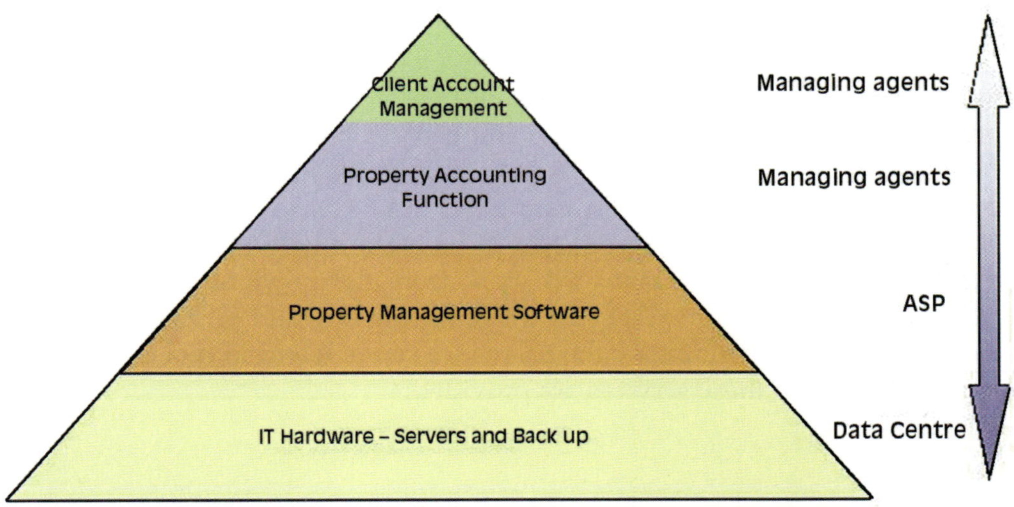

RemitConsulting
Improving information in property

Figure 6.1 Range of potential service providers supporting each element of managing property.

process the invoices – his company designed the software and the training manuals so he should be in a good position to carry out the process. At least one property software company in the UK is doing this for a property client and it is interesting that this is perceived as treading on the toes of the traditional property-managing agents.

The fact that software companies can imagine providing this type of service in competition with managing agents suggests that it is a short step from providing remote access for your property system to outsourcing your property management or property accounts team.

The diagram above shows the different system and process support levels for the property management accounting function. You may wish to control all of these levels by directly procuring staff, software and hardware. Alternatively, you may wish to control the top level, strategic client management (or property management strategy if you are the client) and outsource the other parts of the support.

This may not be the position you expected when you started out looking at systems; splitting the functional areas like this often provides new insights.

However, if you have arrived at this stage of the process and are only now considering whether to outsource your estates management team, you have come too far. In an outsource contract, much of the process detail you have determined will be the responsibility of the contractor and it would not be necessary to have reviewed this. However, the comparison of services and software here allows you to take a reality check.

The process you have followed to get to this stage has established the benefits of reviewing the team's processes. This understanding of where the value lies within the process also allows us to consider whether the process has to be done by the existing internal accounts team at all. If service providers are available to undertake only part of this process, it may still be worth investigating this at this stage.

The analysis required for outsourcing part of your team will differ only slightly from the approach we have already taken; the work from the previous chapters will have answered the relevant questions to tender for both software and services. However, the actual tender will differ depending on the balance of services and software to be provided and the manner in which these services are provided.

The Tender

Whichever procurement route is selected, the work done in the previous chapters will provide the following information necessary to progress the tender.

- What the current situation is and a description of the problem that needs to be addressed.
- The current technical platform.
- The critical processes which must be effectively supported by the system.
- A statement of the measure of improvement that is sought through the new system.
- A list of features which are graded as must have, should have and could have.

Not all this information will be sent to the suppliers but it will all be essential in developing your understanding of the project. To develop the structure for the tender into a useful document, it is worth looking at the problem from the view of the supplier.

The view from the supplier

Imagine that you are a software supplier. You have developed some software and, although you know it has its limitations, you are proud of it; it changes the way that property managers manage their property for the better and there are some neat features which could save users time in their daily work.

Your software has been implemented successfully in property management companies and you are therefore convinced that with very little modification, you have a good chance of winning this tender. However, you need to be sure what is required by the customer can be satisfied by your system.

Firstly, how big is the customer's property team, in how many offices, and how many properties does the company manage? The number of transactions/activities required to be undertaken by the software and the location of the team(s) will determine some of the requirements of the system. This will give some idea of the complexity of the required system.

A software solution developed in Microsoft Access is unlikely to be adequate for a team of 20 users spread across five offices, especially if they have a need to collaborate on the same portfolio of properties. MS Access is not built for that type of solution and the supplier could stand down from the tender without further waste of his time.

In the same way that you will have developed an understanding of the processes you need covered, the software supplier will have developed his system around several key processes. With luck, they will be the same ones and his view will be that regardless of the way you currently conduct your business, your change to his system will greatly enhance your processes.

The supplier will be fairly unwilling to change the processes he has developed because the easiest way to maintain software in the long term will be to stick with the system as it has been built. This approach will also help the users because each time the system is upgraded (and you are in this for the long term, remember), it will be less costly if the system does not have to be rebuilt around "non-standard" processes.

So, the supplier therefore looks at the opportunity to sell you software as part of your change process to adopt the way he has designed his system. However, he will not want to put off potential customers and so will explain that the system can be completely reconfigured to the customer's needs. Once the system is sold, he knows that the implementation and training stages provide another opportunity to change the customer's processes.

This is not a deception, nor even sharp practice – it is simply the application of the necessary change management as applied by a different stakeholder in the process. We have approached this process from the point of view of a customer wanting to conduct a tender across several suppliers. If we had started from the equally valid position of choosing a leading supplier and moving straight to implementation, we would probably apply much of the supplier's approach.

The supplier therefore assumes that whatever starting point you have, the end result will be broadly in-line with the processes he has developed in his system.

You may not want this. In fact you will know exactly what you want because you have mapped, and made obvious improvements to, your current processes. The supplier therefore needs to see what you expect the system to do. This can be both good and bad news for the supplier.

First the bad news: this is clearly not a simple sale where the promise of being able to use the same software as a market leader will produce a sale, after which the system can be implemented in the same way as last time. The supplier will have to read the documentation and work out which requirements need work and whether the changes are feasible. The potential client also has a better understanding of the detail and so the supplier may have to be more open about any shortfall in the specification of the system.

For all these reasons, it is less likely that a tender to more than two or three suppliers will be greeted enthusiastically. Putting more effort than usual into a tender for less than a one in three chance of winning is unattractive and may even result in the supplier declining to tender, especially when he is busy. It may also push the tender towards higher priced packages where the margin for the supplier can cope with the higher cost of sale.

Set against this for the supplier are the positive points of this approach. The potential client obviously understands the issues and what he wants to achieve. Therefore the sales cycle is likely to be shorter, albeit more intense. It will be clear that the client has defined a business case for the solution and there is a greater likelihood that the budget is adequate for the project. The measures applied both to the tender and to the resulting solution are also clear and the supplier can be in little doubt about the improvements that the client expects to arise from the new system. If the supplier wins the contract, he has a better chance of a successful implementation, higher chance of incremental revenue and a first class reference site and credential.

The supplier knows that his competitors will have the same set of problems to solve and may be inclined to decline the invitation to tender. This gives a better than average chance of winning if the system is either close to requirements or can easily be configured to suit.

Furthermore, the tender documentation will provide far more relevant detail than most of the tenders he receives and this will give a far better insight into the real needs of the client. This is an early stage of the project for the supplier to become involved and start to influence the shape of the solution. Although the client will have defined many of the requirements around their preferred processes, there will be many gaps that will have been left for the supplier to fill in the details. A sensible and effective approach to solving these issues will win points in the tender and set their solution apart from the competition.

Finally, if the supplier believes that there are other factors that need to be addressed to produce a successful result, this can be introduced to the tender process.

From the supplier's viewpoint, the more relevant detail provided, the better their opportunity to show that their system should be chosen.

Similarly, from the point of view of a services provider, the same holds true. He will not need to know all the same details as above; the fact that he is taking over the service means he will have some latitude over how the service is performed. The critical elements for a service contract are in explaining the objectives of the service and how it will be measured.

Elements of both contracts will be the same. Other elements will have different weightings. The trick is to balance the contract in the right proportion of software to services supply. All contracts will have an element of both, even if it is as simple as a help desk for desktop software.

The Tender Document

There are a number of different terms used for the document which is sent out to suppliers and on which they will base their quotation. There are subtle differences between each and the definitions I will use here are as follows:

Request for Information (RFI) – The intention of an RFI is to ask for suggestions about how to solve a particular issue. It is often used at the start of a selection project to find out what types of solution are available. This is the most flexible document for the supplier since the solution can be almost any style of product or service as long as it satisfies the objectives of the customer.

It is usually difficult to compare the responses of different suppliers but this approach is useful for gauging the range of solutions available.

Request for Proposal (RFP) – An RFP is more detailed than a RFI but still gives some flexibility for the supplier to suggest leading practice solutions that the customer has not defined. This is the style of tender that is most common and a suggested format is set out later in this chapter.

Invitation to Tender (ITT) – Where a customer knows exactly what solution or service is required and has a detailed understanding of the technical requirements and limitation, an ITT can be used. This approach gives the supplier little room for changing the specification and therefore can be a risky approach if elements of the ITT are ill defined or missing. Companies with experienced IT teams are the most likely to use this form of tender document but many of these still prefer the flexibility of the RFP.

The public sector can also use an Invitation to Negotiate (ITN) where the services element of the contract will be large or the eventual solution is unclear.

Each approach has a particular objective and these definitions further help to achieve the right type of response from the supplier. By defining the objective of the document as one of the above, a key element of the introduction to the tender is already partly written; the supplier should be able to match their response to what is required.

Template RFP

It is probably a good point to review the work we have done so far.

We started by identifying the areas of the business that would benefit most from improvement; first we looked at the Three Clouds and the Five Globes diagrams and then we translated this into critical processes using the RPM.

During this process we have attended demos from the software suppliers used by our colleagues or those we met at the trade shows. Having now defined our critical processes and a list of prioritised features and functions, we have the raw materials to put together the RFP.

In real estate, by this time, there will be a relatively small number of software suppliers able to provide the reassurance that their product will survive the RFP. Given this fact, the RFP can be focused on reducing the time taken to select a system and you already have sufficient knowledge of your processes to test the solutions offered quite comprehensively.

If your organisation is likely to choose the real estate element of one of the enterprise systems, the RFP approach will differ from a packaged real estate system. If your RFP process includes both types of solution, your approach will need to integrate elements of both approaches.

Packaged real estate systems will compete effectively with enterprise systems where the client company is in the real estate sector. However, where the client is a corporate occupier of real estate, there is little chance of the real estate system being able to manage other areas such as general pay roll or logistics. In pure integration terms, a successfully implemented enterprise system should provide significant benefits across the whole company and the one-system approach will often prevent industry specific applications from being selected.

In these situations, the objective of the selection project often changes. The IT team responsible for selecting and implementing the enterprise system for the rest of the company usually insist that the relevant real estate module is the only choice. In these cases, the estates team can be concerned that the new system will match industry specific systems.

Although the estates team tends to think of this project as a selection exercise during which the best system will be chosen, the IT team often use the process to validate that the enterprise solution can offer sufficient functionality to prevent the estates team making a case for an industry specific application.

Let's look at each in turn.

Industry specific solutions

There are a wide variety of structures for RFPs. Our approach is to base the RFP around those processes that give maximum value to the users and these are the processes that have been defined in the course of the project.

The RFP will therefore include:

- background details of the requirement
- critical processes – description, maps and test scripts
- prioritised list of features and functionality (to be scored)
- reports and data-maps.

You will need to tell the software company what you are trying to achieve for the business both now and in future phases of the software. You should also provide a set of reports and details of where the data for those reports currently sits or where it comes from (the Data Map).

Additionally, there are a set of features that you have already prioritised which should be listed. Many of these features will be tested in the scripts but this will allow you to broadly check the presence of other features. However, don't rely on this test alone and if something really is essential, make sure that there is a test script to cover it.

Part of the RFP process will be the demonstration of how the system delivers the Critical Processes. The test scripts are the means by which you will compare "apples with apples" if there is more than one system to choose from. They also show how *your team* would use the system, not the standard generic demonstration.

Finally, there are the administrative details of the RFP – format of the proposal, timescales, addresses, and details of how to ask questions.

The key elements of the RFP are described in detail below. At each stage you will recognise the elements of the specification that has been developed over the last few chapters.

Introduction

The introduction sets the scene for the selection process, and defines the expectations and the parameters within which the vendor will need to work during the proposal submission process and the evaluation that follows. It is likely to include.

- Background – general information regarding the company that is likely to help the vendor prepare a better proposal, eg nature of the business, location of activities, operations, current systems and equipment, system being sought, etc.
- Submission details:
  - where and to whom the proposal should be sent
  - the deadline for delivery of the proposal
  - any special delivery instructions (such as plain sealed envelopes)

  - the number of copies of the proposal required (including one in loose-leaf format for photo-copying)
  - it is useful to put the submission dates on the cover of the RFP so there can be no doubt.
- Contact details – for the person in charge of the request, and any others who should be contacted if the vendor wants further information.
- Confidentiality – The extent to which any of the information in the RFP should be considered confidential.
- Important dates – The dates and important events in the selection process, eg period for conference room pilot demos, deadline for submission of the proposal, evaluation period, plus likely implementation dates.
- Disclaimers – These can include:
  - a statement that the company reserves the right not to choose any tender and, specifically, not to choose the lowest price tender
  - a statement that the company will not be responsible for any costs incurred by the supplier in preparing the tender
  - a statement that an accepted bid will be considered to be contractually binding and those responses are considered to be a binding statement of capability. (This may discourage vendors from changing prices after they have been awarded the contract but before the contract itself has been signed).
- Description of the evaluation process and the expected involvement of the vendor.

Description of Requirements

The RFP will describe in detail what the company wants the system for, what features and functions the system will have to provide, and the services the vendor will have to supply during implementation and thereafter. The key elements of the requirements description include the following.

1 Processes – An overview of the processes that the system will be expected to support, with the critical processes described in detail and accompanied by test scripts which the vendor will be expected to use to demonstrate the capability of the system.
2 System Functions – a checklist of the functions that the system will be required to carry out in support of the processes.
3 Reporting and Data Requirements – the key data items and the relationships between them. The reports that the system will need to generate and the source key data items for each report.
4 System Features – Any specific non-functional aspects important to the system selection should be detailed, eg technology constraints, user interface preferences, security, performance and system response requirements, interfaces with other systems, and any standards with which the system needs to comply.

5 Description of how the system will be used – now and in the future, in terms of users, where they will be located, what processes different groups of users will require, and anticipated growth in user and data volumes.
6 Implementation – any specific requirements known at this point, for instance target implementation dates (perhaps linked to business critical events), and migration of data from legacy systems.
7 Contractual Issues – if the company has any specific requirements for specific contractual provisions, or particular preferences for payment schemes. The company may also state how long they expect the prices quoted to remain valid (say three months).

Form of the Vendor Proposal

A key part of the response will be the demonstrations of the system, designed from the test scripts provided by the customer, where the vendor will be expected to show how their proposed system can support the critical business processes.

The RFP should specify to the vendors the outline form for the written proposal to be submitted in addition to the demonstrations. This is likely to include:

- A proposal and costs summary.
- Implementation schedule and methodology.
- System and data migration assistance.
- Proposed software solution in detail:
  - a response to each of the requirements detailed by the company in the RFP
  - bespoke versus package elements.
- Hardware and infrastructure requirements.
- Vendor support.
- Other vendor services, for instance:
  - implementation project management
  - training
  - *ad-hoc* bespoke work.
- Contractual arrangements – a copy of the proposed contract, including warranties on the products and the implementation.
- Costs – an itemised breakdown for all hardware, software and services, categorised as one-time costs, lease costs, ongoing maintenance and support, and installation and implementation. Any other incidental costs should also be stated.

Enterprise systems

How will this differ for enterprise systems? The key area that will not be feasible is the running of test scripts to check that the functionality built into the system matches the team's processes. This is never satisfactorily replaced but elements of the following activities can be used to minimise the risk of a non-compliant system.

1 Ensure that the implementation team has an in-depth understanding of the processes involved and that they have direct, relevant experience.
2 Check reference sites and credentials in as much detail as possible – preferably to the same level of detail as if the reference client were to be selling you the solution. Remember that the reference site has achieved that status for one reason – they support the product and they are unlikely to tell you the major problems. After all, they chose it themselves and a failure would reflect badly on their team.
3 Work with the supplier using your future state process templates to develop an understanding of the base functionality and where most of the work is required.
4 Use your reports analysis to establish variance from other implementations and check how the data-map would fit the new system.

Without the preparation for the Conference Room Pilot (CRP), some of the timescale outlined below will be available for these activities. However, in our experience, it will take far longer to validate the case for an enterprise real estate solution because of the time taken to set up sufficiently detailed meetings with the supplier, the implementers and the reference clients.

The Tender Process

The tender process, from the issue of the RFP to commencement of contract negotiations, is unlikely to take less than three months. This is one reason why companies sometimes opt for a preferred supplier approach. The main areas where time is taken is waiting for responses, and discussing the outstanding issues following the CRP.

The other time consuming element of the tender will be the contract negotiations. By this point there will be time pressures on the customer to start the implementation and further delay through extended contract negotiations will be unwelcome – however, the only time that the customer has the stronger negotiating position is before the contract is signed. The moral here is clear: do not underestimate the time this process will take and retain the upper hand in negotiations.

The detail of the RFP has been described in this chapter and the questions raised by the supplier should not by now cause much of a problem.

The CRP is the part of the tender where the supplier shows how their solution fits with the customer's requirements. This is the opportunity for the users to see elements of the system in action using data that they recognise.

Test scripts

We developed a number of test scripts for the functional requirement in the last chapter and this is where they are put to good use. The RFP will brief the supplier about the CRP and the timescale will allow time for the supplier to develop a demonstration around the scripts and with your provided data.

A typical timescale for the tender process will be as follows:

Activity	Description	Timescale
RFP issued	Supplier reviews RFP and develops set of questions.	2–4 weeks
Questions to customer	Customer meets supplier to answer question and provide further details.	one week
RFP Response	Supplier submits response to RFP and prepares for CRP. Initial contact with reference sites, if possible, may help to establish questions for the CRP.	2–3 weeks
Conference Room Pilot	Full demonstration and response analysis.	1–2 weeks
Pre-contract negotiations	Customer selects preferred supplier and begins negotiations on aspects of solution non-compliant with the specification. Reference site visits will usually be run in parallel although timings are often difficult to arrange. Queries arising from these investigations will need to be answered before proceeding to the next stage. Always assume that this stage will take longer than you think.	2–3 weeks
Contract negotiations	Detailed negotiation on the software licence and services contract.	4 weeks.

A typical score sheet for one of the critical processes in the demonstration is shown in Figure 6.2 and this, together with background and an agenda, is circulated to all attendees of the CRP beforehand.

The attendees will be the main selection team and any relevant users who have been involved during the development of the functional specification. The agenda will allow for an introduction, an overview of the features of the system and a number of demonstrations. The CRP may take a full day and for this reason it is important to get the right combination of people from your business and to allow the supplier reasonable opportunity to hone his presentation through questions beforehand.

There should be adequate time for questions to the supplier and the opportunity to test the software by example throughout the day. It is not unknown for suppliers to write code specifically for a demonstration and you should be aware of inconsistencies. The classic case is where the field demonstrated only recalculates with a specific figure for a report, eg whatever input figure is used, the same result is produced in the report.

The chart in Figure 6.2 takes the basic format for testing the system set out in Chapter 5 and simplifies this to show the key elements of feedback you will require from your users in the CRP. The briefing document you hand out to the users before the CRP will also need to set out the background to the requirement, the expected results and other details to help gather the required feedback.

No.	Exercise	Outcome as expected (Y/N)	If no, why (Comments/issues)	Estimate %age pass
Demand Raising				
1.	Raise rental demands			
2.	Raise service charge demands			
3.	Raise utility demands			
4.	Raise directly recoverable demands			
5.	Raise demands using different templates for different scenarios, eg one property where S/C paid to Agent while rent payable direct to Landlord			
6.	Revise charges following rent review			
7.	Send demands to tenants			
8.	Receive monies for outstanding charges			
9.	Generate banking summary report for monies received			
10.	Transfer monies as required			
11.	Allocate/post monies received			
12.	Post unallocated cash			
13.	Generate arrears listing			
14.	Generate aged-debtors report			

Figure 6.2

Following the CRP, make time for a debriefing session with all those people from your team who attended, and collect and analyse the marking sheets. Test and challenge the responses to get a thorough understanding of the issues that may arise and go back to the software supplier if anything needs to be resolved.

This is a time-consuming process for both sides but you will learn much about the supplier's approach over this period. It is also important to recognise that the supplier will be spending more time with you than other prospects and will not be keen to go through this if you intend to test more than two or three vendors in this way.

References and site visits

To get the most from references treat them in the same way as for the CRP process, prepare question and answer sheets and take along a (small) number of key users. The following tips may be useful.

- Interview all references face-to-face so that you can discuss matters around the main subject.
- Seek a demonstration of the system at the reference site and ask to see your critical processes in place (if these have been implemented).
- Seek out the current chair of the system's user group (most systems will have one) and ask him for views on the system, the supplier and alternative reference sites.
- Try to conduct the reference site visit without the supplier present.
- Try to talk to users of the system at the reference site who were not part of the core team who selected the system – check to see if there are any tips to take account of during implementation and rollout.
- Ask about the implementation team and post implementation account management. Ask how the relationship has developed since the system went live.

Negotiations and Contract

On the basis of the users' feedback from the CRP and answers to queries of the reference sites, negotiations will centre on the areas of the supplier's proposal that do not meet expectations. Assuming that the outstanding queries to the supplier have been answered to the users' satisfaction, negotiations can now focus on the contract.

Typically, when people talk of "technology procurement", they are referring to either or both of the following.

- Procuring software or hardware and/or
- Procuring technology services from a third party.

Both procurements have their own idiosyncrasies and challenges as shall be seen below. Buying hardware is not included in this chapter but many of the issues that are relevant to software will also be relevant to hardware.

1. Procuring a Software licence

Off-the-shelf software

When you buy a piece of software off-the-shelf (such as Microsoft Office), you are not actually buying the program itself, but rather you a buying a right to use somebody else's intellectual property.

The licence is often known as a "shrink-wrap licence" (because it is often only accessible once you have opened the shrink-wrap) or, if downloading from the internet, a "click-wrap licence" (because you need to click to confirm your acceptance of the terms of the licence).

Bespoke software

Alternatively, if your needs are somewhat more specialised, you may require the skills of a software developer to write the software for you. Depending on the terms of the commercial agreement, you may own the software outright at the end, or, more unusually, you may be given a wide licence to use the software, with the developer retaining ownership.

A word of caution: with few exceptions, where a customer engages a contractor to develop software for it, *unless the contract states a contrary position*, the contractor will retain ownership in the software.

To confuse matters, where a company engages an *employee* to develop software for it, unless you have agreed a contrary position, the company will own the software.

Since few property companies or advisors have their own in-house development team, they will often rely on contractors. Even if the software being built by a contractor could only ever be used by that company because of its uniqueness, a contractor could end up with its ownership. If that is intended, you should negotiate something from the re-sale rights.

While informal arrangements are prevalent in this field, time and time again disputes arise. For example, a company may ask its in-house team to write some software, only to find that the team consists of consultants *and* employees. From an intellectual property rights perspective, who owns the software? Things become messy.

The Licence

Let us assume that the customer is not to own the software outright, but that the supplier is providing the customer with a licence. Licences vary dramatically, in language (from the very legal to the plain English), length and complexity. However, at the core of all licences, the following clauses are almost ubiquitous.

Scope of licence – as explained above, a licence is merely a right to use. A clause in the licence will set out restrictions on such right. These may include:

- geographical restrictions (where can you use the software?)
- volume restrictions (how many people can use the software? How many items of equipment can it be installed on?)
- time restrictions (is the licence perpetual, or does it terminate after a length of time?)
- usage restrictions (often the software can only be used for specified purposes, such as "internal business purposes" – whatever that means…)
- upgrade rights (do you have rights to new versions of the software, or could you be stuck with an out of date, unsupported platform?).

Charges – at its simplest, the charges clause will set out how much a customer will pay to use the software. A word of caution: often charges are expressed to be "as set out in the supplier's current price list". In theory, the supplier can set out *any* price in its price list! In practice, prices are negotiable and you should be aware of your negotiating position long before you sit down to discussions.

Term and Termination – these clauses set out the duration of the contractual agreement and how the licence can be terminated, if at all.

Limits and exclusions on liability – in the event of a dispute, this clause states the maximum amount that the parties can sue each other for. While suppliers will often try to exclude almost everything, under English law certain statutes prevent unreasonable exclusions or limitations of liability under certain circumstances. This is one for the lawyers – every word in this clause tends to have case law or a statute behind it, clarifying its true legal meaning.

Intellectual property rights indemnity – a supplier has supplied a user with a licence to use some software. A third party claims that it owns the software, and that the supplier had no right to grant the licence. The third party can sue either the supplier of the software, or the user. If the third party sues the user, it is usual for the supplier to indemnify the user for any costs (etc) it suffers as a result.

Distinct from the licence, is the service contract, discussed below.

2. Procuring Technology Services from a Third Party

Perhaps you want someone to take care of all or part of your technology function. If so, you will engage one or more third parties to carry out this function.

The service contract has (at least) three important functions:

- it clarifies the requirements of the parties, eg in drafting a schedule setting out the required services, the parties can fully understand each other's needs, minimising ambiguity and therefore disputes down the track

- it apportions risk. If something goes wrong, who is responsible for the error and by how much?
- it provides remedies in the event things do not go to plan.

The Contract

A service contract will consist of a number of complex elements, but at the heart of the contract, you would expect to see the following.

Terms and Conditions – the legal framework under which the commercial, operational and technical content follows.

Service description – as detailed and clear as possible. Services descriptions can be:

- input based (which answers the question, "what is the supplier going to give us?)
- output based (ie "we don't care how the supplier is to do it, this is the result we require" – popular in outsourcings)
- a hybrid of the two – becoming more popular all the time.

Service levels – performance requirements in respect of the services.

Exit provisions – the terms of the hand over at the end of the contract.

Charges – how much will the services cost and how are the services to be paid?

Transfer issues – where you transfer a function you are currently providing in-house, you will be outsourcing that function – a specialist form of the services contract.

As part of a traditional outsourcing, the biggest single issue is often dealing with the transfer from the in-house function to the third party provider of any or all of the:

- assets
- people
- software licences
- equipment
- services.

Other Issues

Here I have summarised two common technology procurement contracts. The reality is there are many variants on a theme, eg the services contract often will contain software licences.

Many licences, in turn, contain support and maintenance (ie service) provisions.

And we haven't even touched on hardware…

Perhaps the most important aspect of contracts is that they set out what should happen if things go wrong. Even the best agreements are subject to things changing over time: account managers leave and are replaced with different personalities; companies merge or are sold. Any number of changes can trigger differences of opinion and no contract will cover all eventualities.

If things go bad, how do we resolve matters? The contract should help.

Before the contract is signed both parties are eager to close the deal. The balance of negotiating power often sits with the client. This is the time to ensure that the contract suits the client should there be a disagreement. It will not be possible to attribute blame in advance but there are numerous ways of ensuring that any dispute is resolved as quickly as possible.

For example, one useful contract term is an attendance clause: should there be an issue about the contract, the supplier's managing director, for example, is required to attend the client's offices every week for a meeting until the dispute is resolved.

This soon concentrates the mind of some very senior people at the supplier. It is unlikely to work with IBM, but for a supplier for whom your sale is one of only 20 each year, this term may well survive pre-contract negotiations. There are many other examples of clauses that at the time of the contract may seem unimportant but later in the day will come to be worth their weight in gold.

While both parties believe that there will be no cause for discontent, there is a good opportunity to load the contract in your favour.

Do you need a lawyer?

For low value, strategically unimportant procurements, it is not unusual for customers to "take the plunge" and sign up to potentially onerous standard terms and conditions. Frankly, if you are buying 10 licences to use Windows XP, you are not going to achieve much in attempting to negotiate with Microsoft in any event.

However, where goods or services are strategically important, or are of a higher value, it is likely to be worth negotiating the terms of the contract in order to apportion the risk and clarify the requirements as set out above.

While some would take this task on without a lawyer, here is a further word of caution. The supplier is likely to have done this "once or twice" before – as a customer, you may well be less familiar with the contract and subsequent negotiations. While the supplier will often ask its customers to rely on the "spirit of the relationship" (which is fine unless the relationship goes sour) a lawyer can redress the balance, and guide the customer through the legal maze of some of the more complex clauses. In some clauses, such as limitation of liability – an "and" rather than an "or" can make an awful lot of difference.

Conclusion

We have taken a standard approach to buying new software and turned it on its head. The journey we have taken has involved the users, it has redefined much of the way your team works and has developed a specification which allows you to test some generic software against your own detailed needs.

We have split the contract into software and services and considered whether we need to own software at all. Now we have a set of contract terms that will allow us to manage the disputes that will arise to our satisfaction.

The contract is signed; the implementation is about to begin. What can possibly go wrong?

Let's see in the next chapter how to make it work.

7 Making it work

The tender process has been successful and your team awaits the first meeting of the implementation phase. This is the part of the project that instils fear in the minds of most property managers: the disruption, the risk of failure, the constant apologies to managers and clients about late reports. It is the fear of the unknown and the placing of trust in strangers.

Why are the users afraid? This is not the first time you have involved them in the system project and the solution is intended to make their lives easier. You will have sought their views when you developed the early specification and no doubt will have discussed some of the issues as the project developed.

However, it is often easier for the core team to make decisions without explicit help from the users during the specification period – a theme we will return to later in this chapter. Users can often lose track of what the project will deliver, especially when they are concentrating on delivering their own work with the sub-optimal systems already in place.

Up to now, we have concentrated on developing the specification for the system. This focus was chosen on the basis that most projects are poorly scoped and most systems are poorly specified. Our approach has made this element of the project less "difficult" and with clear vision and strong attention to detail, we have by now selected a system that matches a well thought out specification. This in itself will provide a far better chance of success than would be the case with the majority of system projects.

Yet there is another, and more obviously "difficult", part of the project still to be addressed. This is the delivery of the solution itself.

I do not intend to go into the detail of the implementation of software because the approach to this stage will depend on the solution chosen. For example, bespoke software will require a team of developers and a software development phase; packaged software will need to be configured to suit the specification and integrated with other systems; hosted software will require a different project approach again.

Instead, this chapter develops ideas around minimising the risks in this stage of the project and in order to deal with many of the issues raised, we will need to go back to the beginning of the project. Despite the robust approach we have taken in developing the specification, further actions can be taken early on to improve the ease with which users adopt the system. Addressing implementation issues early on will help the success of the overall solution because even the best specified system will not bring business benefit if staff do not use it.

(Therefore I give my apologies if you have been reading this book as a recipe and have already selected your system without attending to the issues about to be discussed).

The five areas of delivery with which we will deal in this chapter are:

1 Project management issues.
2 Project risks.
3 Disagreement over functionality and achieving consensus.
4 Change management.
5 Communications.

Project Management

To recap, we have concentrated on the preparation necessary before implementation. We have decided what will improve the business, obtained strong sponsorship, developed a functional requirement around the critical processes and tested the software in a way that reflects our proposed use. Because of this we already stand a better than average chance of achieving success.

There are two elements of the project management that will now need attention.

1 The quality and experience of the supplier's implementation team. We know what to expect from the software but you are still reliant on their project team. If the supplier's team is small (and many property software suppliers fall into this category), you may need to be very firm over the quality of staff you allow to manage the project.
2 Your own approach to project management.

We will therefore need to decide the resources and management style of the home team for the project in preparation for negotiations over the supplier's team. If you understand the gaps in your team's knowledge, you should be in a better position to judge what gaps remain after you have selected the software supplier's team.

There are plenty of texts about effective project management and plenty of methodologies, both practical and theoretical. Many specialist project and programme management consultancies have their own methodologies that tend to combine features from the best-known approaches.

The methodology applied to your project will depend on many things: most obviously, whom you appoint as a project manager, his style, experience and training.

If we resource the role internally, the project manager should have some basic training in project management and there are many weeklong courses available. The most common approach is to use a methodology based on Prince 2. This is one of the most common project management approaches, widely used in the UK public sector. It has its critics because it can be inflexible and is often bureaucratic. However, experienced project managers often rely on large elements of the approach.

In a bespoke development project there will be lower level methodologies applied to the actual programming such as Extreme Programming, Rational Unified Process, or OMT++. The approach to software development is complex and if your team has no direct experience, hiring a specialist project manager to run a directly employed team is risky. Often it is better to hire a software company and concentrate on managing their contract with you rather than undertaking the work itself.

There is a big difference between managing the actual software development, which needs specialist experience, and managing the overall business project. The trick is to balance the skills of the team as a whole to ensure that the programming or implementation team has sufficient experience, and that the overall project manager understands both the business requirement, and how to report progress effectively to the Board.

In simple terms a project structure that has a project board and project team may be useful, similar to the structure of a Prince 2 project. The project board is made up of senior stakeholders who cannot take day-to-day part in the project but who can sponsor the project and challenge the approach. The project board may comprise people from both inside and outside the company including, for example, the business sponsor, company board members, head of IT, internal audit, software supplier director, and an independent industry expert.

The project team comprises the full time and part time staff and contractors who are responsible for individual aspects of the project.

Between these two groups is the project manager, who ensures that the project is delivered and that an appropriate level of information is transmitted between the two groups.

Above all, there are three key elements that must be in place.

1. A dedicated Project Manager (PM) who will not be distracted by day-to-day work is essential. Ideally this PM will be from inside the company because he/she will retain the knowledge of the process developments during the implementation and provide continuity. The PM will understand the quirks and foibles of the organisation and will be able to work with the PM appointed by the supplier to resolve issues. The PM must have the respect of the project board and the ability to communicate with them effectively.
2. The PM must have an in-depth understanding of the requirements and the objectives of the project. Ideally the PM will have been instrumental in the prioritisation of the system specification and developing the tender documentation.
3. The project board must give the PM and the project team strong sponsorship and must be prepared to support the team to resolve issues which arise. If this project has

successfully cleared the business case hurdle, it must be delivered in accordance with that case. Without strong sponsorship the project will fail.

Project Management is an immense subject but it can be learned. It is quite possible to take a respected staff member and appoint them to this position and, with prior basic training the experience will develop their management skills. It will also provide them with an even more thorough understanding of what elements are critical to the running of their business.

Using an internal resource for this – perhaps from the team of users – not only develops your team's skills, it saves money. To hire a contractor as a project manager is expensive because it is likely that he will be dedicated to the project for six-nine months. At the end of the period, the contractor will leave with a significant amount of knowledge that then will be unavailable to your business. At the very least, the contractor will need to spend additional time at the end of the project managing the hand-over; however, lack of a central focus after this stage often means that further development of the system, and sometimes even training, goes unattended.

Clearly, if you have no way of releasing a member of staff for that period, external help is an option. The ideal PM will have worked on the solution you have chosen in the recent past and have good credentials in the property industry. There are some independent contractors in this market and fewer consultancies specialising in property systems and you may have to compromise. This is where attention to detail in the prioritisation process will pay dividends.

One tip to bear in mind: if your PM has not developed an outline project plan for delivery of the system within the first two weeks, it is unlikely that you will ever have a plan for the project. Without a plan, the project will fail. Therefore, if your PM has not produced a plan within the first two weeks of his appointment, hire a new one. Do not delay in doing this or accept excuses; there is too much additional risk in delay at this stage.

There are clearly many things of which to keep aware of and many risks. However, the implementation stage of your project will be easier than for most companies. You have a plan, a budget, a specification and detailed measures of success.

Project Risks

There are a number of further elements in this next phase that will require special attention in all projects. Once again, allowing the necessary time for each of these at the outset of the project will reap dividends later and at the very least will ensure that the team manages the expectations of the project sponsor. Briefly, these include:

- **Data migration** – The time taken to do this properly is almost always underestimated. The data will need to be cleaned and checked and this is a great opportunity to re-establish control of the information you use on a regular basis. The usual project rules apply – it will take twice as long and cost twice as much as anticipated.

- **Training** – Another area that is underestimated is training. It may be sufficient to nominate two or three "super-users" from your staff who will learn enough about the system to be able to train the rest of your staff. However, it is far better to develop a role-based training programme where the system is applied to each user's job in a way that allows the user to work through a fixed sequence of events. This approach also minimises the time taken to hand over the role when there are staff changes, and to train new joiners.

  The downside to role-based training is that more preparation work is required but the majority of this will be in analysing the workflows; you have already done this to specify the system.
- **Scope creep** – The basic rule to follow is that, "if you have agreed the specification, and bought a system based on that specification, don't mess with it." However, at some point in the implementation, changes will inevitably need to be made. For example, the software may not work in quite the way predicted in particular circumstances, or there is a change to your company that requires a change to the software.

  It is essential that the project manager has a robust approach to change control. If the change control is not in place, the risk is the implementation phase will take longer, cost more and the software supplier can use any change to the specification as an excuse for poor performance in executing their role.

If we address this at the beginning of the project, we can resource these elements effectively and allow sufficient time so that they do not delay the overall project.

Now, why won't it work?

Assuming that the system will be implemented by experienced PMs and the main risks have been addressed, the users will be happy, right? Wrong.

Depending on whom you believe, estimates of the percentage of IT projects which fail to achieve their objectives or are delivered over time and over budget is 60%–80%. This is a staggeringly high number and even in situations where the system has been used as a case study, it is easy to find disgruntled users who claim that the system is a retrograde step; it never works and it was better the old way.

It is safe to say that very few implementations are a complete success and many do not appear to work at all. The first REMIT survey[1] undertaken at Ernst & Young found that the average life of a property system was three-four years. We joked that this was one year to implement, one year to discover it doesn't work, one more year to fire the person who chose it and the fourth year to carry out a selection of a new system. I am sure that this was actually the case in many companies.

1 REMIT Survey 1998, Ernst & Young

You have set up the project well and have a good understanding of what is needed. The principle reasons for projects still failing are:

- disagreement over functionality
- change and disruption.

Disagreement over functionality and Achieving consensus

Professional services teams are focused on providing a service to clients and, apart from marketing and training, they are expected to have a high proportion of hours chargeable to clients. This is typical of all professional services firms and I mention this because it will provide some context in the next story.

One of the departments where I once worked provided advice on property finance and to do this they needed to conduct appraisals of development opportunities. The team leader, in passing, asked me what type of valuation software was available in the market and which package they should buy. He agreed to gather his team together and a few days later all six team members sat around a meeting room table with me.

"So, Andrew," started the team leader, "You know what we do, what software should we buy?" A simple enough question but this needed some qualification and so I asked each team member in turn to describe what they wanted from the software.

"It has to deal with development calculations."

"It must value existing buildings with long unexpired leases."

"It must show discounted cash flows"

"It must incorporate Spanish land taxes."

And so it went on with each team member creating yet more detail in each diverse aspect of the valuations they needed to conduct. After about 10 minutes, the team leader said, "So there you have it, it's clear that we need a software package to do development valuations – which one should we use?"

I observed that the requirement seemed a lot more complex that that – for example, his colleague had said he did no development valuations but needed to value other situations. I suggested that we spend some time prioritising the requirements before looking at suitable software to which his answer was, "Look, we can't waste any more time on this. We have to earn fees, you know." And they left.

Four weeks later they placed an order for the software they first thought of – the market leader. Six months later, only two members of the team used it on a regular basis. Much of the specialist functionality that had seemed so essential was still incorporated in various versions of MS Excel spreadsheets and the team would occasionally ask if there was any other software which would be a closer fit to their needs.

In this case, the team's expectations were out of line with what was needed to select software and the story shows how important it is to manage the expectations of the team when you organise the first meeting. It also shows the difference between what users want to experience in a software selection and what is usually possible. Here the requirement to get on with making a decision without spending too much time away from projects over-ruled the need to get a consensus on what was actually needed.

The construction industry, as an analogy, has a tradition of jokes about the difference between the client's requirements, the architect's plans and the builder's delivered project. It is no different in the software industry and even with valuation software packages (relatively inexpensive in comparison with property management systems) the scope for choosing incorrect software is quite large.

Looking more closely at the last situation, the team leader clearly expected that one meeting would be enough for everyone to agree on a specification. When it became apparent that alternative specifications were needed, and compromise may be necessary, he tried to force a decision. Whether that decision was the team leader's own choice or whether he simply tried to gauge the majority requirement and push that through to save time does not matter: the result was software that was not accepted by the majority of the team and after a few months had largely been abandoned.

Combine the effects of IT and business change

Reinforcing the concerns about IT projects, management consultants McKinsey points out that 60% of IT projects examined in 2002 went over budget or failed[2]. This was partly through a lack of focus on what they were meant to achieve.

IT cannot achieve success if the underlying business process is flawed. This is why we have looked at developing a tender based on the needs of the business. More than this, though, we have looked at changing the processes in the business and supporting these changed processes with IT.

Companies often start with the IT solution and work from there rather than work out which business processes need to change first. At one property company I worked with, each manager was processing information differently. One might send it to accounting and then asset management departments, while another did the reverse. This approach compounds problems of flawed data and poor training and the positioning of IT as the key part of the solution usually has little impact on the business.

It is a combination of changing and improving the way people work, coupled with improvements in IT which make the main difference. Individually, neither approach is as effective on its own, a point made by McKinsey in the research study mentioned above.

In the case study about Equity Office Properties[3], this is all too apparent. The original plan to automate the company online was not possible without process re-engineering throughout the business. The combination of process improvement and new systems has produced significant overall improvements.

2 Stephen J. Dorgan and John Dowdy – The McKinsey Quarterly, 2004 Number 4

3 Equity Office Properties Case study p 45

It is clear that on its own, even the best IT will fail to achieve its full potential and, involving the full team at an early stage will not only allow all the users to buy in to the new systems, it will improve the chances of success.

Why not ask the users?

In any team situation, gaining acceptance of new software by the whole team is critical in ensuring that the software is used as it is intended. We have described in previous chapters how to prioritise functionality but this is only useful if everyone agrees the priorities. If even one person in the team thinks that their need has been over-ruled, at best the new system will be less efficient, at worst, the user will not change to meet the needs of the team.

It is obviously essential to gain consensus over the specification for software before implementation and this is where many projects fail. They fail before the software has been loaded onto the PCs, before training and before the old data has been loaded on to the new system.

This is an element of a systems project that is often badly covered by traditional methods of selecting software. Despite the best intentions of a project leader the desire of the department head to continue with business as usual leads to the project team being a small subset of all the likely system users. This leads to two potential problems.

1. As a small subset they have only limited access to the varied opinions of the users.
2. Equally as important, the project team will be concerned that too many arbitrary requests should not distract them; this might leave them unable to move forward because no clear decision between conflicting requirements can be made.

It is better still, they reason, to avoid confrontation and "sell" the results of their own selection process when the users can trial it for themselves.

The project team is therefore under pressure to provide an acceptable solution in a cost-effective manner without distracting the department from day-to-day business: a tall order by any standards.

Personal agendas become important; the project team has been given the chance to show how well they can manage this investment and in extreme cases the users become an obstruction. Users can be unreasonable in their demands and unwilling to change the way they have always worked.

Thus, many failed implementations are blamed on the users. I am often surprised at the difference in opinion of the success of new software between the project team and the users – it can sometimes appear that they are talking about different systems entirely. Are these the same users for whom the system was designed for in the first place?

Facing the pressures of a department head controlling costs and high expectations of a rapid implementation, it is often difficult to remember that this is an opportunity for the whole department to gain a new tool to work more effectively. Those obstreperous users are not just your fellow workmates – they are your customers! Would it not be better to establish a project that is successful for both users and the project team?

Achieving consensus

We need to go back to the beginning of the project to encourage things to go smoothly. There is only one way to get consensus about the new specification and that is by properly involving everyone.

This is a scary concept. How can the project team remain in control when everyone is allowed to contribute his or her own pet requirements? Most of the users will be well-spoken intelligent people who can carry an argument and they may overcome resistance from less forthright individuals. Some may use political nous or connections to get their way. Others may just avoid getting involved until they realise the implications of what is being done and then be obstructive.

In any case the possibilities for the project team to lose control are manifold. Failure at this stage through loss of control or woolly decisions may be fatal to the individual careers of the project team.

But think about it. How many different ways are there to manage property for example? Or how many different reports could an investor possibly or reasonably expect to see on a website? The possibilities are finite, not infinite. It is probable, if not certain, that the users will all require similar functionality. They may differ on the detail but most detail is decided by the particular software chosen.

The trick will be to get the users to concentrate on the big decisions and big wins and allow them to understand that how they get these benefits will require some compromise. For example, let's imagine a new system that scans invoices and electronically posts them to surveyors for approval, and posts them back to the accounts team for payment. This might save all users one-two day's work each month and would pay for itself in less than six months.

Any dissenting user would have to put forward a serious set of issues with the system to persuade the other users that this should not be chosen. Subjected to the spotlight of open discussion by their peers, many dissenters will agree to progress the idea. It is through focused open discussion by the whole team that many obstacles can be overcome. Minor detail issues can often be resolved with the software provider who is likely to have dealt with legal and practical issues in previous implementations.

These exercises to achieve agreement can be conducted through interviews but it is often best to use a large meeting or workshop, facilitated by a third party. The third party need not be a consultant; they could be from another part of the business that has no direct interest in the outcome of the project.

In the example in the introduction to this book, I described a workshop that gathered some 20 senior managers and directors in an investment agency to decide how to harness e-business to benefit their company. This was a brave decision from the sponsor; there were participants who were hostile to his attempts to push forward his team. Some participants had significantly more knowledge about the technical difficulties involved and some experts from overseas were likely to say that e-business could not be made to work in their market.

Nevertheless, all who were invited attended the workshop and the first difficulty was how we might level the playing field. Almost all the participants had a view on the best way forward and, being department heads, they were all used to getting their own way. They would at least be able to barter their agreement for a solution they favoured.

The key to success with this workshop was to allow enough time for everyone to have his or her say. Here, this meant allowing them each to make an introductory speech about what they thought was important. Although this took over an hour, the participants were much more relaxed for having expressed their concerns and doubts to everyone at the start. The whole team was able to start within a shared context and the group would not make further decisions without reference to the existing concerns. The proof that this worked was that by the end of that day the whole team had identified three key elements of e-business that they all agreed should be the focus of their work.

Obviously, several different techniques will usually be employed in a workshop context to keep discussions focused and enable the team to form a consensus, and formal training for facilitators is invaluable.

The facilitator need not be an expert in the subject being debated and many people will argue that a lack of knowledge of the subject is of benefit to the facilitator. The reasoning is that the facilitator is present as a catalyst to the discussion. He is there to provide a framework for the discussion and remind the team to keep focused on the question in point. He may help formulate the question and will provide group exercises to draw out the detail of the various suggestions. If expert knowledge on the subject is required, and that knowledge is not present within the team assembled, a Subject Matter Expert (SME) can be present for the workshop to challenge assumptions and add content to the discussion.

I am not convinced that using a facilitator without specialist knowledge of the subject is the best way to run many workshops. Introducing an SME is not always practical, especially in small groups and, where one is present this does not absolve the facilitator from being able to challenge proposals. As long as the facilitator does not seek to influence the debate, the knowledge, for example, that a particular topic may need further investigation is, in my view, essential. The workshop is intended to produce a decision in a short space of time and, if that decision is flawed and later needs further work, the workshop process is undermined. This situation would be remedied if the facilitator can recognise possible technical difficulties with the decision and amend the structure of the workshop to compensate; that the facilitator has specialist knowledge is useful.

Workshops are sometimes unpopular with senior managers. It may well be that much of the criticism of workshops which has been voiced in the past few years has stemmed from poor decisions (or no decision) being taken after a day of poor facilitation. Workshops need plenty of preparation and I recommend undertaking individual interviews with participants beforehand to identify any key issues that might prevent important decisions being taken on the day.

It is often difficult to find an experienced facilitator with sufficient understanding of the issues to be able to bring the group to a series of important decisions and this is why companies often resort to external consultants. If the workshop is successful it may save weeks of negotiation and the best facilitators will be able to achieve this. In my experience, a combination of individual interviews and workshops will provide the basis for agreement.

Finally, and to reiterate earlier comments, strong sponsorship is essential at this stage; ultimate agreement may prove difficult without a senior manager taking responsibility for taking dissenting users on one side, but only as a last resort.

Simple disagreement with ones peers is a key problem area in getting new systems implemented; fear of change is the next.

Change Management

The management of change needs to be addressed as a separate topic because people react badly to change, even if they agree that the change is necessary. The following passage[4] illustrates the key issues about change and why this is a difficult area to get right.

> I am delighted to discover that there is an organisation called "Non-Extremists for Moderate Change in Finland". It appears that they are vilified in all countries apart from Finland and when they joined an animal rights protest in Paris, they were set upon by the Police, animal rights protesters, researchers, medical administrators and bystanders. Clearly, moderate change is neither a popular concept with supporters of the status quo, nor campaigners for radical change.
>
> We live in a constantly changing world. Business evolves and people in businesses have to adapt to new circumstances. We are told that change is good and to reject change is at best anti-social and at worst irresponsible or the act of a traitor.
>
> You would expect that as a consultant, I would promote change, perhaps even "embrace" it. I think change is great when other people have to adapt through my own ideas being adopted. However, when I have to adapt to a new way of working, my routine is disturbed, simple tasks take twice as long as usual and I am often less than enthusiastic.
>
> There are usually two main reasons for people's aversion to change. These relate to competence and control.

4 First published in Property Systems Review, October 2003.

Competence

There are four main levels of learning any given task. The first, "unconscious incompetence" is when I have no idea that I cannot complete a task satisfactorily. I may think I am a good driver and therefore capable of driving a racing car. However, I am unaware of my incompetence and as soon as I try to drive off, I reach the second level, "conscious incompetence". It is clear I cannot drive the racing car efficiently, if at all.

With training I might reach the third level, "conscious competence". At this level, I am able to drive correctly but each lap of the race circuit is physically draining with the concentration required to co-ordinate all I have been taught.

In a racing car, I am unlikely to reach the fourth level, "unconscious competence". Michael Schumacher is able to pilot a Formula 1 car with such skill he needs only to think about how he might shave a tenth of a second from an already blistering lap time. It is hard work but 90% of his driving effort is unconscious.

In any new situation at work, we are asked to move from unconscious competence in our current task, to at best conscious incompetence. The implications for the individual are significant.

We are all overworked and most of us have no time to learn new things. Presented with a new IT system, for example, not only do we have to learn how it works but we will only be able to work at half the usual speed. This will impact our workload, increase stress and allow more mistakes to slip through. It is much easier in the short term to stay with the current, outdated systems and processes.

Control

The other reason why people are resistant to change is because they often feel they are losing control of their environment. Most people feel comfortable if they have a degree of control over the way they work. Once they are unconsciously competent at their job, they can control emergencies and new situations that arise.

However, if new systems are implemented which change working practice, staff often start to feel that they have less control, become anxious, and less enthusiastic about the changes. Let's illustrate that using an example of an exercise from a change management workshop.

In my experience, the most hated warm-up exercise for this type of workshop is one where participants are told to pair up and stare at their partner for two minutes, in silence. Nobody knows why they are doing this and they are uncomfortable. They are then asked to change five things about their appearance and stare at their partner again, this time noting what changes have been made.

Everyone is then asked to make five more changes to their appearance but none of these should reverse previous changes. This increases anxiety because most participants barely managed to change five things in the first place. The resulting discussion about the exercise relates to the responses to each change.

First, there appears to be no good reason to stare at your partner. People are left wondering what, if anything, will come next. There is brief relief when they are given a set task – the task of changing clothing. It appears clear that this is a memory and observation test.

However, stress levels rise when people learn that they have not changed enough and need to change more. They cannot do it – many claim, "It's impossible". This often brings out polarised reactions in the group. Some are inspired to be as creative as possible – they need to win the game. Many just give up and refuse to change anymore. Most just do the best they can, merely going through the motions but becoming disenchanted with the whole exercise.

Compare these reactions to the response that the implementation of a new IT system evokes.

- The key to the above example was that the group had no knowledge of each change. Lack of communication often hinders the rollout of systems.
- New instructions were given without prior warning but clearly to someone else's plan. Functionality in new systems has often been signed off before most of the users get to see the system.
- The participants were not in control and many resisted the final set of commands. Users often fail to attend training sessions and ultimately use the system at less than full efficiency.

A simple communication structure is therefore essential when imposing changes on an organisation. Regular clear communications will help staff prepare for new situations and this alone can take a long time to get right. We use a simple template structure to define the right level and frequency of communications in an organisation but often this can take two-three weeks to agree. Regular communications, even within departments, are often *ad hoc*.

However, getting the communications right is not enough. I may know, thanks to NASA, that an asteroid is heading towards the Earth and is likely to make impact in 2015. I am not happy about it and there is little I can do to improve my position.

Thankfully, it is possible to make a difference to IT projects so that they are more easily accommodated by staff. By involving users early in a project, they will begin to feel that they have some control over the final product. Most have strong views on the way they want to work; or where they want to work. Given that IT systems are enabling radical change in how and where people work, the users will be able to define what is required far more effectively that a small traditional IT team.

Managers responsible for new systems are often worried that by telling people about the changes, and allowing them to get involved, this will result in a talking shop, wasting valuable time and reaching no conclusion. Far better, they think, to spring a perfectly formed new system on the users who will be forced to use it if it doesn't quite meet their needs.

In my experience, the time spent up front facilitating discussions amongst users reaps rewards in the later parts of the project. Once involved in the process, users eagerly anticipate the new functionality that is due to arrive and realise that training will ultimately reduce the time spent on repetitious tasks. More importantly, users can understand why compromises to functionality have been made – they can see the negotiation process going on in the workshops. As a result, the new systems are adopted more quickly, leading to earlier payback on the investment. Training is well subscribed and snagging and proposals for Phase 2 are enthusiastically supported.

Radical change is a way of life for many but resistance leads to moderate change. Those who only strive for moderate change appear to be, if anything, worse off than their extreme counterparts, as our friends in Finland can attest. We can, however, learn to "embrace" change by good planning, good communications and seeking agreement from users at the start.

Communications

We have dealt at length with planning and seeking agreement from users. What about communications?

We have seen how lack of communication causes distrust and lack of commitment. However, effective communications are difficult. It is not how the message is given but how it is heard that is important. The internet has shown how too much information is as pointless as too little and may have a worse effect. If you are bombarded with information that at best is of passing interest, you will switch off – you will assume that all communication is spam and park it in the delete bin.

Seth Godin, author of *Permission Marketing*[5], suggested that we see an average of 4,000 advertising messages every day and advocated that marketing should be sent only to people who have given permission to receive your message at a certain level of detail. In this way, your message is more likely to be read and absorbed. Elements of this approach are important to bear in mind when considering the communications on a systems project.

As soon as you ask, "What am I trying to achieve by this communication?" it is clear that there is no simple answer. Firstly, each message may need to be given in a different

5 *Permission Marketing*, Seth Godin – Free Press

way to different stakeholders. At one extreme, the fact that the tester has failed a software component may be an important element in the timeline for delivering the software; the users do not need to know this level of detail and this information would sow seeds of doubt in the user base, possibly undermining their faith in the solution.

A less extreme example would be that the users need to know the delivery date of the software so that they can begin to quietly market to key clients. The finance director may need to know the same date so that he can commence his analysis of actual costs in time for the annual audit. Sending the same message to both these stakeholders may confuse, and will certainly be less precise to each without further explanation.

Of all the elements of project management, the area of communications is the most difficult and much has been written on this subject. To keep this as simple as possible at this stage, we use a model that forms a framework for discussing the issue. It will usually take two to three weeks to establish the first framework and it will be constantly under review throughout the project. However, the framework allows discussions to take place early enough in the project to make a difference. If a communications framework is dealt with only when it becomes necessary to communicate with the stakeholders, the messages will not be effective.

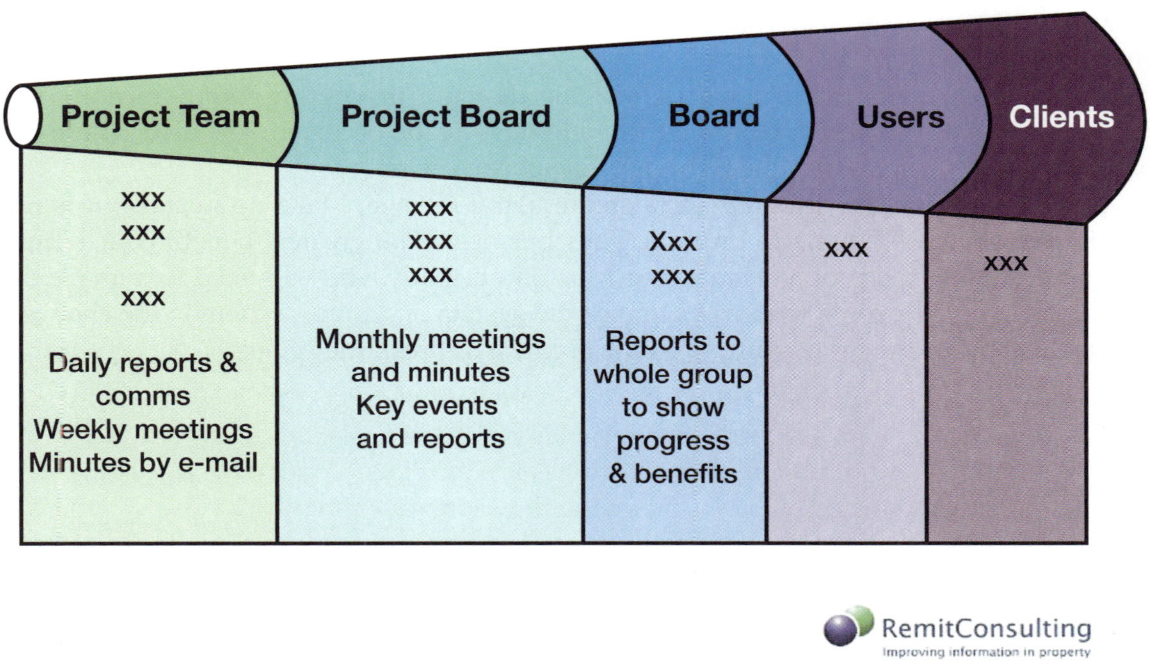

Figure 7.1 Communications megaphone

A megaphone symbol seems appropriate to this subject. At the smaller end, the project team need only "whisper" lots of detail between themselves. The project board will need less detail, less frequently. They in turn will need sufficiently focused information to be able to report on progress to the company board. The user groups, users and, ultimately, clients and public at the loud end of the megaphone need decreasingly frequent and yet more carefully composed messages.

The project team can get the occasional unclear message between them explained in a whisper. The "shout" to the general public that a new system may affect share prices needs more care. Everyone will hear the message and may act on it.

The definition of the groups at each stage of the megaphone usually takes time. Individuals need to be asked about their information requirements – think of permission marketing. As we work through the megaphone, there may be groups of users or clients who need differentiated messages. At the start of the project it is impossible to consider every possible type of message but this broad framework will help establish early regular contact with important groups.

Regular contact is one of the key elements of this approach. Once the first version of the megaphone is defined, communications can be almost automatic. The notes of meetings, the release of project updates, and the requests for information from users can be dealt with from a regular agenda in meetings and sent electronically in an agreed format.

What format? Make use of e-mail, intranets and extranets. However the team wishes to work should be incorporated in the framework. This is not set in stone; if it doesn't work it can be changed. The basic rule is: identify the audience, decide the message, and then choose the medium.

The key element is that a great part of the decision process in communicating has become automatic because much of the thought has already occurred. The team's time can better be spent on achieving the right message at each stage.

At the end of the day these projects are all about change. Make no mistake; it is not possible to change IT alone to improve your business. The greatest benefit comes from changing both IT and processes together. Most importantly, you will need to manage the expectations of the people who will use the new system and involve them in the changes.

It is this part of the programme which will make or break the project.

8 Setting a Long-Term IT Strategy

"Strategy comes first."
"Without a strategy, you may as well not start."
"If you don't have a plan, how do you know where you will end up?"

It is a universally agreed truth that any business, department, or project needs an agreed strategy in order for it to be successful. So how have we arrived at Chapter 8 without setting an IT strategy? Surely this means that what we have developed may not fit well with overall business aims; perhaps we will have to rebuild large parts of the solution as soon as we realise what else there is to build.

Before answering this apparent anomaly directly, let's have a look at what strategy means in practice.

The use of strategy

The meaning and application of "strategy" in most companies is hard to pin down. It is one of those words that can mean a great many things to different people. I always like to remember the Dilbert cartoon where Dilbert was able to choose his job title: he eventually decided upon "Head of Global Strategy" because it sounded very important without defining what he was meant to do.

For many small businesses, the overall strategy will be inside the head of the founder. No matter how often the bank requires him to produce a business plan, the direction of the company will be effectively at the whim of the MD and his directors. As companies grow, so does the exercise of determining a strategy and creating a business plan. The two months before the year-end is usually a frenetic rush to set plans and budgets for the forthcoming year.

Are these plans reviewed six months or 12 months later? Often not, because business is forever changing and there is usually a good reason why the plan was exceeded or not met.

Individual department strategies can also be difficult to relate to the strategy of the whole company and, the larger the company; the more problems there are in formulating a coherent plan.

Where does IT fit?

For many property organisations, IT was, or is, an afterthought. The company muddled through until it reached the size necessary to employ its own specialist to run the servers and network that had built up. Sometimes, the IT manager had no formal background in IT and had been trained to deal with the various issues that need maintenance. IT in the growth phase of a property organisation is rarely seen as a strategic requirement and, if it is, much of it is outsourced to specialist companies who would not be privy to the company strategy deliberations.

For corporate estates departments, the IT strategy may seem even more opaque. The central IT team may seem remote and, although they are well versed in business IT requirements, the needs of the property team can seem obscure or arcane to them. The IT team are tempted to provide generic solutions despite protestations from the estates team that specific solutions exist.

In both landlord and tenant companies the decision makers usually have little technical IT knowledge and the IT manager will often report through a non-cognate director or partner. This leaves little room for discussion about why changes are necessary.

If the IT manager is more of a technician than a politician, a deepening distrust of the reasons for spending vast amounts of money can develop. The money is spent on "invisible" improvements to the network or servers that appear to provide no immediate benefit for the users.

To many business managers, IT is like insurance – a necessary evil that should be minimised wherever possible. As a result the IT strategy is often, by default, "to react quickly to new situations with as limited a budget as possible".

Users, that is, you and I, seldom help the process of defining an IT strategy. We tend to approach IT with an attitude of almost learned helplessness. In other words, it is so difficult and time consuming to correct the malfunctioning system that it is easier to go through a partly manual, partly automated process and check it by hand. The alternative is to call someone to fix the basic problem that may take more time than is available.

When IT is needed, it is needed in a hurry and taking a day to fix the problem is an impossible luxury. Once the task is complete, there are other business priorities to deal with and the problem IT is left until next time.

Eventually, when things get sufficiently difficult to use, users take their case to the Board and the scale of the difficulties makes it easy for the directors to understand how much time and money is being wasted through using the old system. A new project is approved and a team set up to develop a new solution to the problem. However, as soon as the new IT is implemented, the difficulties of justifying new IT spend return and the Board concentrates on more pressing business issues.

The Planning Process

It is this common sequence of events that militates against the creation of a coherent IT strategy. High-level support for change only becomes available when each isolated IT problem escalates; a point solution is developed and the support wanes until the cycle of disruption repeats.

This is why I have left a discussion of IT Strategy until now. Most companies start with the solution of a single problem and at that point, it is difficult to justify a holistic approach, let alone taking three months to prepare an overall strategy.

To avoid this cycle of individual, unconnected projects, it is clear that IT does need to be planned strategically; it needs to be an integral part of the business planning process. There is clearly a gulf in many cases between the perception of the need for IT strategy by the Board and the actual need. It often takes time to embed the process of relating core business strategy to IT strategy, but it is no less important than developing human resource strategy or corporate communications.

Where to start?

Should IT drive the business or should it be responsive to the needs of the users? In some circumstances, such as when new technology allows a dramatic decrease in cost, IT can drive business improvement. However, in most cases, the business should drive IT.

At the development stage, the questions should focus on the business. Some initial questions to ask which will help to start formulating a strategy might include:

- **What will make the most difference to the business?** Would an improvement in investor reporting yield a greater return than a project to collect rents more efficiently?
- **How should key business processes be supported by IT?** Would it be more effective to implement a document management system or to provide all managers with hand-held computers?
- **What size will the business be in five years?** Will it be possible to link together all your current systems with a browser interface or should you start planning to implement a large integrated system?
- **Are there any new technologies that would give us competitive advantage?** Will property portals dramatically reduce marketing costs or increase the number of credible buyers? Can referencing of properties be done more accurately, more cheaply and more quickly with new technology?

Let's go back to the beginning of this book. We looked at the different types of IT that could help a property organisation. We started to relate the core and critical needs of the business to the types of IT functionality available and then defined solutions around these needs. In other words, we started the process of developing a solution for the first individual project by using strategic tools for defining its scope.

We asked questions of the business which would draw out the processes critical to increasing sales or reducing cost. We prioritised the functionality for the solution around the aspects of the software that would make achieve most benefit.

In fact we used the first project to ask many of the questions we need for an IT strategy; we now need to develop what we learnt.

The process of developing the specification for the first project will have exposed the Board to questions that suggested ways IT could help develop the business. It will have drawn out ideas for using new technology which otherwise would have found little time for discussion. It will have created a wish-list for parts of the business unaffected by the immediate project. This wish-list can now be revisited and help to form your strategy.

Assuming that this first project is successful (you have been paying attention, haven't you?), this whole process of developing the specification for a single project will have been instrumental in raising the profile of IT in the organisation. With luck, other departments or teams will have seen the benefits provided by this project and will be eager to develop their own projects. The success of this project, and the measurable gains in efficiency will also make the business case process easier for other teams.

The potential to improve other parts of the business released by a successful project should have justified this first project in itself (although this is clearly not part of the original business case). However, the request for funds for a series of new projects will now emphasise the need for a co-ordinated approach. The question on the mind of the Board should now be, "How many of these projects should we sanction?" rather than the original, "Why should we spend money on IT?"

Before we get carried away with this project success and the largesse on the part of the company directors, we should remember that the success has been achieved through a visible project in an under-performing part of the business; within a strategy document we will still need to address the issue of planning infrastructure upgrades. These may never be seen, let alone understood.

Still, the favourable environment delivered by a successful IT project should help the IT team, and I have discussed planning for IT support in more detail in the next chapter.

The constituent parts

The word strategy is too vague to be of help here. A definition from Princeton University describes a strategy as "an elaborate and systematic plan of action". However, a search of the

Web[1] reveals a definition more in keeping with many people's views: "A long-range plan whose merit cannot be evaluated until sometime after those creating it have left the organisation."

Many of us have sympathy for the latter definition but we cannot get away from the fact that without an understanding of where we want to get to, it will be difficult to make progress.

Current State Analysis

Before we look at where we are going, let's look at where we are. We need to analyse the current situation and look at the strengths and weaknesses of where the business finds itself.

Some organisations call this element the Current State Analysis (CSA) and others, the "As Is" state. This is probably the easiest part of the process because, although there might be disagreement over the size or priority of current failings, most businesses will agree that they exist.

The danger here is that the current state becomes over-analysed. In any meeting to discuss the elements of the CSA, navel-gazing can be rife if not well controlled. The objective is to identify issues, both good and bad, not to resolve them at this stage.

As mentioned above, the bad points that need resolution will come easily. It is just as important to identify the elements of the organisation which work well and which, if lost, will create problems.

The principal objective of the CSA stage is to define the where we are and what needs to be done. There may be significant elements of the business that require little improvement. Parts of the business may not be included in a strategy because it intended to sell them: further investment in IT in those teams may not achieve a greater sale price.

The most effective way of determining the issues most relevant to the IT strategy is to convene a meeting of the senior directors or partners of the business and seek their views. This is not easy to arrange because of other pressures on their time but the achievement of this gathering is essential for two reasons.

1 There is no better way to discover the correct balance of key issues facing the business.
2 It shows that there is sufficient sponsorship of this project to attract the organisations attention.

In the case of a corporate occupier, it is often even more difficult to convene a meeting of the non-property directors to discuss this one aspect of the business and it may be more realistic to retain this discussion within the team and select key directors from other parts of the business to attend where necessary. These directors will be from IT and operations

1 www.netfunny.com/rhf/jokes/new90/glossar.35.html

(property management, development and acquisitions in a property company) and, if possible, the chairman and/or managing director.

Often a board meeting can be extended to allow time for a discussion about the impact of future plans on the need for IT but these sessions are typically short in comparison with normal workshops. It is rare to get more than half a day from these senior people and so the workshop environment must be well structured and preparation will be extensive.

Early meetings to prepare for the workshop will include an estimate of the scope of the IT strategy. This may be done through individual meetings with key directors. Once documented, this is the first element of the strategy to be validated at the workshop.

The meetings to prepare for the workshop will also allow the collection of views about the current positive and negative points which need to be dealt with by the IT strategy. Firmly held convictions and personal agendas can be flagged early so that these can be sidelined if necessary during the workshop.

This preparation allows the presentation of a great deal of the information as agreed (if that is the case) allowing the workshop to concentrate on the areas where agreement needs to be reached. In itself, this process will have reduced the discussion by about 70% in most cases.

Agreement on the CSA should be achieved quickly in the workshop, and time must be made to move forward to the next stage, sometimes known as the Future State Vision (FSV) or "To Be" state. Setting up a workshop that merely seeks to agree how deeply we are "in the chocolate" is often career limiting. The FSV logically follows the CSA closely and there will always be overlap in the discussions between the two.

Future State Vision

In developing the FSV for an IT strategy, we need to discuss the issues of the company at the highest level. A good starting point is the corporate business plan and better still, any document setting out the long-term vision for the company. The typical timescale for selecting and implementing IT is between one-two years and so the future direction of the company and the market in which it works will be a key input to the process. Some examples of changes in business that may affect property organisations are set out below. IT will have an impact on each of these.

Business Development	**Implication**
Call centres and shared service centres for many financial organisations are being established in India.	Many property processes, particularly in accounting may prove to be more cost-effective by following this example. Online access to these centres will be essential.

The possible introduction of tax transparent property investment vehicles will encourage the private investors into the property sector	Far more detailed investment performance details will need to be provided to a far greater number of individual investors. The internet will be key in distributing these reports
The potential for changes in retail environments may alter the balance of property types in retailers' portfolios.	Landlords may need to develop logistics services for their shopping centre tenants. The increasing complexity of their contractual relationship will require improved and more regular reporting.
Shopping centres will have a far greater requirement for wireless infrastructure allowing retailers to compete in attracting shoppers, as shoppers increase their use of wireless devices and mobile telephones.	In addition to the wave of investment in broadband to offices, landlords will have to understand how to implement and recoup the cost of wireless infrastructure in their buildings.
More outsourcing of non-core IT activities will lead to companies depending on hosted technology solutions.	Even if property managers are retained inside client organisations, their IT support will be accessible from any web-browser equipped PC. Teams will become more mobile, changing their requirement for space and other services.

The element of the workshop that tackles the FSV will inevitably generate a significant number of ideas on its own; the management team now have an opportunity to discuss their own visions for the company and describe their aspirations for new information systems. Many of these ideas will have been waiting for the right discussion forum and this is it. In addition, the various requests for particular IT resources or solutions that are generated in the course of business can be added to this wish-list and considered in more detail. This reduces the risk that more ideas are raised as possibilities after the strategy has been signed off.

Despite the fact that the input to this process seems quite comprehensive, the ideas generated internally are not normally enough.

This is an opportunity to look at how new technology from other sectors could enable the company to work more efficiently. The ideas above are just a starting point and an important part of a session to discuss FSV is a presentation of new ideas. These can be property technology from other parts of the world or generic solutions from other industries that can be adapted.

Where can you find these ideas? The internet is a good starting place and there are many forums for IT discussions. Property related forums in the US include Pikenet and Realcomm and these are good ways of keeping up with new developments. In the UK look at www.itforpropertypeople.com and the Estates Gazette's Vision section is another useful resource for researching the latest developments in management and technology. Most of the major newspapers also carry IT supplements from time to time that will carry overviews of trends with case studies – the Financial Times is particularly useful in this respect.

Prioritising ideas

Suitably primed with external ideas, the workshop should generate a good number of potential solutions to current issues and, in addition, will provide a vision of the future some way ahead of the current state. In order to be able to focus on the achievable, the workshop should be structured to allow the participants to prioritise the drivers of the

Company type	Initiative
Property Company	In order to prepare for REIT style investment vehicles, internal property systems will become able to export key data automatically to web pages which can be accessed by individual investors. This will attract more investors to this company because they will feel more in control of their investment
Corporate Occupier	Because the company is fiercely acquisitive, systems and processes will be agreed and documented so that newly acquired portfolios and staff can be brought into the management team as smoothly as possible. This will reduce the time taken to resume the smooth running of the portfolio after a merger and minimise risk of errors.
Property Advisor	A disparate number of property data systems has developed over the years leading to lost opportunities to sell work. The company has decided to join all the property data together so that every team can access all relevant data. This will allow teams to share knowledge on every property in a way that will encourage teams to bid for further work.
Local Authority	As part of the Government's initiative to allow public access to Local Government data, all property data will be accessible over the Web on the Council's website. This will reduce the time taken by the property team in answering mundane questions about property ownership and will satisfy the Government's objectives in this area.

business and the potential solutions. This is done in much the same way as in the workshop described in Chapter 7.

A set of agreed priorities then forms the basis for the needs of the FSV and allows the development of a strategy to provide solutions. The FSV provides the basis for the strategy and by now there will be broad agreement from senior management what the key elements of the strategy will achieve.

For example, the following initiatives could form part of the strategy:

In each case there will be a number of business-led initiatives. The opportunity for the initiative may have come about through better technology becoming available but in each case, the strategic initiative takes the form of:

Business Opportunity – Overview of Solution – Benefit Statement

This is a long way from providing all the information necessary to develop the initiative but it provides clear terms of reference so that the detail can be developed.

Each strategic initiative will need to be developed and each will therefore need a business case to justify the expenditure. In order to progress this, each will need a sponsor and the sponsor needs to be selected at the IT strategy workshop.

This is a good way of reducing the number of initiatives if the discussion produces too many. The requirement of a Board level sponsor ensures that only the most important initiatives are selected. The sponsors have limited time to spend on initiatives and if an individual does not support an initiative, it can be dropped. If it is deemed by the board to be too important to drop but no resource is available, this can be addressed; addressing this issue at this stage provides a far greater chance of success than later in the project.

A thorough risk analysis will also remove some opportunities from the selection list. Many of the projects will be high profile and high cost. Sponsors will want to know the chances of things going wrong and the implications if they do.

The sponsor will be responsible for co-ordinating the development of a business case to support the initiative's inclusion in the strategy and this process filters the number of initiatives still further.

Although not a large part of the strategy process, the initial business case is essential to gauge the size of the benefit available and estimate the amount of resource required. So far, in the same way that we developed the initiative in Chapter 3, we have looked only at the business requirement. Using the Three Clouds diagram (Figure 3.1) as a reference, this business requirement may need support in the office applications and infrastructure areas and the initial business case will rely on information on these areas from the IT team.

Infrastructure strategy

The business cases will start to arrive back with the head of IT and it will be easier to gauge the breadth of the initiatives in terms of the technology they require. The initial business case will have filtered a few of the solutions from the strategy and the rest will have been approved to go forward to the next stage. The IT team will need to assess the technology implications.

The same process applies: there will be a CSA of the IT infrastructure to establish weaknesses and current benefits. The collection of initial business cases will together provide an indication of the FSV for the business applications. The IT team will now have to develop a full FSV for the IT infrastructure. Some of the costs for infrastructure upgrades may be provided by the business case for an individual business project; this is often a key discussion in obtaining approval to proceed.

Various options will present themselves in terms of infrastructure. Questions will be raised over the basic systems: should the company depend on Microsoft with the inherent costs attached? Should we develop a strategy based on Opensource software; that is, software which is free to use and can be developed by the company on the basis that whatever is developed is freely distributed. The attractions of the strong functionality within Microsoft are clear. However, it is estimated that 70% of the global market for operating systems and web servers is now taken by the probably more secure, and free, Opensource offerings.

Very large organisations, particularly those in which property forms only a small part of their operations, may choose an enterprise system such as SAP, Oracle or Peoplesoft to manage the entire business. The property team will use only some of the functionality available but they will be able to access data from all other parts of the organisation. This is not a quick decision to make and one of the following scenarios is more likely.

1 The company already uses an enterprise system in other departments and the request to improve the property team's systems provides a useful opportunity to add the property modules to the system.
2 The company is growing rapidly and the IT team start to investigate whether the large collection of IT solutions they already have could be better managed by buying and implementing an enterprise solution over the coming years.

The latter situation may require two solutions to be developed because it is unlikely that a new enterprise system will provide the requisite solution within the timescales planned in the initial business cases. The first solution will be developed as cheaply as possible to be temporary. In parallel, the specification developed for the temporary solution will be used to test and develop the appropriate modules in the enterprise system.

For many organisations, new IT initiatives will mean that the number of unconnected solutions will grow and an essential part of the IT team's brief will be to minimise the costs of supporting these systems and integrating them where possible. It may be possible to integrate all of the systems using one set of tools and the potential list of suppliers for this is huge.

Essentially, there are four main ways to integrate data across systems and these are shown in Figure 8.2

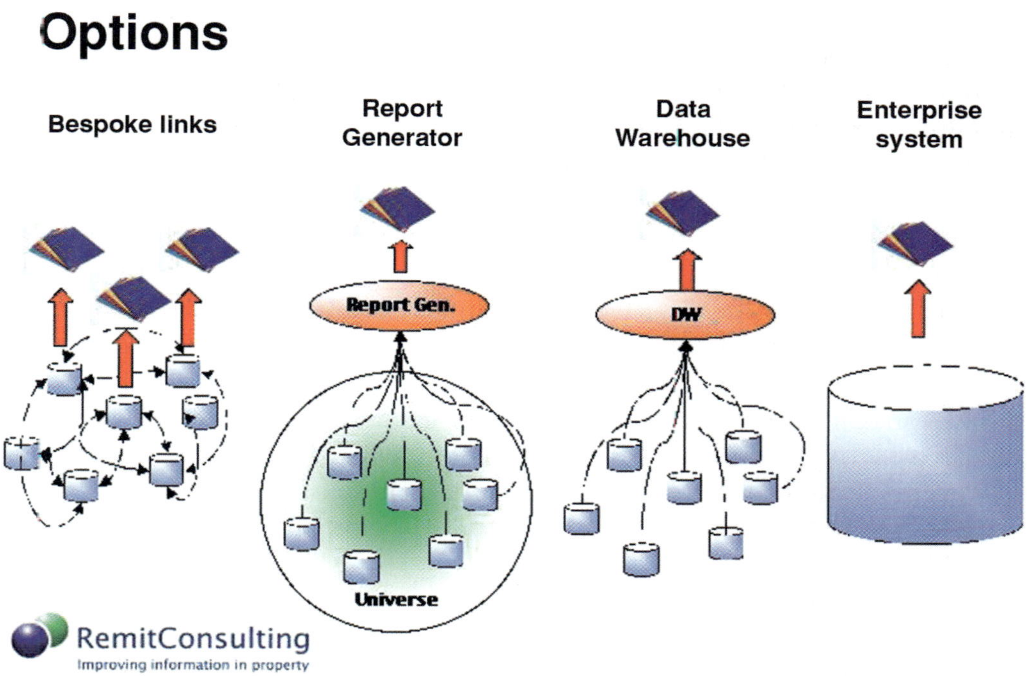

Figure 8.2

We have covered enterprise systems above where all the data is contained within one database (or set of databases) and integration appears to be seamless.

At the other extreme is when an IT team develops bespoke links between all systems. Depending on the specification of the links, it may be possible for reports to be produced in each application using data from many different applications. This method of integrating is time-consuming and expensive. It is also inflexible because often, when an application is upgraded, the links need to be re-written. Pisces (OSCRE in the US) mentioned previously may provide some help here.

However, this is a common solution within IT environments that have developed on a piecemeal basis over time. It also the arrangement that leads most companies to consider enterprise solutions as a radical alternative to the problems it produces.

In between these two solutions lie a large selection of options that differ slightly but can broadly be divided into two groups.

1 **Report Generators** – A report generator provides a set of tools to map information held in a number of different systems so that it can return to those data fields every time it needs to. The map is often known as a universe since this is the term used by

one of the more common report generators, Business Objects. Once the universe is mapped, the software can use any information in the universe to produce reports.

The software provides tools to produce the reports and, although these tools are user friendly for those people using the software regularly, users who rely on a few templates and only need new reports occasionally often find these tools cumbersome. However, this need not be a problem if reports are specified effectively at the outset.

2 **Data Warehouse** – A slightly different approach is used by data warehouse applications. Here a completely separate database is configured into a structure that makes it easy to reference and report data. Data from many different systems is regularly loaded into the data warehouse and this set of data is manipulated and used to provide reports. This dataset can be changed without affecting the source data and updates can be taken a frequently as every few seconds.

However, data warehouses are usually updated at frequencies of over an hour and often once per day, and so the data being reported may be out of date. These solutions are large, powerful and expensive to implement. They also require extreme discipline to be effective and companies often use separate teams to manage them.

The area of integration is one of the biggest dilemmas for all companies and the IT team will want to be fully involved in these early stages of setting strategy. It might be that some initiatives are severely compromised by the current or proposed IT infrastructure and this clearly will need further discussion if it is the case. The fact that this discussion has been flagged as necessary would be an improvement for many organisations that might be used to developing a series of *ad hoc* solutions and storing up trouble for later.

There is likely to be far more discussion and research required the first time that an IT strategy is developed. The Board will agree the key long-term initiatives; the sponsors of each initiative will develop a business case; the IT team will review and define the infrastructure they will need. The following year, the CSA will involve an assessment of the success or otherwise of the initiatives undertaken, a review of the initiatives which were seen as being second phase and a new set of business cases. There should be less need for intensive work on the infrastructure strategy unless the first year's plan was to make do for another 12 months.

Setting the strategy

The major difficulty in setting an IT strategy is co-ordinating the various inputs. The head of IT will want to take control of the process but the main driver for the strategy will be the decisions from the business. The skills required of the head of IT are unlikely to be those often expected, ie blue-sky strategic thinking and innovation. More likely, they will be co-ordination of disparate ideas, the ability to achieve consensus between conflicting views and an awareness of how each element of the overall strategy can add to the corporate vision.

All participants should be involved in the creation of ideas and external influence at this stage is important. Specific tasks and responsibilities should be assigned to the research and business case stage. The development of the strategy itself, with its supporting costs, benefits and detail, needs to be thorough and able to stand rigorous intellectual challenge.

By the time the strategy document is submitted first to the IT strategy team (those from the initial workshop) and then to the main board, the only gaps should be in resourcing and these should be sufficiently obvious for the Board to decide whether additional resource should be made available.

The decision on resources will clearly be made on the basis of the strength of the business case put forward and therefore the role of the individual project sponsor is essential. This is why any initiatives proposed at the first workshop that do not have a sponsor should be dropped at that stage. Without a sponsor, they will not find a strong business case and therefore will not pass the final stage of the strategy development. The time wasted on that initiative should be spent more wisely on the other, well sponsored, projects.

Timescale

The IT strategy is often developed at the year-end when budgets are being considered for the following year. Most teams in the business are doing the same thing and therefore it is unreasonable to expect to benefit form large chunks of people's time when they are concentrating on their own problems.

You may therefore consider that another time of the year is more suitable for starting this initiative. This has the added benefit that by doing this well before the year end, the majority of the IT budget will have been developed by other teams (with developed business cases) and the year end season of budget setting will be straightforward.

However, the luxury of a timescale without a deadline will also kill the project. Other teams will not take it seriously if this process drags on. It is therefore essential to set timescales around individual Board meetings when the results will be presented and further decisions requested. It is unlikely that the IT strategy development will be successful if it takes longer than three months from beginning to end and, a well organised project can produce a strategy in one month.

Other elements of the strategy

We have dealt with the main business requirements for IT and also the infrastructure. Depending on the structure of your organisation, there are other elements that need to be addressed.

These include:

- training

- help desk
- upgrade management
- office applications.

It is important to remember that the result will be change mainly within the business and therefore communications and change management (covered in Chapter 7) will require explicit resourcing and funds.

Many of the IT fundamentals are dealt with in Chapter 9 and will be part of the on-going management of the IT support function. The strategy may be to outsource the whole range of services or alternatively you may have a strong in-house team. For either of these approaches, or any combination, the strategy document should clearly state how this will be approached and may include a plan to change the current structure over time. This would be particularly relevant if a new enterprise system is proposed or, for example, if the property management team may be outsourced in the next few years.

Conclusion

Unfortunately, the setting of an IT strategy does not only involve discussing the need to buy new mobile telephone gadgetry. Some "blue-sky" thinking will be involved at the beginning but this is mainly aimed at getting the business users to elaborate on their needs to develop the business.

Most of the strategy development will involve persuading overstretched executives to delegate the task of producing business cases for new initiatives. It will need the co-ordination of often-divergent opinions and requirements and the presentation of a coherent, well-structured argument to invest in an area many perceive to be a drag on resources.

The first year is the hardest but that is the opportunity to establish a change in thinking and make the next few years far easier to manage.

9 Setting up and running an IT support service

Contrary to the popular perception that an IT support team is comprised of techno-obsessed geeks, IBM's research labs have found that 95% of an IT manager's job is communication and only 5% is "twiddling knobs".

Their job is not that different to yours or mine. So why do we get this impression every time someone comes to fix a malfunctioning PC that they have no real idea about what is going on in the business?

Even in the best-run businesses, IT can sometimes stop play. One company I know complained that their property management system, albeit rather dilapidated, crashed on average seven times each day. This involved everyone switching off his or her machines and starting again. Thankfully, for most organisations this is a thing of the past but the stray niggles in every system only ever seem to occur when you most need the computer; and you need it in a hurry.

Consequently, the IT team is fixing the machines when tempers are at their worst. The support team is stretched (as most are) and the users never see them at a time when business needs can be discussed.

Perception is everything and if the IT system causes problems, the IT team will be perceived to be techno-geeks who are failing to serve the company, however unfair that is.

So, IT teams get a bad press and have little extra time to spend on the PR necessary for every internal support team. There are, however structural problems within a traditional IT team in a small organisation; by that I mean that small companies cannot hope to use an internal IT team effectively. The team is too small to solve all the problems thrown at them and it is too expensive to hire a team large enough to manage all the IT.

As we have seen, the majority of real estate owners and managers run small and medium sized businesses. Government and occupiers, on the other hand, are part of large organisations that tend to have IT departments that manage IT on behalf of the whole business. The majority of this chapter deals with the approach that smaller businesses can take to manage their IT support. Although this will provide a useful understanding of what is involved for those with IT departments, there may be little that can be done to influence the structure of corporate services. I have added a section at the end of the chapter that suggests ways of preparing for such a situation.

Therefore, given that most property companies are small – they have relatively few people who make large amounts of money for the company – I have firstly concentrated on the problems of IT within small companies.[1]

Too much to do

Before we think about resources, let's consider what we actually need to do to manage and run IT – irrespective of the size of your business.

To do this, we can apply a simple model for analysing the processes in the IT function (Figure 9.1). You will recognise this model as a version of the RPM that we discussed in relation to the functional areas of a property company. Here the RPM is set up to reflect the functional areas required within an IT team.

At the very highest level, the blocks shown in yellow are the mega-processes that categorise the main areas. Here they run from setting the IT strategy through to providing the technical support.

For each of these we then define a set of major processes. At this slightly lower level, the tasks within each mega-process start to become clearer. For example, "User Support" groups those tasks which involve interaction with the users and these include the Helpdesk, User Liaison and User Training; "IT Management" will deal with the business end of the IT support function and will include Supplier Management and Legals.

In practice, and in the same way as we dealt with property processes, we could continue to subdivide each block to lower levels.

Whether the processes are done formally or informally, this shows the wide range of activities typically involved in IT. Of course, this model will change in detail for each organisation, particularly at the lower levels. This example for instance doesn't have a slot for bespoke software maintenance and if this is an important area for the company, there will need to be agreement over where this fits within the structure.

The four mega-processes to the right, IT Management through to Technical Support, represent the areas of ongoing IT operation.

1 Much of this chapter was developed from a presentation given by Mark Jones of Remit Consulting at the PCS-Expo in 2004.

What do you need to do to run IT?

Set Strategy	Implement Strategy	IT Management	User Support	Technical Management	Technical Support
Business Plan	Procurement	Supplier Management	Helpdesk	Problem Determination	System Administration
Development Plan	Development	Contract Management	User Liaison	Incident Management	Security
Strategic Resourcing	Tactical Sourcing	Asset Management	User training	Configuration Management	Backup & Recovery
Budgeting	Management of Change	Licence Management		Technical Portfolio Mgt	Capacity & Performance Mgt
Business Continuity	Policies and Standards	Legals (DPA data retention etc.			Storage Maintenance
	Project Management	HR			Software Maintenance
					Hardware Maintenance

RemitConsulting
Improving information in property

Figure 9.1 RPM for IT Support

These mega-processes cover both non-technical management aspects, and technical issues.

Now, if we're in a large company, we can easily start to structure an in-house IT team. It's clear we need a team with a wide range of different skills.

We will need:

- managers who understand the business and external factors. They will need to manage staff, relationships with suppliers and work with users
- user support staff who need to have a knack for dealing with people (although you wouldn't always think so)
- the technical team. Some will be supervising the installation as a whole, while others will have skills that only apply to a subset of systems.

The range of people skills in this team spans a vast spectrum. Technicians are often fantastic when it comes to "fire fighting" behind the scenes, they will stay up all night or work weekends when a particularly nasty virus gets past the firewall and anti-virus measures. They will take great pride in having worked such long hours and solved a difficult technical solution – especially if they are among the first of their peers to do so.

The next morning, they are often required to be on the helpdesk, advising an IT illiterate to reboot his machine to fix a trivial bug and, even if they have had sufficient sleep, the best technical people are often less good at dealing with users.

It is rare that you will find a technician who can prioritise the most important user queries, who has the encyclopaedic knowledge necessary to provide answers to user's problems, has the interpersonal skills of Henry Kissinger to deal with the problems in the order that suits the company; *and* can also manage a budget which is always under pressure from the management.

If someone like this works in your organisation, you had better keep quiet about them – better still; send their details to me with a brief note about their current remuneration.

So, a wide range of skills needed to undertake all that is required of an IT support team, and that's fine in a big company which can recruit teams of people with a mixture of skills. In large companies, the average number of IT staff tends to be between 25 and 30 for every 1000 end users.

But now let's think about a small company with say less than 50 users.

What you actually need is some fraction of a person in all these IT function areas since, as a small business, you can only afford one (or maybe two) IT people in total.

This is where it is easy to come unstuck.

1 It's really difficult to find an individual with the wide range of skills and abilities needed for the complete IT function. If such a person exists, they'll probably be too expensive.
2 The small team won't normally be able to cope with the complete workload. Most of the time, they will be sorting out problems and fire-fighting. Thus the management aspects, any sort of proactive approach, and standards and formality will go by the board. That normally means risks increase and quality suffers.

In addition, there are the practical issues; for instance how do you provide adequate cover for holidays and sickness, for the extended working day, for training courses and for flexible working?

What can you do? Your first thought maybe to find a service provider to manage all of this. We can use the process model as a checklist and define a service that covers all of the IT we use.

In each area, we will need to identify the separate service requirements and document these. It is important to identify the exact service levels required and the measurements that will be applied to the contract. Your users will need to understand the implications of each service level agreement and it must reflect the actual needs of the business.

One contract that covers all of your IT is therefore potentially very complex.

In addition, you may not feel comfortable with a single agreement for all your IT needs. It may be too risky to put all of your eggs in one basket. For example, can you find a service provider in your area who covers the range of technology and systems you have, but who also deals with small businesses? Often, the smaller IT companies have exactly the same problems of attracting and retaining good IT staff that you do.

Those IT companies that do knock on you door probably can't offer a range of services wide enough to be your only provider. On the other hand, large service providers with complete coverage won't normally deal with small companies.

If that's the case, we need to think about some of the ways to reduce the size of the requirement for a single service provider, and look at different options for decreasing the need for in-house resources.

Options

Let's leave aside the do-it-yourself route. Unless you run a large company with the ability to hire a large, multi-functional IT team, running your own IT is unlikely to provide the most effective answer.

So we can look instead at options for using external service providers; in particular, hosted solutions and managed services.

Hosted solutions are systems run by an external provider that are located remotely and which you would normally access over the internet.

Managed services are an arrangement through which one company looks after all your systems and this works best where the solutions themselves are hosted by specialists. The managed service provider may host some of the solutions but in most cases, they will manage the service hosted elsewhere.

The advantages of using these services to run large parts of your IT are that they hand the difficult time-consuming aspects of IT to specialists, who can then pass onto you the benefits of economies of scale. In addition, the solutions are themselves scaleable, ie as your company gets bigger, even on a temporary basis; the costs of adding more IT support are not disproportionate. It is also possible to stay up to date with the latest software more easily than having to plan your own upgrade path.

Hosted Solutions – Commodity services

As mentioned above, these are systems run by an external provider that is located remotely and that you would normally access over the internet, often using your PC's web browser.

Typically they are priced according to the number of users, and you pay on a regular basis, for instance monthly or quarterly.

These services tend to be commodity services that are not necessarily industry specific. There are some good examples for e-mail, CRM, contact management, collaboration tools, and services for things like automatic data backups.

The great advantage with this approach is that you get to use a system that as a small business you may not otherwise be able to afford. There is usually little start-up cost, the applications usually require little formal training, and the hosting company takes care of upgrades and maintenance.

A further advantage of this approach is that businesses might take this approach to experiment with a system before investing themselves and this is often the case in larger organisations where pilot projects are run in this way.

Even more importantly, the hosted solution is likely to offer a highly available service with built-in resilience, the latest software updates, and it will be properly protected from security risks. Data will always backed up and the hosting company will offer industrial strength firewalls and anti-virus solutions.

In other words it will be maintained at a higher level than you would be able to afford with an in-house team.

Obviously, you will need to have a decent internet connection however and wherever you work. Broadband internet connections have driven the take-up of this type of service and the solutions for mobile workers are becoming effective. Even a hosted e-mail application seems slow over a dial-up modem when you are used to broadband in the office and it will not be until 3G telephony or inexpensive wireless LANs become widespread in public places that anything more than simple hosted applications become the norm for "Road Warriors".

Nevertheless, the advantages of hosted solutions for anyone who finds themselves working regularly with a broadband connection are significant.

Hosted Solutions – e-mail

As an example, we use a hosted e-mail service at Remit Consulting. Our original options were to use free internet e-mail accounts or, because we want to be able to collaborate and share information between ourselves, we could have set up an e-mail server with something like Microsoft Exchange software.

The difficulties are:

1. Free services are rarely reliable enough for business and have quite low limits on the size of files sent and stored. Although it is possible to set up MS Outlook to send out e-mail with a return tag to the business address, when using remote access, clients get to see your basic "free-service" e-mail details. Furthermore, connected filing areas to share documents are rarely available.
2. An MS Exchange server is expensive in terms of software and hardware and is very complex to set up. It also needs to be housed somewhere. In a small consultancy business, most of us are at client offices or on the road and a server in a central office still needs to be maintained. A more convenient answer is to give one of the consultants the responsibility for the e-mail server and allow them the choice of keeping the server in the office or at their home. However, keeping a business critical server at someone's home is not ideal, to say the least.

We settled for a hosted service where MS Exchange is hosted and we access our e-mail and shared files over the Web. Even accessing the service remotely or by mobile phone/PDA is reliable and is fast enough for this type of application.

The hosted service gives us the full facilities of Microsoft Exchange, with the shared calendars, meeting scheduling, and task management and shared contact lists – using the full Outlook front-end, and also Outlook Web Access so that we can get to the system from any machine on the internet. A typical screenshot is shown in Figure 9.2.

Best of all, we never have to worry about any of the support issues: availability, up-to-date virus protection, and backing up the data each night is all taken care of. For a small, highly mobile team it is a much better solution than a traditional e-mail service.

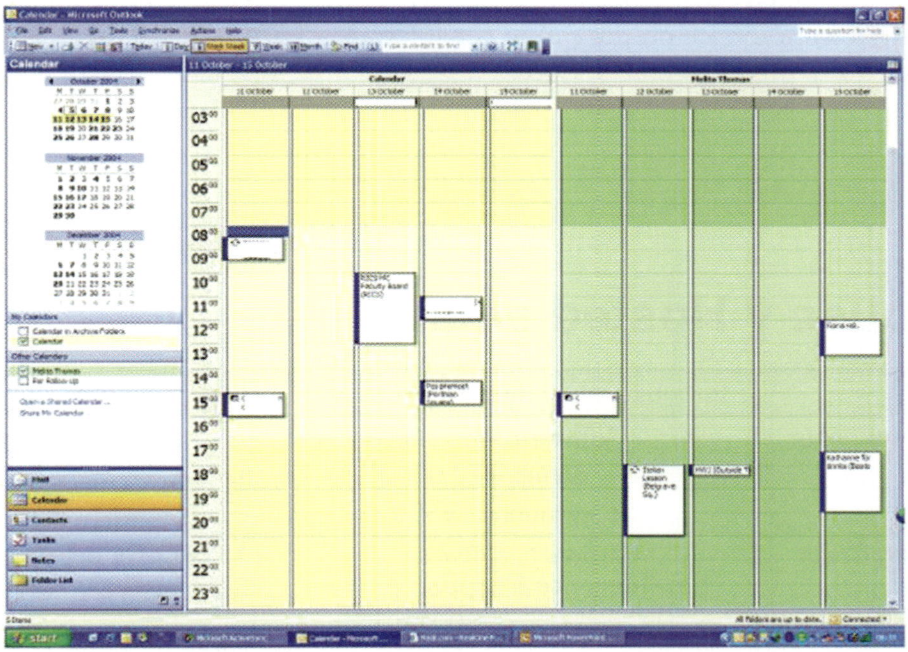

RemitConsulting
Improving information in property

Figure 9.2 Screen shot of MS outloook on a hosted service

So we have removed an element of complexity from our own IT function. And this is essential with something like e-mail which is crucial to our business, but which can cause so many support issues.

In-house v Hosted E-mail Costs

A hosted solution for small businesses can also work out much cheaper than a DIY solution. If we were to set up an e-mail system based around Windows Small Business Edition, the typical start-up costs are shown in Figure 9.3. This is where the majority of cost in running your own system falls.

Compared with the limited ongoing costs of hosting our own server, we'll pay a regular fee for the *hosted* service that may cost more per annum – over a number of years this will work out more expensive.

However, in this example there isn't an enormous difference over two or three years. Obviously, this will depend on a number of factors so, over time, the costs could be higher or lower on either side.

The real advantage with the hosted service is the reduced risk with no technical headaches. We concentrate on providing consultancy advice rather than worrying about upgrading and fixing the e-mail service.

In-house v Hosted email

	In-house email system	Hosted system
Start-up costs	Software - £1,500 Server - £2,000 Installation - £500	None
Ongoing Costs	Hardware, software maintenance & support £500 pa	£15 per user per month. 10 users = £1,800 pa
2 years 3 years	£5,000 £5,500	£3,600 £5,400
	• Higher risk of downtime • Technical management and support overhead • Extra cost to set-up Internet access	• 24/7 supported availability • High resilience • Latest security patches • Latest anti-virus, anti-spam • Internet access from anywhere

Figure 9.3 Typical cost comparison for e-mail services

In the end, if you can reduce the risk of the loss of your e-mail by even one event, that might be the difference between winning new business or not, and this is where the real value of a hosted services lies.

Hosted Business Applications

If this approach works so effectively for a small business using e-mail, can we use this idea for our main business applications?

Hosted services are useful for commodity items like e-mail. They work particularly well where the software will work with many different industries because there are more customers; therefore the costs can be spread over a large number of users.

As mentioned above, these "horizontal" applications include CRM, contact management, collaboration tools, and services for things like automatic data backups. You can see that all these applications could be used by any industry with only minor modifications and as such these are the applications that will be the most readily available.

The more specialised the software, the lower the number of users in the market and the less likely that a company will add that software to its range of hosted solutions. Add to that the fact that the UK property systems market is so diverse, and that each property software supplier has relatively few customers, and the prospect of hosted solutions providers offering hosted property solutions is less likely.

Despite this, solutions are coming forward directly from the property software providers themselves. In the past, property organisations have run these solutions on computers in our own offices. Now however, a number of the property system suppliers are offering hosted services as an alternative.

Just as with the commodity solutions, the systems will run from a data centre and they will be accessed over the internet. However, the services will be much more tailored to the company's specific needs.

This move to a more flexible set of solutions has been driven, and limited, by a number of factors.

1 The customers desire for ever cheaper solutions for back-office support has driven demand for leased software and services.
2 Many medium sized companies have a number of small regional offices. Keeping a traditional software solution in one central office produces many of the typical remote access problems mentioned above.
3 The property industry is, by its nature, very mobile and this should drive the need for remotely accessible solutions. However, with the exception of the recent craze for Blackberry e-mail devices, many property professionals have been reluctant to take property management solutions into the field. This is possibly because of the great weight of paper on which the industry relies.

These factors and the lack of development resource at the variety of small property software suppliers have led to a piecemeal development of hosted services. At present, the UK property software industry's response to the need for hosted solutions is typified by the following features.

1 There is a range of options normally made available to customers that usually focus on purchase cost, rather than accessibility or support. Often the possibility of leasing the software and hardware rather than outright purchase means that the business case can still be justified with minimal change in the way that IT is run in the business.
2 Where remote access is required, for example, in regional offices, the industry has developed software access based on Citrix-style solutions. The detail of this type of solution was discussed in Chapter 6 and, in short, this may not be the answer you wish to adopt. The use of Citrix requires the purchase of additional software and, although more than three million users of Citrix worldwide "can't be wrong", the decision often comes down to the personal preferences of the IT director.
3 There is potential overlap of services between supplying software and outsourcing the Property Management Accounting (PMA) function. Some software suppliers are experimenting with providing a full PMA service and this, coupled with the features mentioned above, confuse the straight comparison of what is being purchased.
4 The enterprise software providers do not yet have the critical mass in real estate to provide hosted software services but, with the advent of offshore outsourcing providers in many related industries, this may become possible shortly.

At present, the options tend to fall into two structures.

- At one extreme, you might purchase the hardware and software outright and pay the supplier for hosting and support services.
- On the other hand, you may simply pay a monthly fee based on number of users to cover all the supplier's costs for implementation and set up, hardware and software, and the ongoing hosting and support.

This somewhat confused market means that there will be more effort required to set up this type of agreement. It will also be necessary to consider carefully other aspects if, for instance, you want to integrate the data from the hosted application with other systems. This may be only the starting point for building all your systems around one provider, so take this into account when starting to develop a strategy.

Despite this, hosted business solutions should be very appealing for a small company because the support of property systems is one of the more difficult IT tasks. This is also a lucrative area for software suppliers to develop because the low start-up costs and long-term revenue from services allow them a better quality revenue flow.

Because of this, this area of software provision will evolve quickly. Nearly all the UK suppliers already claim to offer a hosted solution and most of the larger suppliers can point to relevant and effective reference sites for their hosted services.

Managed Services

The hosted services give options for removing entire systems from your own installation and thus reduce your need to provide IT support. However, you will always be left with some infrastructure and systems on your own site – file servers, firewalls and routers, PCs and printers, and so on.

This can be dealt with through "managed services".

The idea behind managed services is that one company takes responsibility for your IT services as well as the software.

Some companies provide specific services; some total service across all aspects of IT. Let's start by looking at the specific managed services because they are a short step on from hosted services; that is, once you have another company looking after specific applications such as e-mail and property management, an easy next step would be to contract a specialist to look after security or infrastructure maintenance.

This is often easier than it used to be. Usually, the provider can carry out infrastructure monitoring remotely so that they do not need to place staff physically at your premises. However, it is important to ensure that the managed services contract is just that – managed. It should be a proactive management service, not just reactive support.

Specific Managed Services

These services are a cross between hosted solutions and managed services. They relate to specific elements of IT, perhaps one that needs a high-level of expertise. A managed security service is a good example here.

Anyone who connects his or her PC to the internet regularly, or even just listens to the news, knows that security in our online world is a big issue. Most of us have a continuous connection to the internet, using e-mail and web browsing, and perhaps hosted services. Risks are high, threats are always changing, and the impact of a breach of security by a virus or Trojan Horse can have catastrophic effects on your business.

One large property agency was quite candid when, in 2002, the "I love you" virus forced them to close down all their e-mail in Germany because the local offices had not kept up to date with their anti-virus protection. The German offices concerned were without e-mail for 17 days and the effect on business was pronounced.

The agency has a large team of IT professionals with a large IT budget and this virus exposed a gap in their defences. The risks of a similar problem occurring in a much smaller company which cannot budget for new threats in the same way is much higher.

This is a highly technical area, and one that needs constant monitoring to ensure proper protection. Fortunately, there are firms who offer security as a managed service and you can rely on them for the expertise, for managing security devices, for monitoring, and for software updates. They will also work with you to develop a security policy as well.

Other examples of specific managed services are as follows:

1 You might consider a specific managed service for your wide area network.
2 If you haven't used a hosted service option for e-mail, you might put in place a managed service to look after your own e-mail system.
3 As telephony migrates from analogue, to digital to VoIP, a managed service might be the best way of ensuring that you lower your telephony costs but keep capital spending within reason.

The IT support process model – review

At this point, it is probably worth looking back at the RPM we set up at the beginning of the chapter to see how much of the IT support we are now managing effectively. The diagram in Figure 9.4 shows the areas that are now contracted to a managed services provider in red; those shaded red receive advice and ongoing input from the same supplier.

Figure 9.4 shows that, by using hosted solutions and specific managed services, we have dealt with maybe half of our responsibility to provide IT support in about one third

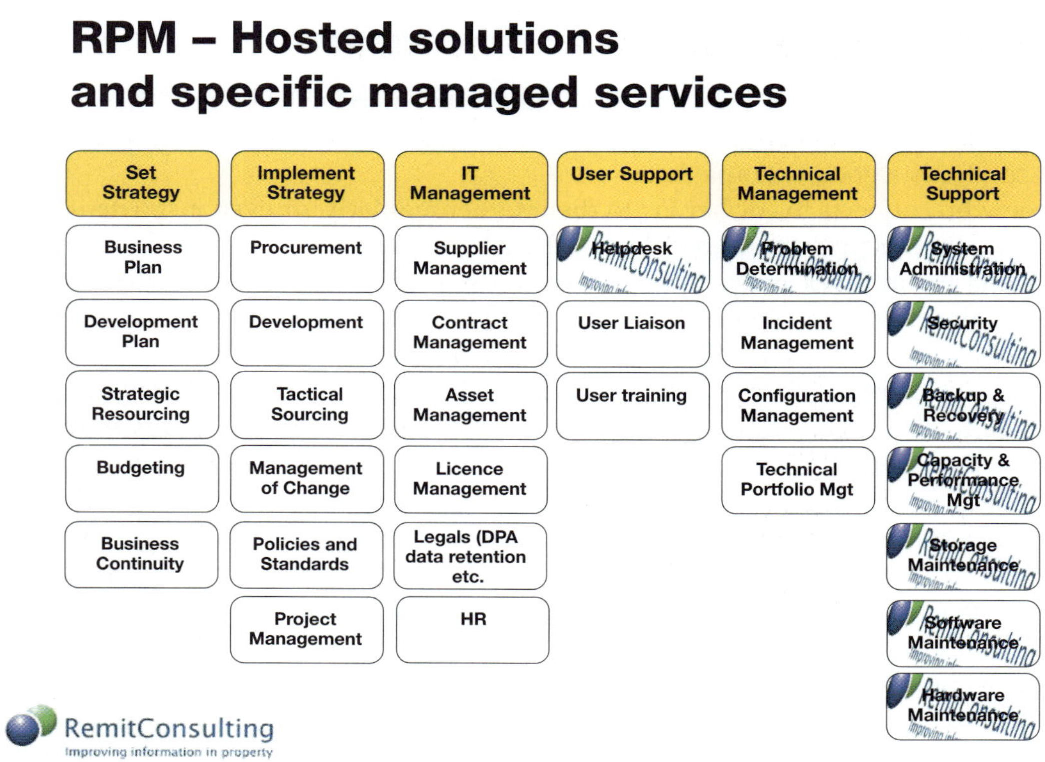

Figure 9.4 RPM for IT Support showing outsourced managed services in red.

of the functional areas. Despite the fact that we now have e-mail, security and infrastructure supported effectively this does not look that impressive and it shows how useful the RPM diagram is at identifying weaknesses.

The options we have considered so far have removed some direct in-house responsibility for:

- technical support and
- some technical management.

However, at best this is only on a system-by-system basis or for specific parts of the infrastructure. This leaves a good deal of co-ordination and management with the client company and importantly, the IT team will still be the first point of contact when users have problems.

That may be enough for your organisation but it hardly counts towards reducing your in-house IT team. What we are really looking to do is completely remove the need for in-house IT resource in the technical areas; we will also probably do the same in the user support functions, and as far as possible in IT management.

The goal is to be able to populate the RPM diagram as shown in Figure 9.5, below.

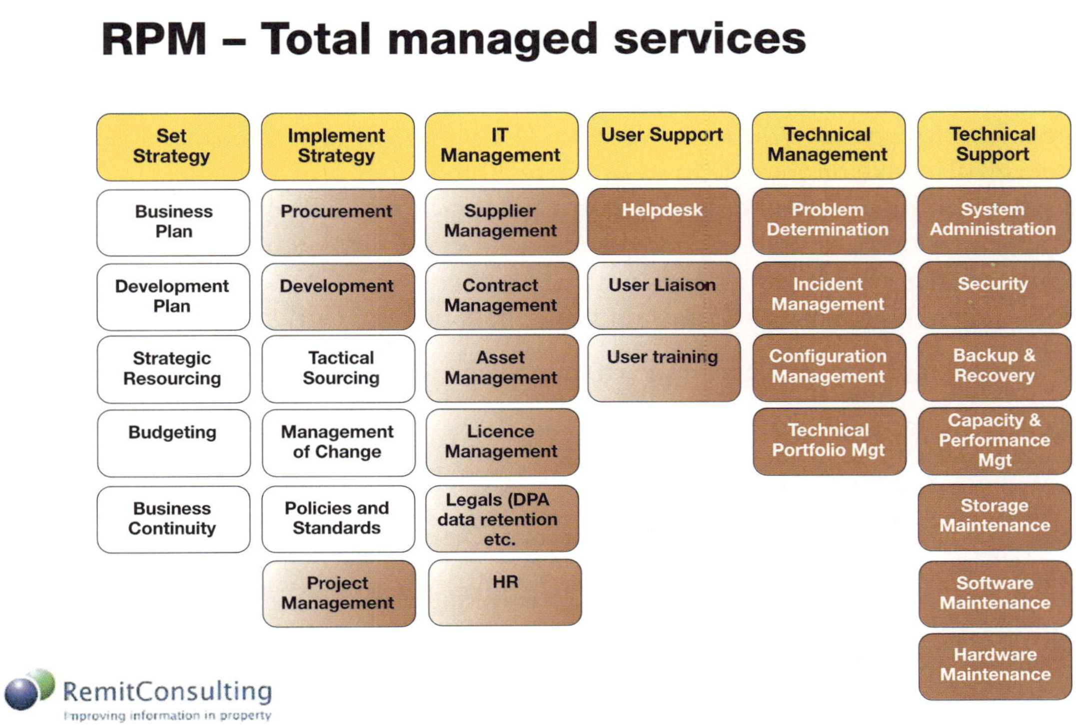

Figure 9.5

Total Managed Service

We can do this by extending the managed service concept beyond specific contracts to a managed service contract that *oversees* all of your IT. This sounds great but didn't we start by saying that one company is unable to show the strength of skills in-depth across a number of different IT areas?

This is where the managed services idea works well. The service supplier takes your existing contracts with a number of specialists and provides one point of contact for all of them. The client gets its services through a single contact, reducing the complexity inherent in multiple contracts; specialist companies that on their own do not wish to provide an entire range of services perform the contracts.

In addition, the managed services provider takes care of the infrastructure in your organisation. Much of the infrastructure you use may now be hosted elsewhere; this reduces the management to that of ensuring that you can use your PCs to access the relevant applications and data.

A total managed service is likely to provide most of this general infrastructure and office application management and support. It may also take on existing hardware maintenance contracts.

The intention is that it will also absorb many of the IT "management" activities at a level above day-to-day technical support.

You'll probably still consider making use of one or more of the other options we've discussed and you will continue to use, for example, the hosted e-mail service or the managed security service you have already set up. However, a total managed service provider can also take on the role to co-ordinate all the other providers.

This approach has a variety of benefits, some of which we have already discussed. One of the biggest difficulties with IT today is that systems are delivered across a variety of components that are expected to work with each other.

There is an old joke, which will be familiar to anyone who works on an IT helpdesk:

Q – How many software engineers does it take to change a light bulb?

A – None. It's a hardware fault.

Q – How many hardware engineers does it take to change a light bulb?

A – Two. One to look at the light bulb, the other to convince you it is a software fault.

In the real world, if you aren't receiving e-mails properly, is it a problem with your own router or firewall, the physical comms link, your ISP, or your e-mail provider?

You just want one point of contact and to know that the problem is going to be sorted. So incident management and problem determination is a key part of the main managed service.

Let's summarise what we can expect with a total managed service provider:

- a central point of contact for users for any IT related query, from a request to a specific technical problem. In other words a help desk
- proactive technical management as well as reactive support
- aspects of the non-technical IT management such as asset and licence management, procurement and
- a single co-ordination point for all IT contracts.

This combination of providers can really reduce your need for in-house IT support. It allows you to retain flexibility and minimise your risk. It's a feasible way for a small company to outsource its IT.

Considerations

IT contracting is not that simple, I hear you say. If it were that easy and cost effective, nobody would run his or her own IT department. If you're going to outsource the running of your IT function using a combination of the options discussed here, what other considerations are there?

Hosted Solutions

The commodity-hosted services are normally going to be almost shrink-wrapped; there may be some options, but you won't have too much opportunity to vary the contract or service.

However, you still need to be very clear about what you're buying and that means asking lots of questions. I hope that by now you believe that most of IT is about business, not technology; it follows that if the service or contract from an IT supplier cannot easily be understood, there may be problems hidden behind the terminology. Make sure that you understand the answers from the IT supplier and if not, seek out a supplier that can provide straightforward descriptions of what they will provide.

Secondly, make sure you know whom you're buying from; some suppliers simply sell on the services provided by an apparent competitor. It will probably be possible to get a better service and price from the direct provider.

Hosted business applications will need to be customised to the company's business needs. Here, there is an interesting balance to maintain.

- Hosted services should aim to be as simple to use as buying a book on the internet. This means having standard processes and workflows for all users.
- However, despite major similarities, no two-property management companies, for example, use exactly the same processes. The business application will provide some flexibility in the way it is used and therefore it needs to be selected and implemented with the same care as with a traditionally deployed system.

One advantage of buying a hosted application contract form the software supplier itself is that the supplier will completely understand the application they are selling. They have far more control over how the application is deployed and direct experience of customising the solution. This is far more control than the reseller of, say, Microsoft Exchange has over his solution. Use this experience to develop the solution you need.

Managed Services

Managed services will also need to be customised to match your needs. The first task is to define the processes in your IT function and decide where you want the dividing line between internal and external responsibility to lie.

As with business applications, this needs a detailed requirements document, a formal tender process and relevant scoring of provider's responses during the selection process.

Much of the detail of selection and tender processes is dealt with within Chapter 6. The service descriptions, service level agreements and contracts are key. Taken together, these define the service and its scope, how it'll operate and to what levels of performance, and the terms on which you're buying it.

The service provider will be experienced in negotiating a service; he does this every week and knows his standard contract backwards. When you pick up a point in your favour, you need to know that you have not given away two more against you.

Our advice is that you should level the playing field on both the IT and the legal matters, and take advice – maybe just speak to a mate who's done this successfully in another organisation; but more probably you need to take professional advice.

The devil really is in the detail when it comes to these sorts of agreements. There are a whole host of aspects of which to be wary. Here are just a few examples:

1 Make sure to set performance measures which can actually be measured (and that they motivate the right behaviour in your provider).
2 Create flexibility in the contract to cater for changes to your business – also, agree upfront what the changes will cost. Increased flexibility creates extra contract cost. However, it might be possible for the provider to create savings through proactive management of change.
3 Where does data ownership lie? Who will be responsible for security?
4 What happens if things go wrong? For example, are service credits available? Additionally, do the problem escalation procedures reach senior management?
5 The exit strategy needs to be considered in minute detail.

Your company might be relatively small and therefore might seem to have little negotiating power. There is, however, one moment when you will have the maximum negotiating power – that is just before the contract is signed.

Do not be browbeaten into signing a contract if there is any negotiating point outstanding. Trust is the foundation of every good deal but these contracts run for many years and relationships between service provider and client can change for many reasons. Achieving a fair and comprehensive contract takes time and therefore the definition process needs to be started up to a year before you need the service to start.

It is also worth considering managing the changes that will be perceived by the users of the service. Defining the level of service you need is therefore an important point.

With an internal team, service levels will often be informal. We have all seen (maybe been part of) a situation which starts with a user who rings IT to say, "I've got a problem, come here now and fix it". With an internal IT team, if the person with the problem is senior enough, the problem will be fixed immediately regardless of how important it is in the plans of the IT team.

If that happens often, it's difficult to formally detail the level of service really *needed*. Some providers suggest implementing a trial period to discover what should be in the SLA before the service is finally agreed. This is a useful idea but sometimes breaks down because once the contract is let, there is too much day-to-day work to let the more strategic aspects be addressed properly.

It is therefore also important to manage the change in users perceptions to a more formal regime. Implement a change process that allows them to understand that their demand for service "NOW" may be put in a queue or dealt with in a few days time.

IT management and the IT Strategy

The rest of this book has concentrated on providing solutions to business issues and developing a business IT strategy. The policy for resourcing IT on an ongoing basis is also a key part of the IT strategy and in this chapter I've discussed some options for minimising the need for an in-house IT team.

These two strands of the strategy are clearly related and, in reality, strategy is never created in a vacuum. Developing the right overall strategy is always complicated by the different options available. These include:

- basing your strategy around your existing infrastructure
- defining your strategy around business needs and creating a new infrastructure plan regardless of existing technology
- asking a managed service provider to build an infrastructure for you, either based on your business requirements (preferred) or on their existing technology partnerships and skill sets.

So, when discussing how to develop an overall strategy with your supplier, which comes first: the business IT strategy or the IT support? Let's look at the implications of each approach.

Business Strategy first

It is possible to take your current support to a total managed service provider, discuss the overall strategy and the detailed requirements for business applications. The provider will then work with you to create a formal IT strategy and the IT to support it.

However, while this is possible, most suppliers will have different options for implementing your business strategy; how do you choose one supplier with the right strategy for you when other considerations such as cost and personalities have an equal share in the decision process?

Furthermore, few suppliers will compete for the contract if there is too much work to be done in defining the service as part of the tender. This option falls foul of the number one rule in outsourcing – do not outsource a mess.

Setting the strategy first is feasible but it would be wise to take independent advice before going this way.

IT Support first

In developing the IT support first, you may be able to outsource the solution rather than the problem. There are two ways of doing this:

1. You may enter into a managed service contract early on and use the provider's resources to assist you with further projects.
2. Alternatively, you might do a series of enabling projects and only enter into a managed service contract when you've reached some kind of steady state.

This approach takes longer but allows you to develop an understanding of your supplier and build up to a co-developed overall strategy. This will not prevent you from developing a business IT strategy that can be shared with your supplier and may allow a managed approach to change in the organisation.

Both approaches have their pros and cons and, ultimately the choice will be shaped by the timescale for change and the budgets, resources, and advice available.

Corporate occupiers and Government

The above represents an effective way of dealing with IT in a small organisation but in a large company there is likely to be an IT team already in place whose role it is to make to the decisions outlined above. In this case, we cannot influence general IT policy and our objective is to help the IT team support the real estate team as effectively as possible.

Here are a number of actions you can take to improve your IT support:

- **Educate your IT team.** Most IT teams appoint a member of their team as the representative for the real estate team. Make sure that this person is part of the planning process for the real estate team and that he/she fully understands the demands on your team.

Invite them to attend industry conferences such as the PCS-expo where they will see the range of specific solutions for the real estate industry. As soon as the IT team realises that specific solutions exist for many real estate issues, they may try to integrate these into their overall solution.

- **Understand your processes.** Much of the software in use in the company will be generically applied across all departments and real estate teams often believe that generic solutions will not work in real estate. Through gaining a thorough understanding of your processes, as described in previous chapters, you will be ready to test any new solution which is proposed centrally. This will put you in greater control of deciding how well the solutions fit your part of the business and gain you a stronger negotiating position should you wish to object.
- **Be enthusiastic about change.** Keeping abreast of the latest developments in information systems will enable you to request change rather than have change forced upon you. If you can be part of pilot schemes, you will have a far greater chance of influencing the outcome of the test, and gain new systems that work better for your team. Furthermore, the discipline of looking forward at new technology will allow you to challenge the basis of your existing methods and improve performance.

Conclusion

For smaller companies, there is now often little need to keep a full time IT support team. Care should still be taken in awarding contracts but the discipline of structuring a formal arrangement will in itself benefit the company's understanding of how it uses IT.

Larger companies will already have a significant investment in IT resource and the skill is to leverage that existing resource to improve the team's efficiency.

I started the book by saying that IT is not about technology. Even though this part of the book has dealt with "real" IT, I hope that it has demystified this function sufficiently for property people to feel in control.

CASE STUDY

Realm

My colleague at Remit Consulting, Mark Jones, was head of IT at MEPC, a large UK property company, which, as part of a transformation in its business, sold one part of their organisation to the management. The new company, REALM Limited, manages large retail centres on behalf of investor owners.

They have about 35 staff who are based across a number of sites in the UK. The approach Mark took was based on the ideas set out in Chapter 9 and a series of projects allowed them to gain control of their IT without the creation of a formal IT department.

The individual projects which allowed them to do this were to:

- set up a hosted Exchange e-mail service
- implement a property management and accounting system. A key factor in the selection of this system was the ability of the supplier to host a remotely located system and carry out all technical management and support.
- select a managed service provider to look after the desktop and network infrastructure, and the IT admin and management tasks.

The company now have no internal IT team and IT responsibility falls to the Project and Facilities director. He reviews the service with the managed service provider on a regular basis and the finance director does the same with the property system supplier on application issues.

The total cost of services which substitute for an in-house IT team is less than £50k. To give an idea of the scope of the work and costs involved, within this, £4k covers both the maintenance of e-mail and the "hire" of software and hardware.

Their experience has been very positive and the directors consider the service to be better than if they had their own small IT team; it is more reliable, there is less management hassle, and, of course, no human resource issues.

Mark Watts, finance director of REALM comments, "We are particularly pleased with the helpdesk support, the support team can remotely take control of our PC screen to fix the problem. This is much quicker and more effective than it would be to rely on overworked internal staff to fix things when they have a moment".

IT management activities as well as IT support are undertaken effectively and there is access to an available pool of resources for project work.

The key to their success was detailed preparation and, in this case, an initial hand-over period to the managed service provider. It should be noted, however, that it was a large amount of work to thrash out the Service Level Agreement (SLA) and the contract.

Mark Jones added, "The key parts of this project were to detail the service levels and really understand how the service being proposed would work. It was the detailed development of the SLA and the contracts which produced a successful outcome. We did the service level analysis ourselves because we had just been through a similar process elsewhere in MEPC but we relied heavily on legal advisors to ensure the contracts were fair."

The company is very happy with the outcome and is now at the point of contemplating an extension of the original three-year contract.

The future 10

In the year 2000, Microsoft started marketing their Tablet PC concept[1] and over the next three years the actual tablets started to become available. In essence the machines look like the screen of a laptop but without the keyboard. The theory is that users write on the screen and the writing is translated into typed text in the tablet.

What is remarkable about this launch is not that the technology was so advanced, but that it had been possible to create this type of computer for 10 years. It had been trialled and used by scientists, and many pilots were tried for specific data capture in mobile situations.

However, market research told the manufacturers that general commercial users could not yet grasp the concept of writing directly onto a screen. During those 10 years users became accustomed to using PDA devices and learnt to use the screen for inputting data instead of a keyboard. Hence, it was not until the year 2000 that the Tablet PC was likely to become popular.

Ten years previously, the concept of a tablet must have seemed fantastic. We could use the tablet in just the same way as paper; slow typing would be a thing of the past. It would be easier to write things on a tablet while standing up than finding a flat surface on which to type, PCs would finally become more mobile.

Many people familiar with the tablet concept at that time must have been convinced this was the way forward and frustrated that the hardware was not made widely available. All this time, laptops became smaller and faster and people continued to type using conventional keyboards.

Now, of course, tablets are widely available but in the past five years they have failed to significantly dent the sales of laptops. You could have bet on market domination for this significant new technology and, 10 years later, you would have been wide of the mark.

The opposite was true of SMS messaging or texting using mobile phones. Personally, I could see no merit in using SMS messages when this technology first became available. To

---

1 www.microsoft.com/prepass/features/2000/nov00/11-13tabletpc.asp

me, using your thumbs to tap out short messages that took quite some skill appeared to be heading up a blind alley. As mobile telephones became more sophisticated I reasoned, better ways of inputting text would be developed – perhaps using screens you could write on. But I was very wrong.

The telephone companies marketed SMS so well to young people as a virtually free messaging service, that take up was huge, spawning a global texting culture with its own language. So prevalent is the texting phenomenon that it has changed young peoples behaviour; sociologists point out that anyone under 25 now uses their thumb to turn on a light switch rather than their forefinger like their parents.

SMS is now possible with PDAs using a pen stylus on the screen but this is irrelevant. People have learnt to use an inefficient way of typing because of the low cost and exceptional convenience.

What this shows is that it is not only easy to misread technology trends but that given a few years, many of the brightest ideas become almost irrelevant. People find effective ways to use what they have. They learn to love 80% – sometimes they learn to live with much less than 80%.

Predicting the future

Bill Gates of Microsoft once said that we overestimate what will happen in the next two years and underestimate what will happen in the next 10 years. This rule of thumb works well. In 1989, a UK telecoms company undertook a survey where 85% of respondents said they would not use a mobile telephone; they did not want to be available to contact at all hours.

By 1997, 65% of the UK population owned a mobile telephone and the percentage was still growing. Given the data to hand in 1989, a prediction indicating a population of texting, always available, phone addicts who consider these devices to be fashion items would have been hard to support; but that is what has happened.

If we look at history, there are at least two versions of most major events. If there are different versions of what has already happened, how many possible versions of the future can be imagined? For anyone considering how to plan for the future, and in particular, plan IT, the variables are numerous and hard to grasp.

So, there are many possibilities for the future of IT and many more events that influence the final answer. However, this is not obvious when speaking to an IT company. IT companies are particularly good at spinning their version of the future and the dreams they sell are seductive and compelling.

While broadly similar in long-term vision, the detail of what each company is selling differs depending on their own history. For example, Enterprise solution suppliers will sell you a vision of the future with an enormous, "one-size-fits-all" software implementation that links together manufacturers, suppliers and customers. Companies selling middleware to join up disparate systems will eloquently explain why that scenario is doomed.

Both types of company start with the same idea that linking data across all stakeholders is the way forward but pick different ways of providing a solution. With many different versions of the future, from many different suppliers all selling their own unique approach, the chances of the customer winning seem slim.

Typically, users of technology will want to know:

- How do I future-proof my IT investment? If I buy into the latest version of Microsoft .Net, Java, Linux, SAP, or whatever, what will prevent the need to throw it all away in five years time? I want my decision to stand the test of time.
- How do I know I have picked the right IT? My business is constantly changing in response to the market and new legislation – how can I be sure my IT will adapt as rapidly?
- Should I spend more to keep on top of this change or could I reduce my investment but remain effective?

We have looked at how to answer much of this within the rest of this book and it is tempting at this stage to repeat that it is best to look at the business needs and prioritise around those. The principal cause of software failure is poor adoption and management of change in the business – not the software chosen.

Therefore, if the IT projects are well chosen and well implemented, the majority of the cost will have been invested in the people, not the software. This makes the actual life span of the software largely irrelevant: once the users have adapted to a more efficient way of doing things, a change in style of software should cause little problem.

Look at the relative ease with which people change their mobile phones every one-two years. The new features, such as cameras included in the new phone, make the change worthwhile to the user and the pain of learning the quirks of new software seems acceptable. The lifespan of the hardware itself is even shorter than the software and obsolescence is a real issue.

While this might sound glib, it has to be the foundation of an approach to managing obsolescence. The lifespan of an individual business system may be as little as three years; the life of hardware may be as little as 18 months (eg mobile phones). It is a fact of life that technology in five year's time will look little like that of the technology today. The hardware will be smaller and lighter, the interface will be different and the software will reflect more modern design.

Companies will update their technology, partly because the old technology will cease to be supported. This fact puts an increased burden of change upon the users and, consequently, a flexible workforce will be more effective at adapting to whatever is best for the task in hand.

The previous chapters have concentrated on business needs and seeking agreement among the users because this approach breeds less reliance on the actual IT. IT cannot be about IT: technology will change and devotion to one solution will stifle innovation. Better to ensure that the users are focused on working better, minimising costs and increasing profitability, than rigid adherence to a single technology. The business cases you have developed will take care of the costs of change or upgrade; if they do not make the case, the priorities need to be re-examined.

This re-emphasises that there is no one answer the questions posed above. Get the overall approach right by including the users and helping them innovate, and IT will support and enable the business.

IT – a driver or enabler?

Yet, prioritising business issues and developing the business case only deals with the short and medium term; it does not help us look beyond this time horizon to get new ideas and plan for change. To do this, we need to consider whether IT is:

- driving change or,
- enabling businesses to change.

In a very simplistic example, if it is the former, the fact that a new connected PDA device is launched which lets us stay in contact more effectively might provide the possibility of making all your staff mobile. This could reduce your office costs by disposing of accommodation; if your staff are on the road, they do not need a desk. The technology has created a shift in working practice that makes your team more efficient.

However, in all probability, there will be alternative technology along within the next six months that will change your opportunities again. Stretching this example, your company discovers new knowledge management software that might produce a four-fold increase in productivity. The only problem is that, until reliable broadband wireless is available, the amount of data needed to flow to a desk top is so high that you need to give a desk to all your workers again.

But you've just disposed of your offices and have no desk spaces; to take advantage of increased productivity, you need to buy and equip new ones. If this costs too much, your tardy competitors, whose high cost base you taunted when your teams became mobile, may have the last laugh.

If you follow the very latest thinking and continue to pioneer as early adopters, there is a higher risk of failure. It is always risky to buy "Version 1" of any new technology.

This set of examples is extreme but in every business similar decisions occur every few months. It must therefore be better to plan your strategy around business drivers and see what technology is available at that point, than constantly chase the latest IT concept. All other things being equal, IT should enable change, not drive it.

That is not to say that developments in IT should be ignored. The innovations from any number of new devices or software applications can suggest radical improvements which may well lead to a change in the way a company does business. It also helps that many people will want to use the latest gadget and, properly managed, the enthusiasm for the most up-to-date piece of kit will aid adoption of new ideas. Like the ever-changing mobile phones, if staff want the gadget enough, they will change the way they work. We can harness this enthusiasm to get the users to justify the business case.

Yet, regardless of the drivers and constraints, we should make time to imagine how business will change. Let's look at the likely innovations in technology, possibilities for business drivers that will change the property industry, and see if we can draw some conclusions of what to expect.

New Technology

Most people in IT seem to be focusing on mobility as the great change of the next few years. There are a number of reasons for this and the reality is that, at last, mobile computer power is actually a reality.

While I do not completely believe the "fact" that there is more computing power in a musical birthday card than there was in the early US space programs, my current PDA with its built-in phone, messaging and synchronisation with a remote Microsoft Exchange server is nothing short of miraculous. It means that I do not have to carry around a laptop, I am always using my e-mail and calendar as if I am at my desk and I don't have to worry about backing up the database – it is done automatically when I connect.

This really is a step forward from the early days of laptops and provides genuine business benefits. The various technologies it leverages are the improvements in telecoms (GPRS), software (Microsoft Outlook in its many versions), and in hardware (PDAs are now robust, reliable and have reasonable battery life).

The coming together of phones and computers is a key point in technology development and, as we have seen through developments in internet technology, connected computers will fuel major improvements in the way we can work. A lawyer friend uses his PDA (a Blackberry) to deal with his e-mail on the train into work and estimates he frees up at least an hour each day in the office. Clearly, the addition of useful time to the working day should reflect in a higher number of chargeable hours and will repay the cost of the IT investment.

We can see the start of real variety in the types of mobile devices available. Simple text handlers for SMS messages and e-mails; more complex devices with larger memory and the ability to edit documents; similar devices aimed at the games market or for media files; devices designed to browse full-sized web pages on a small screen; mobile phones with built-in video cameras.

Combinations of all these features (except, maybe, the gaming) will be useful for many aspects of the real estate industry and the memory capacity, the power of the processors and the speed of connectivity will continue to improve. However, the current line-up of gadgets only hints at what may be next. Three developments are converging which, if successfully integrated, will bring enormous changes to the way in which we can work.

These three developments are:

- telecoms/wireless connectivity and bandwidth
- screen technology
- grid computing.

Telecoms development continues apace. Without going into too much detail and at the risk of the descriptions being only superficial, the main technologies are as follows:

1 The current most common technology is General Packet Relay Service (GPRS, sometimes known as 2.5G) that can deliver data at approximately 60kbps – not much faster than a dial-up modem[2].
2 3G technology (UMTS) is now more widely available, delivering data at speeds of up to 1920kbps (but frequently no more than 360kbps).
3 4G (used to describe two different but overlapping technologies) is expected in 2010 with data transfer speeds of up to 1Gbps, about thirty times faster than 3G.

3G can already deliver passable video across a mobile network and we will become accustomed to using moving images, just as we now demand full colour photographs as standard over black and white images.

3G is accessible through the supplier for your mobile phone and other wireless technologies such as Bluetooth™ and Wifi (802.11) are also competing aggressively to allow mobile gadgets to communicate wirelessly.

Many of the latest PDAs now have all these technologies built-in which currently makes sense. Bluetooth™ works at short distances and Wifi slightly longer distances. Typically Bluetooth™ will connect your wireless earpiece to the phone and Wifi will keep you hooked up to the internet around your home/office or at the coffee shop. GPRS or 3G take care of everywhere else that is not close to a Wifi or Bluetooth™ node.

It may become even easier to connect wirelessly when away from the home or office. New technologies such as WiMax[3] have potential ranges of up to three kilometres overcoming any shortfall in current Wifi range. At this range it becomes a direct competitor to mobile telephony and 3G, but there are issues yet to be resolved in some countries about operating frequencies that may clash with existing public services.

Significantly, the increase in data transfer rates is not so much about computer power and more about memory, ie photographs and videos. The long celebrated Moore's Law, which suggests that computers will continue to increase in processing power at a great rate,[4] appears to be coming to an end.

Let's look at the way we use data before examining the possibilities for processing power in more detail.

2 en.wikipedia.org/wiki/GPRS
3 www.wimaxforum.org/about
4 en.wikipedia.org/wiki/Moore's_law

Paper to data

One thing that holds us all back is the amount of information we need to carry with us. Paper is heavy when carried in bulk – in fact, paper storage is second only to an iron foundry when engineers calculate weight limits in industrial buildings. It would be useful to minimise the weight we carry around and one way to do this is to carry it in digital format in your laptop or PDA.

Often the information we need has been produced or sent out on paper and it therefore needs to be digitised before it can be used in an IT network. However, now that most documents are produced digitally, much information is stored electronically and therefore can be carried on portable devices. This should lead to a reduction in the amount of paper carried but, more often than not, it doesn't.

People have a fear that the wrong document will be loaded on the laptop and that the right one will be inaccessible on a server somewhere – or worse, on someone else's laptop. Taking all the documents on a PDA would take up a lot of memory and it is tedious exchanging data between machines each time we visit the office.

Now that memory is becoming cheaper, we can take most of the files we would ever need on a USB memory key but it is still something that needs regular updating to ensure the most recent documents are carried with us.

What is needed is access to the server where all the documents are held. This would mean that we need not worry about updating files on the server. New files would be written to the server, even if working remotely; all other files are available at the click a mouse (or whatever we next adapt to).

Increasing speeds of wireless data transfer make this possible. As long as the device you are using can access the right server, carrying paper could, in theory, be a thing of the past. Yet, we cling to paper partly because we find it easy to use, and partly because reading from a computer screen is still less easy on the eyes[5].

Screen technology

The second of the developments I mentioned above is seeking to resolve the unpopularity of reading information on a screen. New developments such as Polymer Light Emitting Diodes (PLEDs) allow screens to be "printed" onto almost any material[6]. This means that folding electronic "newspapers" are a realistic prospect[7]. The applications using PLEDs need little power and could revolutionise how we use computer screens. Gone will be the days of carrying around 1-2 kilos of plastic and glass. Screens could be very small on items such as watches or even worn on t-shirts. Of course this will be dependent on the screens requiring little power and on batteries becoming smaller; yet claims to this effect are being made.

5 And, as a friend pointed out, because paper is less dangerous in the bath

6 www.cdtltd.co.uk/technology/38.asp

7 www.innovationmagazine.com/innovation/volumes/v4n3/features3.shtml

It remains to be seen whether we will find reading from these screens any easier than from a PC monitor but the flexibility and mobility afforded by this technology will make it very seductive. At present, many early adopters find that the convenience of downloading newspapers such as the Financial Times[8] to their PDA from Avantgo[9] outweighs the discomfort of reading the news on a screen only four inches tall.

If that same news was on a screen the size of a tabloid newspaper that you could fold up and keep in your pocket, perhaps many more people would be converted from old-fashioned newspapers. Furthermore, the ability to create a screen almost anywhere on almost any surface means that all information, not just your business data, could be available wherever you are.

If you could use these new screens to call up any document from your server, or create a letter and save it wirelessly to the same server, this may be an attractive alternative to carrying paper around.

Grid Computing

The world's largest particle physics laboratory, CERN, in Geneva has a data problem. The organisation has a huge tunnel running through the mountains, around which they send particles at close to the speed of light. When these particles collide, they give out 40 million pieces of data each second and the scientists need to analyse all this data to find three pieces of interest.

The exercise requires a lot of computer power – so much that CERN cannot fit all the computers they require on site.

Back in the 1980s CERN developed the World Wide Web so that their scientists could collaborate around the world on projects. The Web was intended to be a method of keeping their files so that they were accessible but did not need to be on everyone's PC. The success of the Web when it became mainstream is self apparent and now most computer users rely on getting information from the Web rather than buying it on discs or keeping it on their own computer memory just in case.

What CERN have now developed to deal with their "lack" of computer power is a "web" for computer processing power. If the computer in Geneva needs more processing power at a certain moment, it can borrow power from PCs that are currently being used at less than full power; this could be on the other side of the world where the computer users are asleep. They have named this technology the Data Grid.

The technology has been used by the SETI project[10] that is the Search for Extra-Terrestrial Intelligence. How this works is that if you wish to sign up your computer to the project, the SETI team will use its processing power when it is sitting idly in your study; all you need to do is leave your PC running day and night. In this way, SETI gain significant amounts of

8 www.ft.com
9 http://www.ianywhere.com/avantgo/aboutus/index.html
10 setiathome.ssl.berkeley.edu/

extra computer power worldwide for their analysis and it costs them nothing other than the cost of setting up their grid.

If this is applied across businesses as a whole, such as suggested by CERN, it could be very useful for computer applications that require large amounts of processing power. In the area of fluid dynamics, for example, companies need massive computers for their calculations. For a few years, the Jaguar Formula 1 Racing team operated without a wind tunnel and they used a computer to calculate the effects of aerodynamic modifications. They used the most powerful supercomputer available but the calculations still took four days to complete. If their computers were linked via the Grid to every PC in Ford (Jaguar's parent company), they could have reduced the time these calculations took without buying an expensive one-off computer.

Similar benefits have been proposed for financial modelling and many large companies, especially with offices all around the globe, have been investigating the potential of this innovation. However, at a smaller scale, the implications are even larger. If one computer has too little processing power for a modelling calculation, it can call on the power of other computers. This assumes that the PC usually has enough power for its day-to-day activities and requires a boost every now and again.

So far, the thinking about Grid computing has been concerned with applications that need huge amounts of computer power. However, it gets interesting if we think about the use of Grid computing on handheld devices:

- What if the device you want to use has almost no processing power to start with?
- What if the device is a greetings card and requires nearly all its processing power from the grid?
- What if that PC now needs only a very small battery to power a flexible screen and a transmitter?

This would mean that the "PC" could be very small indeed and possibly integrated in reading glasses or in an earpiece. Coupled with a screen that could be large or small, rigid or flexible, the computers that we know now will look very dated.

All this needs an effective communications network and this could be provided by 3G, 4G or WiMax. Our data could be stored on servers almost anywhere, maybe at the same place that provides the processing power and whenever we need to check facts or read the most recent version of a document, we simply click through to the relevant page on our foldable "newspaper".

Since the communications technology is already available and the Grid is only four years away from public use, this vision of the future may be closer than we imagine. What this means for business is a profound change in the way we work and the Grid is the least of our problems[11].

11 See also, www.smartmobs.com for author, Howard Rheingold's views on how these devices might be used in a social, rather than business context.

The immediate future will be mobile in some form and many companies are already making plans for this. The implications of dealing with data while mobile are far reaching and will be much more difficult to manage.

Organising data

Let's imagine that, using this new wireless technology, we can easily gain access to any document on our company server or elsewhere on the various collaboration tools or subscription services we use. Will this make us more efficient?

It will if we can find the information. However, more information being published electronically inside and outside the organisation, and further innovations in software will make integration a moving target. Information management may put some of your data into order and document management may take on many of the more informal data storage issues. Yet all these solutions will change and develop over time and many of the current batch will be superseded.

Where are we currently in the development of the necessary infrastructure? Most property organisations have databases that hold the majority of their building data and they also have rudimentary structures on their servers for tracking documents.

The next step being taken by many larger organisations is to implement some form of document management system. These are still relatively expensive: the fact that Microsoft have dropped their plans to incorporate more extensive and flexible document storage in their next operating system[12] (known as Longhorn), indicates that easy answers to linking groups of documents will not be around anytime soon.

P2P

An alternative technology solution is rapidly gaining ground and appears to be developing a neat solution to the problem of data sharing. Peer-to-Peer (P2P) networks started with music websites such as Napster. Although Napster itself was taken to court for assisting the infringement of copyright material, the basic idea has relevant applications to business.

In essence, the problem Napster tried to solve was this: if you wanted to create an online library of music, you would need a huge amount of data storage for all the tracks. If you imagine that Google has more than 6,000 servers just for meta-data, ie information merely giving clues to where other data is, the storage requirements for every piece of music in the world would be huge. It would be far simpler if the owner of the music track simply told a central server what the music track is and where it is stored. As long as the track is located on a server that is available to the internet, someone looking for that track will be directed by a central server to the track, which they can then download.

12 news.zdnet.co.uk/software/windows/0,39020396,39165023,00.htm

This is how Napster worked. Computer users worldwide were encouraged to upload a list of their music, video and any other document that someone else might find useful onto Napster's servers and then leave their PCs ready for anyone else to share their files. One problem with this was that giving other people copies of music that you have legitimately bought is probably illegal under the copyright laws and Napster found itself in trouble. Another was the patchy service, and having to wait while your download fails and finds another version of the file to use.

The basic idea, though, is sound. Files owned by one organisation will solve the copyright issues and new technology such as BitTorrent, which allows several versions of the file to be stored and downloaded simultaneously, will overcome some of the technical issues.

If I am working on a large consultancy team and am usually working remotely from the office, I probably do not know the details of the projects of my colleagues. However, if I send a request to a central server asking a question about, say, oyster farming, any report logged on that server on that subject will show up on my search. As long as the report is held on a PC connected to the internet (or intranet), I can download it and carry on my work.

This system has several advantages over a document management system, not least that it uses the storage on individual PCs and laptops rather than central servers that replicate all that data. It also means that individuals can fail to copy files to the server, keeping them on their hard drives, which many of my colleagues consider a crime worse than murder.

However, this approach does rely on access to those hard drives and fast data transfer. The technology described above deals with the fast data transfer but also throws up the possibility that individual devices will be "dumb" and will have limited processor power. Maybe they will also have limited storage too and require large server farms elsewhere. See what I mean about the possibility of backing the wrong technology? Either solution may win in the long term.

Regardless of where the files are stored in the short-term, there are several competing technologies which provide a better solution to data management than we have presently and if users demand, or can be persuaded to adapt to open sharing of files, the efficiency improvements will be plain to see.

Knowledge

For those who manage to structure their electronic documents in a way that helps share information effectively, the major change will be in the way their organisation works. If document management is about technology, knowledge management is about culture. True knowledge management is often described as a seven-step process where only the first three steps are concerned with implementing the right technology and populating the knowledge bases. The top four steps deal with persuading the whole organisation to rely on the knowledge base to make both strategic and tactical decisions.

Very few companies are yet tackling the latter steps of knowledge management and even at Hewlett Packard, considered one of the best knowledge organisations, Lew Platt, former chief executive officer observed: "If HP knew what HP knows, we'd be three times more profitable."

Nevertheless, there will be little choice but to organise the company's information and turn it into knowledge. Information currently in the heads of the industry experts will increasingly become available online through subscription services. The levelling of the playing field for information at a basic level will be comprehensive.

At the other extreme, investment of time and money will be required to co-ordinate internal and external knowledge sources. Companies will be forced to invest in systems and culture change by the reducing value of basic information.

The winning companies in the future will be those that are able to change their culture to one where the use of knowledge systems is ingrained in the work they do. Basic information will not add value on its own. Combining different pieces of this information may not be enough either – if clients have access to the same information, why would they not do this?

Our businesses will have access at any time in any place to any amount of information. To give an example of how far this might go, it has already been suggested that the search engine Google might be able to search through all your e-mails, voicemails and instant messages; coupled with voice recorders around the home, this would augment your own memory[13]. Craig Silverstein, Technology Director of Google says, "Five years from now people will think about searching everything". Since all new business documents will be created electronically, why not?

The competition between search engine companies is intense and improvements will be made in the way answers to your questions are structured and how many types of media can be searched. After aligning business processes to capture the information, using it effectively will be the next big challenge.

One thing is certain: the improvements in technology will force changes in our behaviour. An infrastructure that captures knowledge is of no use if the organisation's culture does not use and refresh the knowledge. Technology changes may also affect us for the worse. Bill Clinton, the ex-President of the USA apparently wrote only three e-mails in his term of office, and we may not want to record the details of our own lives in as much detail as will be possible.

Business Drivers

If the IT developments just described are merely the enablers of business improvement, then what are the drivers?

13 FT – 31.01.05 "Friendly" engines that manage the data of daily life – Richard Waters

Let's go back to where we started. Real estate is an information business. Much of the value created is because one party has a different view of the information to the other. Even if both parties had perfect knowledge, trades would occur; for example, one party might believe he can design a more valuable building than the other and be willing to pay more for that opportunity.

At present, real estate market knowledge is imperfect and that leads to more value being created by individuals. However, the lack of transparency is off-putting to many potential investors and liquidity suffers as a result. Many other financial markets have found that when transparency increases, greater volumes of trades occur and liquidity improves.

From an investment point of view, there is the potential to increase the availability of real estate information but until prompted, the close-knit market will be maintained. That prompt is likely to happen in the UK through the forthcoming introduction of REIT style investment vehicles since both the US and Australia have seen greater investment in the real estate market through this type of vehicle. Greater transparency demands better information, and better information delivered effectively produces a more attractive investment.

Just as other markets court investors who will be able to track stocks and carry out analysis wherever they are, so too will real estate fund managers, who will make available investment details in the same way as do, for example, retailers. Real estate companies will find new ways of automating the collection of details that investors want to see; if they don't, they will find their entire lives governed by collection and analysis of data.

New roles in the industry and for the industry

The current vogue is for professionals to aim for what is known as a portfolio career, where the richness of a CV/résumé is determined not by solid employment at one company but by a "portfolio" of interesting and challenging assignments. This may be the case although I personally believe that many people want the security of permanent employment.

Nevertheless, companies wishing to be more flexible and agile are developing their structures to take advantage of a more mobile and flexible workforce. Coupled with the increasing availability of generic market knowledge, it often makes sense to structure a team to tackle a particular project and then reform the team elsewhere for a different task.

In their book *Atomic*, Roger Camrass and Martin Farncombe argue that the shape of companies will change dramatically[14]. Their argument is based on the economics of the firm, put forward by Nobel Laureate, Ronald Coase. Coase reasoned that firms work well when the costs of transactions within the firm are lower than the cost of dealing with external suppliers.

14 Atomic, Roger Camrass and Martin Farncombe. 2003 Capstone Publishing Ltd

For example, buying your stationery from a local shop must be more expensive than aggregating all your stationery buying through a single internal department. When buying externally becomes cheaper than internally, the value of the firm breaks down.

Camrass and Farncombe argue that the cost reductions in finding and dealing with goods lead large firms to be less competitive than small firms which have lower internal costs; they propose a selection of new types of company which will flourish in this new scheme of things. For example:

- Smart companies will concentrate on their brainpower. They will develop and sell their innovation.
- Web spinners will develop networks of business-to-business relationships These networks will allow the web spinners to introduce companies to others with useful and complementary services.
- Customer managers aggregate the end users – they know what they want and how to channel large volumes of demand.
- Asset platforms are the necessary factories that produce to the demands aggregated elsewhere.
- Service platforms do the same but with human resources. These are, for example, the shared services centres of the finance industry.
- Portfolio owners are the risk takers and they are responsible to the shareholders.

All these roles are present within the real estate industry but they tend to be arranged in a traditional structure. For example, we are currently seeing consolidation among the larger property advisors; this is adding to their scale but the global operators still offer a range of services from strategic advice through to implementation and brokerage.

Set against these giants who are all things to all people is the category of investors often known as opportunity funds that have developed over the last five-10 years. These are small, often with few directors and staff, and agile enough to take advantage of new deals that might take traditional companies weeks to analyse. They act like the Portfolio Owners above and show that parts of the real estate industry can adapt to new models.

There is not the space here to develop a theory about how the real estate industry could become "atomic" but it is unlikely that the industry will avoid change altogether. Consider for example the following possibilities:

1. Many of the best brokers are leaving the larger advisors and setting up small companies to reap the benefits of lower overheads.
2. There is a movement among the global advisors away from promoting investment brokers fastest in order to retain the large deal income, and towards corporate property account managers, responsible for annuity income.
3. Middle market advisors are becoming more specialist in the advice they offer to effectively challenge the global coverage of the large players.

4 Publicly quoted property companies that have struggled with analysts setting capital values at less than Net Asset Value (NAV) have been turning private. Those that remain are investing heavily in making their operations transparent so that they are attractive to new waves of investment through REITs.
5 The weight of investment into the real estate sector is set to increase with REITs and will force property companies who traditionally invest in commercial property into the residential market, many for the first time.
6 Occupiers, driven by the need to develop markets in the Far East will shift their headquarters operations away from Europe and the US, playing to the global attractions of the large advisors and speeding further consolidation in the advisory market.
7 Investors will also look to increase investment in the Far East providing an outlet for investment cash but increasing the difficulties of collecting and managing information.
8 Leased accommodation will increasingly be considered by large occupiers as a utility and will be treated as such through short flexible leasing arrangements, possibly through companies like Regus and Trillium.
9 Increasing statutory demands on companies to report liabilities effectively will require frequent review of the amount of accommodation occupied globally at any one time.
10 Corporate and Social Responsibility (CSR) will become an increasingly important reporting requirement. Reputational risk will become a key assessment criteria and details about Health and Safety, disabled access and environmental standards will become essential from the real estate portfolio.
11 Property managers will move their accounting functions offshore to cheaper labour markets, drastically reducing the cost of the service, improving profits for the best, and allowing the property managers close to site to focus on value.
12 Local government, under pressure to improve public access to information will become central coordinators of all local information, especially property details from many sources. It is this sector that will be leading the charge to develop ways of making all available real estate data accessible and this will, in turn, undermine the role of advisors as "guardians of property information". Advisors will thus be sidelined by anyone who believes they can use the information more effectively than a consultant on their behalf.

I have not touched upon the need, or otherwise, for offices because flexible working and flexible location will be features of all industries, not just real estate. However, the main point coming from these various possibilities is that IT will enable changes that better serve consumers of real estate; the providers will adapt to the demands of their customers. Furthermore, the infrastructure of information that allows the service providers to function effectively will be pivotal in this change.

The real estate industry has often been slow to change and has congratulated itself for standing aside when short term bubbles of IT investment have come to nothing. This is no longer an option as the leaders in the industry strengthen their lead on the back of better information.

Leadership in IT is not about technology. It relies on an understanding of where a company makes its money and how it can minimise the cost of providing service.

Summary and Conclusion 11

Leadership in IT is not about technology. It relies on an understanding of where a company makes its money and how it can minimise the cost of providing service.

In this book we have abandoned the concept of merely replacing a system with a better one. We started our journey with the initial identification of the business need; therefore, by the time the implementation started it had a far better chance of delivering value to the business.

The whole approach has been built around how the business works and, as we went along, we have developed and refined better working practices internally before specifying the requirements for the software.

Fundamental to this approach has been the thinking in Chapter 7 about the project management, identification of risks, and communication structure. This must be set up at the beginning of the project and the needs to not only communicate with the potential system users, but also to actively manage their input has been met through the controlled environment of facilitated workshops.

It is essential to gain consensus at the beginning about what the system will provide for two reasons: we need to justify the business case and we also need to prepare users for when the system is rolled out. Adoption of property systems is often through coercion rather than enthusiasm; many of the difficulties experienced with systems come about because users are unconvinced of the benefits of using the new solution.

Once this project structure is in place, a program of workshops leads the team through the various stages.

The first stages of the project are where the Board get the chance to agree their sponsorship for the project as a whole. This is where the overall scope is defined and the business benefits are identified and agreed. The problems of too much choice can be overcome by prioritisation and you will need to facilitate the decisions about which area of the business should be improved first.

As the project team digs deeper into those critical processes that require a new solution, the users help to develop and refine their way of working. Leading practice ideas from elsewhere can be included and the specification starts to take shape. The benefits of a new system are defined in more detail and reporting requirements are reviewed and rationalised. Ideally, the reports from age-old spreadsheets will be incorporated in the new system and data will, at last, be centrally available.

The documentation of the tender documents has become straightforward because the team has agreed all of the core details and has set them out in a way that is easy for the suppliers to understand and relate to their products. It is also straightforward for the suppliers to demonstrate their system in a way that allows you to compare "apples with apples".

Negotiating contracts may take less time than they usually do but there will still be many minor points to agree. However, your knowledge of what you want the system to support and how it will do that job will be invaluable in negotiating the deal.

The main difference brought about by the work done up to now will be in the implementation. Changes can be controlled and targets set and achieved. The ideal of "no nasty surprises" is within your grasp.

You may have started to develop a strategy before the first project or, more likely, when the success of the first one has unblocked funding for new initiatives. The strategy you develop now will draw on key elements of the research done in the early stages of the first project. It will define a current state and its problems; it will develop a vision of the future state and will identify a prioritised list of projects that will be resourced and costed.

Supporting this will be changes to the IT infrastructure. There are too many areas of IT support for one person and you might develop an outsourcing strategy to help ensure that the increased reliance on IT is ably supported by specialists. If you do this, your suppliers will shape elements of your IT strategy and the support you choose.

And what of the future? To misquote an old adage, we can be sure of three things in life: death, taxes and change. You will need to balance the opportunities provided by being the first to change with the risk that you might start down a technological blind alley. Often it is best to let others pioneer and be agile enough in your strategy and infrastructure to follow those who are successful.

Above all, leave technology alone until you know what your business needs to do, learn to accept 80%, and change the way you work.

Index